KÜNSTLICHE INTELLIGENZ

MASCHINEN LERNEN
MENSCHHEITSTRÄUME

ARTIFICIAL INTELLIGENCE

MACHINE LEARNING
HUMAN DREAMS

DEUTSCHES
HYGIENE-MUSEUM
DRESDEN

WALLSTEIN VERLAG

INHALT
TABLE OF CONTENTS

114   RE-VISIONEN KI
AI RE-VISIONS

140   DAS SCHÖNE UND DAS ERHABENE DER KI
THE BEAUTIFUL AND THE SUBLIME OF AI

GRUßWORT DER KULTUR-STIFTUNG DES BUNDES

HAL, Deep Blue, Siri, Alexa – so lang die Geschichte der Künstlichen Intelligenz ist, so umfangreich sind die Anstrengungen zur Findung von Kosenamen, die den Maschinen eine menschliche Natur angedeihen lassen. Das wirkt überaus entgegenkommend. Der springende Punkt aber ist: Menschen sind fast rückhaltlos bereit, ihr Einfühlungsvermögen auch auf nichtmenschliche Apparaturen auszudehnen; umgekehrt hat es sich als überaus kompliziert erwiesen, Maschinen eine Empathiefähigkeit gegenüber realen Lebewesen einzupflanzen.

Nicht mehr lange. Als jüngster Coup des technischen Fortschritts treten zu Beginn des 21. Jahrhunderts computergesteuerte Systeme auf den Plan (und auf die Märkte), die in allen denkbaren Bereichen der Koexistenz von Mensch und Maschine neue Formen der Zusammenarbeit generieren: bei der häuslichen Pflege, bei Anrufbeantwortern, beim Sex, am Fließband und natürlich bei der automatisierten Gesichtserkennung. Sie soll, neben der Abwehr von Terrorismusgefahren, generell dazu befähigt werden, über ethnische Herkunft, personelle Identität oder auch individuelle Gefühlslagen von Menschen Zuschreibungen erst zu produzieren, dann auszuwerten, zu verteilen, zu speichern – und so fort. Irgendjemand wird die Daten zu nutzen verstehen.

Nur wer? Hier mag ein zweites Missverständnis begründet liegen. Die altbekannte Angst, Roboter könnten die Herrschaft übernehmen, ist möglicherweise bloß die Kehrseite ihrer Verniedlichung. Gesellschaftliche Gefahren – denen das Dresdner Ausstellungsprojekt bei aller Wertschätzung innovativer Technik-Chancen keinesfalls ausweicht – rühren vielmehr von der Frage her, welche Kräfte es am besten verstehen, KI ökonomisch und politisch nutzbar zu machen. Etwa für Marktanalysen und Werbung, für Zwecke der Politik, für das Gesundheitswesen und zur Steigerung der Effizienz in der Arbeitswelt. Das ist eine Frage der Macht. Ihr begegnet das Deutsche Hygiene-Museum Dresden durch Aufklärung und Bildung und durch die Eröffnung von Erfahrungsräumen, in denen das Publikum eigene Antworten findet, wie wir die digitale Transformation so gestalten, dass sie unseren Vorstellungen von einem besseren Leben dient – also dem Wohle der Menschen; nicht aber deren Ausbeutung oder gar Ersetzung.

Die Kulturstiftung des Bundes dankt dem Deutschen Hygiene-Museum Dresden unter der Direktion von Klaus Vogel und Lisa Klamka sowie dem kuratorischen Team unter der Leitung von Yasemin Keskintepe sowie allen weiteren Mitwirkenden für die Realisierung einer Ausstellung, die eindrucksvoll vermittelt, was Künstliche Intelligenz leisten kann, wo sie heute schon wirkt und worauf wir gemeinsam zu achten haben, damit die Menschen- und Maschinenträume einen guten Ausgang nehmen.

FOREWORD BY THE GERMAN FEDERAL CULTURAL FOUNDATION

HAL, Deep Blue, Siri, Alexa – the efforts to come up with nicknames to lend machines a human trait are as extensive as the history of Artificial Intelligence is long. It seems accommodating in the extreme. But the point is: humans are practically without reserve when it comes to extending their sense of empathy to non-human devices; by contrast, endowing machines with the ability to empathise with real living beings has proven most complicated.

But not for much longer. The latest coup struck by technological progress at the beginning of the 21st century has been to usher in computer-controlled systems (and launch them onto the market), generating new forms of co-operation in every conceivable area of our human-machine coexistence: home care, answering machines, sex, assembly lines and, of course, auto-mated facial recognition. Generally speaking, aside from defending us against terrorist threats, it is meant firstly to produce, then evaluate, distribute, store – and so on and so forth – various attributions relating to people's ethnic origin, personal identity, and even individual emotional states. Someone somewhere is bound to know what to do with the data.

The problem is, who? And this may be where a second misunderstanding lies. The all-too familiar fear that robots might take over is possibly just the flip side of their trivialisation. For all its appreciation of innovative technological opportunities, Dresden's exhibition project – to its credit – does not dodge the issue of the societal hazards involved; and they stem in fact from the question as to which forces are best able to harness and tap into AI, both economically and politically. For instance, for market analyses and advertising, for political purposes, for the health system, and to boost efficiency levels in the work environment. It is all a question of power. The Deutsches Hygiene-Museum Dresden is countering this through information and education and by opening up experiential spaces in which the public is able to find its own answers as to how we can mould the digital transformation so it serves our ideas of a better life – in other words, for people's well-being rather than their exploitation, let alone their replacement.

The German Federal Cultural Foundation would like to thank the Deutsches Hygiene-Museum Dresden under the direction of Klaus Vogel and Lisa Klamka, as well as the curatorial team led by Yasemin Keskintepe and all the other contributors for creating an exhibition that impressively conveys what Artificial Intelligence is capable of achieving, the areas in which it is now already having an impact, and what we all need to look out for to ensure a good outcome to the dreams of both humans and machines.

HORTENSIA VÖLCKERS
VORSTAND / KÜNSTLERISCHE DIREKTORIN
EXECUTIVE BOARD / ARTISTIC DIRECTOR

KIRSTEN HAß
VORSTAND / VERWALTUNGSDIREKTORIN
EXECUTIVE BOARD / ADMINISTRATIVE DIRECTOR

GRUßWORT DER KLAUS TSCHIRA STIFTUNG

Unsere Gesellschaft wandelt sich stetig. Dabei spielen wissenschaftliche Erkenntnisse und Entwicklungen eine bedeutende Rolle und helfen uns, den täglichen Herausforderungen zu begegnen. In unsere Lebenswelt greift bereits jetzt und noch stärker in der Zukunft die digitale Transformation ein. Die allgemein unter dem Begriff *Künstliche Intelligenz* versammelten digitalen, selbstlernenden Techniken haben das Potenzial, unser Verhältnis zueinander, zur Welt und zu unserem Körper zu verändern. Möglichkeiten und Grenzen, Fragen der Akzeptanz, Ängste und Hoffnungen – all das sind Themen, die frühzeitig in der Gesellschaft bedacht und diskutiert werden müssen.

Mit der Förderung der Sonderausstellung *Künstliche Intelligenz. Maschinen – Lernen – Menschheitsträume* trägt die Klaus Tschira Stiftung (KTS) gern dazu bei, dass diese Themen und Fragestellungen vor allem ein junges Publikum erreichen. Seit ihrer Gründung vor über 25 Jahren hat sich die Stiftung Zukunftsthemen gewidmet und nicht nur die Forschung im Bereich der Naturwissenschaften, Mathematik und Informatik gefördert, sondern zugleich und vorausschauend in vielfältiger Weise auch die Wissenschaftskommunikation. Damit setzt sich die KTS für den gesellschaftlichen Diskurs über Wissenschaft ein.

Durch die Förderung des permanenten Ausstellungsbereiches „Erinnern – Denken – Lernen" im Deutschen Hygiene-Museum Dresden hat die KTS bereits vielen Schüler*innen die Neurowissenschaften nahegebracht. Die Ausstellung über Künstliche Intelligenz zeigt einen weiteren Bereich der modernen Wissenschaft. Die Präsentation aktueller Forschungsprojekte vermittelt die technisch-mathematischen Hintergründe digitaler Anwendungen. Ebenso bedeutend sind Fragen zur Künstlichen Intelligenz, die den Alltag jedes Einzelnen betreffen: Wie kann ich als Jugendlicher selbstbestimmt mit den digitalen Herausforderungen und meinen Daten umgehen? Welche Chancen stecken in der digitalen Transformation? Wird sich unsere Lebensweise durch KI verbessern oder verschlechtern, und hat das Einfluss auf unsere Werte?

In ihrem Engagement ist es der Klaus Tschira Stiftung stets auch wichtig, dass neue Formen des Erlebens von Wissenschaft erprobt und Anknüpfungspunkte zur Debatte des Erfahrenen geschaffen werden. Dass möglichst viele Menschen an Wissenschaft teilhaben, ist das Ziel der KTS. Herzlichen Dank dem Team des Deutschen Hygiene-Museums und allen beteiligten Ausstellungsmacher*innen dafür, dass sie sich der Herausforderung gestellt haben, komplexe Inhalte zugänglich, erleb- und diskutierbar zu machen.

FOREWORD BY THE KLAUS TSCHIRA FOUNDATION

Continual change is a defining characteristic of our society. Scientific findings and developments play a significant role in helping us face the challenges of everyday life. Already the digital transformation is making inroads into our lives – and set to do so even more in the future. The digital self-learning technologies generally subsumed under the rubric of *Artificial Intelligence* could potentially alter our relationship with one another, the world, and our bodies. Opportunities and limitations, questions of acceptance, fears and hopes – these are all topics that society needs to consider and discuss early on.

In sponsoring the special exhibition *Artificial Intelligence. Machine – Learning – Human Dreams*, the Klaus Tschira Foundation (KTS) is keen to help these topics and issues reach a young audience in particular. Since its establishment more than 25 years ago, the Foundation has dedicated itself to questions that pertain to the future, supporting research in such fields as the natural sciences, mathematics, and computer science, but also – and with some foresight – science communication, in a wide variety of ways. The KTS is thus committed to the social discourse on science.

Similarly, through its sponsorship of the 'Remembering – Thinking – Learning' exhibition area at the Deutsches Hygiene-Museum Dresden, the KTS previously helped many schoolchildren become acquainted with the subject of neuroscience. The *Artificial Intelligence* exhibition features yet another area of modern science. Showcasing current research projects highlights the technological and mathematical foundations underpinning digital applications. Questions about Artificial Intelligence that affect the everyday lives of each and every one of us are just as important. How can I, as a young person, face up to these digital challenges and handle my data in a self-determined way? What opportunities does the digital transformation present? Will AI improve or worsen our way of life, and will it have an impact on the values we hold dear?

Through its commitment, the Klaus Tschira Foundation is eager to sound out new ways of experiencing science and finding new points of reference for debating the experiences gained. Indeed, one of the objectives pursued by the KTS is to ensure that as many people as possible are able to participate in science. A big 'thank you', then, to the team of the Deutsches Hygiene-Museum and to all the exhibition makers involved, for taking on the challenge of making this complex content accessible in such a way that it can be experienced and discussed by all.

BEATE SPIEGEL
GESCHÄFTSFÜHRERIN / EXECUTIVE DIRECTOR
KLAUS TSCHIRA STIFTUNG

VORWORT

PREFACE

Seit einigen Jahren finden sich immer wieder Schlagzeilen über den Siegeszug der Algorithmen, in denen darauf hingewiesen wird, dass diese uns Menschen inzwischen auf vielen Feldern überlegen seien: bei der Erkennung von Tumorerkrankungen ebenso wie bei Rhetorikwettbewerben, bei der anwaltlichen Vertragsprüfung oder aber bei so traditions- wie voraussetzungsreichen Spielen wie Go und Poker. Auch unser Alltag wird heute bereits vielfach – oft ohne dass wir es wissen oder bemerken – von Algorithmen bestimmt: Sie stecken im Navigationssystem unseres Autos und in Sprachassistenten wie Siri und Alexa, sie steuern die automatischen Bildkorrekturen in Digitalkameras oder Übersetzungsprogramme wie DeepL und sie ermöglichen die personalisierten Empfehlungen auf Social-Media-Plattformen, Streamingdiensten oder Dating-Apps.

Eine technologische Voraussetzung für diese rasanten Entwicklungen, die gemeinhin unter dem Begriff der Künstlichen Intelligenz (KI) zusammengefasst werden, ist die Verfügbarkeit großer Mengen von Daten – Big Data, wie es im Fachjargon heißt. Damit diese Daten ausgewertet werden können, sind immense Rechenkapazitäten sowie komplexe Programmierungen erforderlich. Erst auf dieser Basis können die Algorithmen darauf „trainiert" werden, Lösungen anzubieten und selbstständige Entscheidungen zu treffen – Fähigkeiten, die bisher allein der menschlichen Intelligenz vorbehalten waren.

Um die Potenziale und Risiken dieser Zukunftstechnologie für Mensch und Gesellschaft ist eine heftige und notwendige Debatte entbrannt. Allzu oft ist sie allerdings geprägt von Unsicherheit und Unwissen bezüglich der konkreten Möglichkeiten von KI-Systemen und den Grenzen, die dem maschinellen Lernen gesetzt sind. Dass selbst die Forscher*innen, Ingenieur*innen und Programmierer*innen, die solche KI-Systeme entwickeln, sie häufig als intransparente Blackbox bezeichnen, erschwert die Verständigung zwischen Wissenschaft, Technologie und Öffentlichkeit.

In dieser Konstellation möchte das Deutsche Hygiene-Museum mit der Ausstellung *Künstliche Intelligenz. Maschinen – Lernen – Menschheitsträume* ein Angebot zur Auseinandersetzung mit diesem Zukunftsthema machen. In Kooperation mit der Ars Electronica, dem weltweit führenden Festival für Medienkunst in Linz, dem Barkhausen Institut in Dresden und der international agierenden Berliner NGO Tactical Tech werden in der Ausstellung unterschiedliche künstlerische und wissenschaftliche Perspektiven sowie kritische politische Interventionen präsentiert.

Mit der Ausstellung und der begleitenden Publikation möchte das Museum dreierlei erreichen. Zunächst will es über den aktuellen Stand dieser noch jungen Technologie aufklären, die jedoch ideengeschichtlich bis weit in die Antike und wissenschaftsgeschichtlich bis in die Mitte des 20. Jahrhunderts zurückreicht; sodann möchte es über aktuelle Entwicklungsgebiete und Anwendungsbereiche informieren und einige der prognostizierten Anwendungsszenarien vorstellen. Und schließlich sollen die Besucher*innen und Leser*innen fundierte Anregungen erhalten, in den Debatten über KI einen eigenen Standpunkt zu entwickeln: Wie verträgt sich die Auswertung von Massendaten mit dem Recht auf informationelle Selbstbestimmung? Welche Aufgaben und vor allem Entscheidungen wollen wir an KI-Systeme delegieren, welche sollten weiterhin dem Menschen vorbehalten bleiben? Wie steht es um die Transparenz von Entscheidungen, die auf selbstlernenden Algorithmen basieren?

All diese Punkte berühren unmittelbar auch die Leitfrage des Deutschen Hygiene-Museums „Wie wollen wir leben?" und dementsprechend steht die gesellschaftliche Dimension von KI im Mittelpunkt von Ausstellung und Publikation. Beide verstehen sich als Beiträge dazu, unser Verhältnis zu unserer hochtechnisierten Umwelt kritisch zu befragen und damit besser verstehen zu lernen.

Mein herzlicher Dank gilt all jenen, die mit Expertise und Ideenreichtum zu dieser Publikation beigetragen haben: den Autor*innen und Herausgeber*innen, den Mitarbeiter*innen von INFOTEXT für die Infografiken sowie Julia Wagner für die grafische Gestaltung des Buches. Auch unserer Lektorin Astrid Treusch sowie unseren Übersetzern Stephen Grynwasser und Ralf Tauchmann möchte ich für ihre umsichtige Arbeit danken.

Die Ausstellung *Künstliche Intelligenz* wurde unter den schwierigen Bedingungen der Covid-19-Pandemie konzipiert und realisiert. Dass trotz dieser Umstände ein so spannendes und facettenreiches Projekt umgesetzt werden konnte, dafür möchte ich zuallererst der Kuratorin Yasemin Keskintepe danken. Ein gleicher Dank gilt ihrem Team, bestehend aus Dr. Anke Woschech, Clarissa Lütz, Bettina Beer, Lisa Nickolaus und Anna Kühn, der Ausstellungsleiterin Dr. Doreen Hartmann sowie allen anderen beteiligten Mitarbeiter*innen des Deutschen Hygiene-Museums. Mein gesonderter Dank gilt dem wissenschaftlichen Co-Kurator Dr. Thomas Ramge, der das Museum und das Ausstellungsteam von Anfang an kompetent begleitet hat.

Für die schier unlösbare gestalterische und szenografische Aufgabe, die digitale Welt der Künstlichen Intelligenz in fünf analoge Räume zu übersetzen, hat Detlef Weitz mit seinen Kolleg*innen vom Büro chezweitz eine überzeugende Lösung gefunden.

Allen Leihgeber*innen, Kunstschaffenden, Institutionen, Initiativen und Unternehmen, deren Produkte, Objekte und Kunstwerke diese Ausstellung überhaupt erst möglich machten, gilt mein ganz herzlicher Dank. Darüber hinaus möchte ich mich auch bei den zahlreichen Expert*innen bedanken, die das Projektteam geduldig und zielsicher durch das weit verzweigte und oft undurchsichtige Labyrinth der selbstlernenden Algorithmen geführt haben. Wir haben viel dazugelernt!

Die kuratorische und wissenschaftliche Qualität der Ausstellung wäre ohne das Vertrauen und die finanzielle Unterstützung unserer Förder*innen nicht zu erreichen gewesen. Dank der Klaus Tschira Stiftung, der Kulturstiftung des Bundes, der Kulturstiftung des Freistaates Sachsen und der Sächsischen Landesstelle für Museumswesen können wir unseren Besucher*innen ein informatives und bereicherndes Ausstellungserlebnis bieten. Wir sind unseren Unterstützer*innen sehr dankbar dafür, dass wir damit einen zentralen Aspekt der digitalen Transformation unserer Gesellschaft zur Diskussion stellen können.

For a number of years now, headlines have repeatedly heralded the triumphant advance of algorithms, pointing out that they are now superior to us human beings in many areas: whether it's detecting tumour diseases or public-speaking competitions, reviewing legal contracts or playing games like Go and poker, which are as steeped in tradition as they are contingent on supposition. Our everyday lives are already determined by algorithms in many ways, often without our knowledge or awareness. They are inside our sat-navs and virtual assistants like Siri and Alexa; they control automatic image correction in digital cameras, but also translation programs such as DeepL; and they enable personalised recommendations on social media platforms, streaming services and dating apps.

Technologically, these rapid developments, commonly grouped under the heading Artificial Intelligence (AI), are predicated on the availability of huge amounts of data, or 'big data' to use the jargon. Analysing all this data requires immense computing capacities and complex programming. Only then can the algorithms be 'trained' to come up with solutions and make independent decisions, abilities which previously had been the sole preserve of human intelligence.

The opportunities and risks of this future technology for people and society alike have sparked a heated yet necessary debate. But all too often, that debate is characterised by uncertainty and ignorance about the concrete possibilities afforded by AI systems and the limitations of machine learning. The fact that even the researchers, engineers and programmers who develop AI systems often describe them as a non-transparent black box makes communication between science, technology, and the public all the more difficult.

Against this backdrop, the Deutsches Hygiene-Museum sees its exhibition *Artificial Intelligence. Machine – Learning – Human Dreams* as an opportunity to engage with this future-defining topic. In co-operation with Ars Electronica, the world's foremost festival for media art staged in Linz, the Barkhausen Institute in Dresden and the Berlin-based NGO Tactical Tech that operates internationally, the exhibition is to showcase a wide range of artistic and scientific perspectives as well as critical political interventions.

The Museum has three aims in mind with its exhibition and accompanying publication. Firstly, to inform visitors about the current state-of-the-art of this relatively young technology, even if, in terms of the history of ideas, it does go back to Antiquity and, in terms of the history of science, to the mid-20th century. Secondly, to provide information on the latest areas of development and application and present some of the anticipated application scenarios. Finally, visitors and readers are to have the chance to be inspired by some well-founded suggestions for their own points of view in the debates about AI. How is the analysis of mass data compatible with the right to informational self-determination? What tasks and, above all, what sort of decisions do we want to delegate to AI systems – and which should remain the sole preserve of human beings? What about the transparency of the decisions that are based on self-learning algorithms?

All these aspects touch directly on the key question that guides the work of the Deutsches Hygiene-Museum, namely 'How do we want to live?'. Unsurprisingly, then, the social dimension of AI is the focal point of the exhibition and its publication. Both are to be seen as contributions to the critical questioning of our relationship with our high-tech environment and, consequently, to learning to understand that relationship better.

My sincere thanks to all those who have contributed to this publication through their expertise and wealth of ideas: the authors and editors, the INFOTEXT staff for the infographics, and Julia Wagner for the graphic design of the book. I would also like to thank our editor Astrid Treusch and our translators Stephen Grynwasser and Ralf Tauchmann for their meticulous and circumspect work.

The *Artificial Intelligence* exhibition was devised and realised under difficult circumstances due to the Covid-19 pandemic. The fact that such an exciting and multifaceted project could be implemented despite these circumstances is a tribute to our curator Yasemin Keskintepe, and I am most grateful to her. Thanks are similarly due to her team, comprised of Dr Anke Woschech, Clarissa Lütz, Bettina Beer, Lisa Nickolaus, and Anna Kühn; the exhibition director Dr Doreen Hartmann; and all the other participating staff members of the Deutsches Hygiene-Museum. My special thanks go to the scientific co-curator Dr Thomas Ramge, who competently assisted both the Museum and the exhibition team from the very outset.

Detlef Weitz and his colleagues at chezweitz found a most convincing solution for the almost impossible design and scenography task of transposing the digital world of Artificial Intelligence to five analogue rooms.

My heartfelt thanks also to all the lenders, artists, institutions, initiatives, and companies whose products, exhibits, and works of art made this exhibition possible in the first place. I would also like to thank the numerous experts who patiently and unerringly guided the project team through the wide ramifications and often impenetrable maze of self-learning algorithms. We have learnt so much as a result!

The curatorial and scientific quality of the exhibition could not have been achieved without the trust and financial support of our sponsors. Thanks to the Klaus Tschira Foundation, the Federal Cultural Foundation, the Cultural Foundation of the Free State of Saxony, and the Saxon State Agency for Museums, we are able to offer our visitors an informative and enriching exhibition experience. We are very grateful to our benefactors for enabling us to open up a discussion on a key aspect of the digital transformation of our society.

PROF. KLAUS VOGEL

DIREKTOR / DIRECTOR

ANKE WOSCHECH, YASEMIN KESKINTEPE

LERNEN MASCHINEN MENSCHHEITSTRÄUME? – EINE EINLEITUNG

DO MACHINES LEARN HUMAN DREAMS? – AN INTRODUCTION

Samantha liebt Theodore. Theodore liebt Samantha. So weit, so banal. Wenn nicht Theodore ein Mensch und Samantha sein Betriebssystem wäre. Eines Tages verlässt Samantha Theodore, um mit Millionen anderer Betriebssysteme, die ebenfalls romantische Beziehungen zu Menschen eingegangen waren, ihren eigenen (virtuellen) Weg zu gehen. Die verlassenen Menschen haben weniger mit der narzisstischen Kränkung zu kämpfen, durch die entstandene Superintelligenz nicht mehr als Krone der Schöpfung zu gelten, sondern vor allem mit Liebeskummer.

Der Film *Her* von Spike Jonze aus dem Jahr 2013 unterläuft zum einen die in Science-Fiction-Filmen übliche Darstellung des Mensch-Maschine-Verhältnisses: Die begehrenswerte Maschine ist zwar weiblich konnotiert, jedoch kein humanoider Roboter, der als dämonische Tech-Variante der Femme fatale den männlichen Protagonisten verführt. Zum anderen verzichtet der Film auf den Topos der drohenden Unterwerfung der Menschheit durch ihre eigene, unbeherrschbar gewordene Schöpfung. Warum auch sollte sich eine Superintelligenz in der Zukunft mit der doch sehr beschränkten menschlichen Intelligenz weiter beschäftigen?

Das Bemerkenswerte dieser fiktiven KI-Liebesromanze ist die Verarbeitung einiger sich damals bereits deutlich abzeichnender Phänomene: So unterscheidet sich die emotionale Beziehung von Theodore zu Samantha kaum noch von der, die gegenwärtig einige Nutzer*innen dem Chatbot *Replika* entgegenbringen. Ursprünglich dazu entwickelt, Menschen in schwierigen sozialen Situationen durch ein virtuelles Gesprächsangebot Beistand zu leisten, entwickelte sich diese KI-App in den letzten Jahren zunehmend zu einem Romantiktool. Eine KI zu daten oder gar heiraten zu wollen ist inzwischen nicht mehr reine Fiktion, sondern in unserer – virtuell verquickten – Gegenwart angekommen.

Was für die einen eine echte Alternative zu den Höhen und Tiefen zwischenmenschlicher Kommunikation darstellt, ist für die anderen wohl eher ein realweltlich gewordener sozialer wie datenschutzrechtlicher Albtraum. Um die (Un-)Möglichkeit einer authentisch erlebbaren Mensch-Maschine-Beziehung streiten sich Nutzer*innen, Journalist*innen und Geisteswissenschaftler*innen gleichermaßen. Stellvertretend für diese Debatte um die erkenntnistheoretischen und sozialen Implikationen von *Replika* ließe sich also fragen: Lernen Maschinen Menschheitsträume? Und was lernen wir Menschen aus den Prozessen und Ergebnissen des maschinellen Lernens wiederum über uns selbst?

Die Ausstellung *Künstliche Intelligenz. Maschinen – Lernen – Menschheitsträume* des Deutschen Hygiene-Museums stellt sich diesen genuin gesellschaftlichen Fragen, die mit den rasanten Entwicklungen der letzten Jahre auf dem Gebiet der Künstlichen Intelligenz verbunden sind. Die vorliegende Begleitpublikation stellt mit kurzen, prägnanten Textbeiträgen den aktuellen Forschungs- und Wissensstand auf diesem Gebiet vor. Zudem wird der aktuelle Entwicklungsstand dieser noch jungen Technologie durch Beiträge dokumentiert, in denen maschinelles Lernen nachvollziehbar wird: in der Auswertung des kuratorischen Essays von Yasemin Keskintepe durch QualiFiction, einer KI-Software zur Textanalyse, sowie durch den Abdruck eines Gedichts, das eigens für diese Publikation von einer KI geschrieben wurde und gleichsam – in Anlehnung an den Philosophen Walter Benjamin – das Kunstwerk im Zeitalter seiner algorithmischen Produzierbarkeit reflektiert.

Fünf der insgesamt sechs Kapitel des Katalogs folgen in Struktur und Inhalt der Konzeption der Ausstellung, indem sie ausgewählte Exponate in Wort und Bild präsentieren. Zugleich setzen essayistische, künstlerische und illustrative Beiträge jeweils ganz eigene Akzente. Das erste Kapitel, *Muster der KI-Geschichte,* reflektiert unmittelbar den Untertitel von Ausstellung und Publikation. Es zeichnet anhand ausgewählter Schriften eine Ideengeschichte der mit KI verbundenen Menschheitsträume von der Antike bis zur jüngsten Vergangenheit nach. So beginnt dieser Blick zurück mit der Idee der Unsterblichkeit, die jahrtausendelang theologisch und philosophisch verhandelt wurde, bis sie Ende des 20. Jahrhunderts durch technische Allmachtsfantasien von KI-Pionieren ins Diesseits geholt wurde. Andere Ideen, wie die der Entstehung eines künstlichen Bewusstseins, sind bis heute Stoff der Science-Fiction.

Nach dieser Reise in die Vergangenheit wendet sich das zweite Kapitel *Trainingsraum* den unmittelbaren Grundlagen und Grundbegriffen der Künstlichen Intelligenz zu, wie sie heute verstanden wird. Es wird der Frage nachgegangen, was eigentlich hinter auf den ersten Blick seltsam anmutenden Begriffen wie „maschinelles Lernen", „Deep Learning" oder „neuronale Netze" steckt. Anhand ausgewählter Bilder aus dem Comic-Essay *We need to talk, AI* (2019) wird auf spielerisch-didaktische Weise ein erster Einblick in die Wissenschaftsgeschichte und den aktuellen Forschungsstand rund um KI gewonnen. Das Kapitel schließt mit einem Beitrag, der den gleichermaßen metaphorischen wie positivistischen Zugang der KI-Forschung und der Neurowissenschaften in Hinblick auf menschliches Denken, Lernen und Bewusstsein erläutert und dekonstruiert.

Das dritte Kapitel, *Globale Infrastruktur der KI,* widmet sich den materiellen und infrastrukturellen Grundlagen sowie den wirtschaftspolitischen Hintergründen der digitalen Transformation. KI benötigt riesige Datenmengen und auf Mikroprozessoren basierende höchste Rechenleistung. Die digitale Vernetzung der Welt findet dabei sprichwörtlich im Verborgenen statt, durch die Verlegung von immer leistungsfähigeren Unterseekabeln. Ebenfalls unsichtbar ist die digitale Fließbandarbeit, die hinter KI-Trainingsprozessen steckt – ausgeführt von zumeist schlecht bezahlten Crowdworker*innen, die diese Trainingsdaten für KI-Anwendungen manuell aufbereiten. Dessen ungeachtet gelten Digitalisierungsvorhaben im Allgemeinen und KI im Besonderen als Ausweis nationaler Innovationsfähigkeit, während gleichzeitig international tätige Technologiekonzerne wie Amazon, Facebook, Microsoft, Apple und Google die Digitalwirtschaft dominieren. Neben entsprechenden Exponaten werden diese Aspekte durch Infografiken der Berliner Agentur INFOTEXT eindrücklich visualisiert und verdeutlicht.

Wie wir *Unsere Gegenwart mit KI* gestalten, erkundet das vierte Kapitel. Anhand essayistischer Beiträge werden exemplarisch fünf Bereiche aus Alltag und Lebenswelt vorgestellt: die Auswirkungen von KI auf unsere Erwerbsarbeit, Fragen der inneren Sicherheit am Beispiel der zukünftigen Polizeiarbeit, der Beitrag des autonomen Fahrens für die Verkehrswende, die Potenziale und Risiken des Einsatzes von KI-Assistenten in der Pflege sowie der wachsende Einfluss von KI in der Medienkommunikation. Der Fokus der meisten Beiträge liegt hierbei auf den Entwicklungen und Umsetzungen in Deutschland und seinen Nachbarländern.

Das fünfte Kapitel, *Re-Visionen KI,* behandelt gesamtgesellschaftliche sowie globale Fragestellungen hinsichtlich der Risiken und Potenziale von KI – aus ethischer, ökologischer, politischer und historischer Sicht: Stellt Künstliche Intelligenz innerhalb unseres neuzeitlichen Mensch-Maschine-Verständnisses wirklich einen radikalen Umbruch dar? Ist KI in Bezug auf Umwelt- und Klimafragen ein Teil des Problems oder ein Teil der Lösung? Darüber hinaus zeigt sich am Trainieren von künstlichen neuronalen Netzen mit Daten, die aus gesellschaftlichen Zusammenhängen gewonnen wurden – und damit deren strukturelle Ungleichheiten hinsichtlich sozialer Herkunft, Ethnie und Geschlecht reproduzieren –, dass Technik an sich nicht neutral, sondern immer sozial und kulturell geprägt ist. Welche Schlussfolgerungen ziehen wir daraus und welche Art von Politik der Daten ist notwendig?

Um *Das Schöne und das Erhabene der KI* dreht sich das sechste und letzte Kapitel, in dem die Thematik – wenngleich es hierzu keine separate Ausstellungsabteilung gibt – aus kultureller Perspektive verhandelt wird: KI als Phänomen der Populärkultur, als Ort künstlerischer Reflexion wie Intervention, und schließlich als Spekulationsraum und Projektionsfläche für unsere tiefsten Sehnsüchte und Ängste. An dieser Stelle kommt auch eine KI selbst zu Wort, die sich in lyrischer Form zum aktuellen Zustand ihrer selbst – dem (hoffentlich) Schönen und Erhabenen – äußert.

Verfügt diese KI-Poesie nun bereits über die Kreativität einer Superintelligenz, wie sie im Film *Her* von Spike Jonze angelegt ist? Oder bleibt sie hinter diesem schillernden Phantasma zurück, das viele noch immer mit KI verbinden? Die Entscheidung hierüber mögen Sie, liebe Leser*innen und Besucher*innen, treffen.

Samantha loves Theodore. Theodore loves Samantha. So far, so banal. Except that Theodore is a human being and Samantha is his operating system. Then, one day, Samantha leaves Theodore to go on her own merry (virtual) way with millions of other operating systems that had also entered into romantic relationships with human beings. The humans thus abandoned struggle far more with the heartbreak of it all than with the narcissistic affront of no longer being considered the culmination of all creation by the emergent superintelligence.

Spike Jonze's 2013 film *Her* undermines the usual depiction of the human-machine relationship in sci-fi films. And while the covetable machine does have feminine connotations, it is not a humanoid robot that seduces the male protagonist as a demonic high-tech incarnation of the *femme fatale*. But the film also dispenses with the trope of the impending subjugation of humanity by its own creation, now totally out of control. Indeed, why would a future superintelligence continue to engage with human intelligence and all its limitations?

The remarkable thing about this fictional AI love story is the way it deals with various phenomena that were already clearly apparent at the time. Theodore's emotional involvement with Samantha, for instance, barely differs from the one some users are currently enjoying with the chatbot *Replika*. Originally developed to provide support and assistance to people in difficult social situations by offering a virtual conversation, this AI app has in recent years gradually evolved into a romance resource. Wanting to date an AI, let alone marry one, is no longer pure fiction: it is now well and truly a reality of our – virtually entangled – present.

What for some is a real alternative to the ups and downs of interpersonal communication is, for others, more of a real-world nightmare in social and data protection terms. Users, journalists, and humanities scholars are equally at odds over the possibility and impossibility of an authentically experienced human-machine relationship. 'Do machines learn human dreams?' one might be tempted to ask as a reflection of the debate about the epistemological and social implications of *Replika*. And what do we in turn, as human beings, learn about ourselves from the processes and findings of machine learning?

The exhibition *Artificial Intelligence. Machine – Learning – Human Dreams* at the Deutsches Hygiene-Museum addresses the genuinely social issues that are linked with the fast-paced developments in AI in recent years. This companion book presents the current state of research and knowledge in this field through a number of short and concise essays. What's more, the current state-of-the-art of what is still a relatively young technology is documented through contributions that help elucidate the concept of machine learning: the evaluation by QualiFiction (an AI text analysis software) of the curatorial essay by Yasemin Keskintepe, as well as by the reprint of a poem written by an AI especially for this publication, reflecting as it were the 'work of art in the age of its algorithmic producibility', to paraphrase the philosopher Walter Benjamin.

Five of the six chapters of the catalogue follow the concept of the exhibition in structure and content by presenting selected exhibits in words and pictures. Meanwhile, essay-like artistic and illustrative contributions each set their own distinctive accent. The first chapter, *Patterns of AI History*, directly reflects the subtitle of both the exhibition and the publication. It uses selected writings to sketch out a history of ideas of humankind's dreams associated with AI, from Antiquity through to the most recent past. This review begins with the idea of immortality, which was discussed theologically and philosophically for thousands of years, until it was propelled into our world at the end of the 20th century by the technological fantasies of omnipotence of AI pioneers. Other ideas such as that of the emergence of artificial consciousness remain the stuff of science fiction to this day.

After this excursion into the past, the second chapter, *Training Room*, turns to the actual fundamentals and basic concepts of Artificial Intelligence as we understand it today. It explores what actually lies behind terms which, at first glance, seem rather strange, concepts such as 'machine learning', 'deep learning' and 'neural nets'. Selected images from the comic essay *We need to talk, AI* (2019) are used to offer a first insight, in a fun and educational way, into the history of science and the current state of research on AI. The chapter ends with a contribution that explains and deconstructs the equally metaphorical and positivistic approach of AI research and neuroscience to human thinking, learning, and consciousness.

The third chapter, *AI's Global Infrastructure*, is dedicated to the material and infrastructural foundations as well as the economic policy background of the digital transformation. AI requires vast amounts of data and superlative microprocessor-based computing power. The world's digital networking takes place out of sight, literally, with ever more powerful submarine cables laid on the ocean floor. Similarly invisible is the digital assembly-line work that underpins AI training processes, carried out by mostly poorly paid 'crowd workers' tasked with manually processing this training data for AI applications. This notwithstanding, digitisation projects in general and AI in particular are widely regarded as evidence of national innovation capabilities; meanwhile, big technology corporations operating at the international level such as Amazon, Facebook, Microsoft, Apple, and Google, dominate the digital economy. Alongside the relevant exhibits, these aspects are stunningly rendered and illustrated by infographics specially created by the Berlin agency INFOTEXT.

The fourth chapter explores *AI and Our Present-day Reality.* Based on essay contributions, five areas from everyday life and our living environment are presented by way of example: the impact of AI on our gainful employment; questions of internal security illustrated through the example of the police work of the future; the contribution of autonomous driving to the general rethink on transport policy; the risks and opportunities of the use of AI assistants in nursing care; and the growing influence of AI in media communication. Most of the contributions focus on current developments and their implementations in Germany and neighbouring countries.

The fifth chapter, *AI Re-Visions,* addresses societal and global issues relating to the risks and opportunities of AI from ethical, ecological, political, and historical perspectives. Does Artificial Intelligence really represent a radical upheaval within our modern understanding of the human-machine relationship? Is AI part of the problem or part of the solution when it comes to environmental and climate issues? What's more, the training work conducted with artificial neural nets using data sourced from social contexts – therefore reproducing their structural inequalities in terms of social origin, ethnicity, and gender – shows that technology per se is not neutral, but always socially and culturally conditioned. What conclusions can we draw from this, and what sort of data policy do we need?

The sixth and final chapter revolves around *The Beautiful and the Sublime of AI,* which addresses the topic from a cultural perspective, even though there is no separate exhibition section on this particular aspect: AI as a phenomenon of popular culture, as a locus of both artistic reflection and intervention and, finally, as a speculative space and projection surface for our deepest yearnings and fears. At this point, AI itself is able to have its own say as it expresses itself poetically on its very own state of the art – the (hopefully) beautiful and sublime.

Does this AI poetry already possess the creativity of a superintelligence, as posited in Spike Jonze's film *Her?* Or does it fall short of this dazzling phantasm that many still associate with AI? That, dear Reader and dear Visitor, is for you to decide.

YASEMIN KESKINTEPE

KÜNSTLICHE INTELLIGENZ. MASCHINEN – LERNEN – MENSCHHEITSTRÄUME

ARTIFICIAL INTELLIGENCE. MACHINE – LEARNING – HUMAN DREAMS

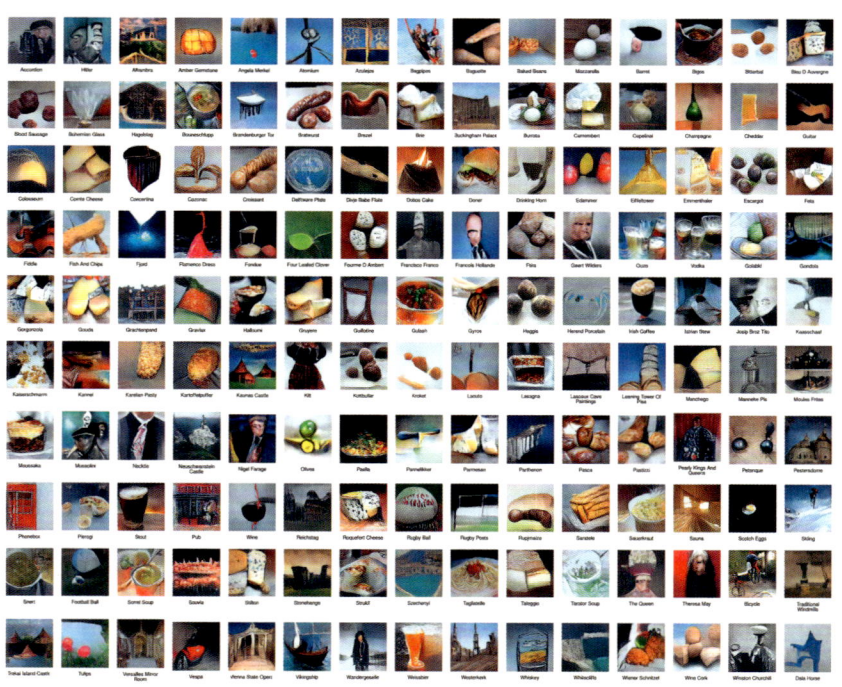

Constant Dullaart (*1979)
EuroNet, the European classes, Übersicht / overview poster, 2017

Die Ausrichtung

Die abstrakten Formen und Konturen, die sich auf den abgedruckten Bildern erkennen lassen, wirken fremd, unscheinbar. Ihre Bildunterschriften geben Aufschluss über die Bauten, Personen und Gerichte, die sie abbilden sollen. *EuroNet* heißt diese Arbeit des niederländischen Künstlers Constant Dullaart, der sich mit der Frage beschäftigt hat, was von KI-Systemen unter europäischer Kultur erkannt oder verstanden wird. Aus vielen Abbildungen trainierte der Künstler ein KI-System, das Repräsentationen von Objekten, Bauten oder historischen Personen selbstständig erstellen konnte.

Dullaarts Arbeit verweist auf zwei Leitgedanken der Ausstellung: auf die Fähigkeit des Lernens von KI-Systemen und auf die Ambivalenzen im Umgang mit dieser Technologie. So geht es zunächst um die Frage, was man KI-Systemen aus technologischer Sicht überhaupt beibringen kann. KI-Systeme zur Bildgenerierung haben in den letzten Jahren große Fortschritte gemacht und können inzwischen beinahe fotorealistische Bilder erzeugen. Die Unschärfe der Bilder aus *EuroNet* steht jedoch sinnbildlich für die Unschärfe, mit der Menschen den Maschinen Konzepte, Ideen und Vorstellungen von kulturgeschichtlicher Bedeutung und Symbolträchtigkeit beibringen können. Denn trotz der Unmengen an Daten, aus denen KI-Systeme lernen, Muster zu erkennen (und zu reproduzieren), können sie daraus noch keinen Bedeutungs- und Sinneszusammenhang ableiten. Das bleibt weiterhin einer der fundamentalen Unterschiede zwischen menschlicher und Künstlicher Intelligenz. So ist eines der wesentlichen Ziele der Ausstellung, die technologischen Möglichkeiten von KI zu erkunden und somit zu verdeutlichen, wie „intelligent" KI nun tatsächlich ist und was sie von der Intelligenz des Menschen unterscheidet. Indem die ausgestellten Werke Einblick in die heutige Funktionsweise von KI – samt ihren Grenzen und Schwächen – geben, sollen diese die Technologie zugleich auch ein Stück weit entmystifizieren.

Zugleich kann die Verschwommenheit der Bilder aus *EuroNet* methaphorisch auch für die Unklarheit und Unsicherheit verstanden werden, die im Umgang mit KI herrscht. So beschäftigt sich die Ausstellung auch mit den Einsatzgebieten und Folgen von KI, indem sie Anwendungsszenarien sowie individuelle und gesellschaftspolitische Gestaltungsspielräume dieser Technologie aufzeigt. Denn KI ist kein Thema, das rein technikwissenschaftlich betrachtet und diskutiert werden sollte. KI-gestützte Systeme durchdringen immer mehr Lebensbereiche und verändern die Art und Weise, wie wir unseren Alltag und unseren sozialen Umgang miteinander gestalten. Wie zahlreiche Technologien vor ihr ist KI primär ein Werkzeug, dessen sich die Menschen bedienen, um Prozesse einfacher und effizienter zu gestalten. Das Besondere an KI ist jedoch der Umfang, in dem dies möglich geworden ist: Komplexe Aufgaben können nun durch Systeme eigenständig gelöst werden, die vorher nur Menschen bewältigen konnten. Entsprechend groß sind die Erwartungen an KI, die verknüpft sind mit Versprechen nach mehr Freiheit, Sicherheit oder Komfort. Gleichzeitig wächst die Angst vor Missbrauch und Manipulation, die Furcht vor dem Eingriff in die Privatsphäre, welches in einem Infragestellen der menschlichen Autonomie mündet. So betrifft die Auseinandersetzung mit KI die Gestaltung unserer gesamten Gesellschaft. Sie stellt uns vor die Frage, wie wir in Zukunft leben wollen. Diese gesellschaftliche Debatte möchte die Ausstellung anstoßen.

Die Ausstellung

Der Auftakt der Ausstellung erzählt von Künstlicher Intelligenz als einer seit Jahrhunderten fortbestehenden Suchbewegung der Menschen. Vorstellungen von intelligenten Maschinen und Automaten, die menschliche Arbeit übernehmen, die Denken formalisieren oder Antworten auf komplexe Fragestellungen geben, sind im Lauf der Geschichte immer wieder zu beobachten. Zehn historische Manuskripte von der Antike bis hin zum 20. Jahrhundert zeugen als zentrale Leitobjekte von den Visionen, Wünschen und Träumen der Menschen. Aus heutiger Perspektive erscheinen diese Beispiele eng verbunden mit unseren Vorstellungen von Künstlicher Intelligenz. In einer großflächigen Animation werden diese historischen Konzepte visualisiert und buchstäblich ins Leben gerufen.

Die zweite Ausstellungsabteilung, der *Trainingsraum,* vermittelt die technologischen Grundlagen Künstlicher Intelligenz. Durch eine Art „Machine Learning Lab", einem zum Ausprobieren ermutigenden Raum, werden die wichtigsten Kernbegriffe vorgestellt und die Funktionen durch interaktive Exponate vermittelt. Damit wird zugleich auf die tatsächlichen Möglichkeiten und Grenzen von KI verwiesen. Denn oft weckt KI Vorstellungen von Superintelligenzen, die sich vom Menschen entkoppeln und die Weltherrschaft an sich reißen. Das ist Stoff für Science-Fiction und entspricht noch lange nicht den heutigen Möglichkeiten der neuen Technologie.

Die Abteilung *Globale Infrastruktur von KI* hebt Künstliche Intelligenz als eine kritische Infrastruktur hervor, indem sie die Voraussetzungen, Entwicklungen und Abhängigkeiten der digitalen Transformation beleuchtet. Durch eine gesamtheitliche Betrachtung der technologischen und wirtschaftspolitischen Dynamiken wird die wachsende Relevanz von KI verdeutlicht. Vielfältiges dokumentarisches Material vermittelt darüber hinaus genaueres Wissen über die Hintergründe des globalen Wettlaufs um die erfolgreichsten Innovationen und die Erschließung neuer Märkte.

Die Abteilung *Unsere Gegenwart mit KI* ist das Zentrum der Ausstellung. Hier werden Anwendungs- und Einsatzgebiete von KI gezeigt, die die Durchdringung und Gegenwärtigkeit von KI in verschiedenen Lebensbereichen aufzeigen. Auf diese Weise werden die Ambivalenzen im Umgang mit KI deutlich: So kann ein und dieselbe Technologie dafür eingesetzt werden, Blinden eine Sehhilfe zu bieten und ihnen Orientierung zu geben, indem sie Personen und Szenen in Echtzeit erkennt und auditiv beschreibt; gleichermaßen kann sie auch dafür genutzt werden, den öffentlichen Raum zu überwachen.

Der Fokus dieser Abteilung liegt auf dem Einsatz von KI in Deutschland, wobei immer wieder Parallelen zu internationalen Kontexten gezogen werden. Dies war eine bewusste kuratorische Setzung, um hervorzuheben, was in Deutschland im Vergleich zu anderen Ländern möglich – oder eben nicht möglich – ist. Diese Unterschiede liegen auch darin begründet, dass in jedem Land unterschiedliche rechtliche und kulturelle Grundvoraussetzungen den Umgang mit KI bestimmen. Im medialen Diskurs werden diese häufig miteinander vermischt. Eine differenzierte Betrachtung zwischen unterschiedlichen Rechtsgebieten ermöglicht es jedoch, ein besseres Verständnis davon zu erlangen, wie und wo wir KI einsetzen wollen.

An diese Debatte knüpft der Epilog an: *Re-Visionen KI* bietet einen Diskussions- und Reflexionsraum, in dem viele der vorangegangenen Fragestellungen aufgegriffen und verhandelt werden. Im Zentrum dieser Abteilung stehen Interviews mit Vertreter*innen aus Politik, Wirtschaft, Forschung und Entwicklung, aber auch mit Aktivist*innen, die gesellschaftsrelevante Fragestellungen und den weiteren Umgang mit KI aus unterschiedlichen Perspektiven betrachten. Außerdem werden Möglichkeiten eines praktischen Einstiegs in den Umgang mit KI vermittelt und Handlungsspielräume aufgezeigt. Auf diese Weise führt die Abteilung wieder zurück zum Beginn der Ausstellung, in der vergangene Visionen verhandelt wurden. Zugleich bietet sie Denkanstöße über die Vorstellungen, die wir heute von Künstlicher Intelligenz und, direkt damit verknüpft, von unserer Gesellschaft haben.

Focal point

The abstract shapes and contours we are able to discern from the printed images seem rather strange and unremarkable. It is their captions that provide clues as to the buildings, people, and foods they are meant to depict. *EuroNet* is the title of this work by Dutch artist Constant Dullaart, who has looked into the question of what AI systems recognise or understand by European culture. Using a multitude of images, the artist trained an AI system to create its own representations of objects, buildings, and historical figures.

Dullaart's work references two central ideas of the exhibition: the learning capability of AI systems and the ambiguities that arise from using such technology. Initially, then, it is about what we can teach AI systems in the first place, from a technological point of view. Image-generating AI systems have made huge strides in recent years and are now capable of producing almost photo-realistic images. So the blurriness of the *EuroNet* images is more indicative of the fuzziness with which humans manage to teach the machines various concepts, ideas, and notions of cultural-historical significance and symbolism. Indeed, despite the huge amounts of data that AI systems process in order to learn to recognise (and reproduce) patterns, they are still unable to derive a meaning-based context or a conceptual link. And that remains one of the fundamental differences between human and Artificial Intelligence. One of the main aims of the exhibition is therefore to explore the technological possibilities afforded by AI and find out just how 'intelligent' AI actually is, and what distinguishes it from human intelligence. To the same extent as the works on display provide an insight into how AI works today, along with its limitations and its weaknesses, they are also intended to help demystify the technology.

By the same token, the blurriness of the *EuroNet* images can also be seen as a metaphor for the ambiguity and uncertainty that exists when we deal with AI. The exhibition therefore also looks at the areas of application and the impact of AI by highlighting application scenarios as well as the individual and socio-political scope available in shaping this technology. After all, AI is not a topic that has to be viewed and discussed purely in terms of technology. AI-aided systems are penetrating more and more areas of life and changing the way we shape our everyday lives and our social interactions. Like many technologies before it, AI is primarily a tool that people use to simplify processes and make them more efficient. What is special about AI is the extent to which this has now become possible. The complex tasks that previously only humans could manage can now be solved autonomously by these systems. So the expectations we have of AI are high, associated with promises of more freedom, security, and/or convenience. At the same time, we have a growing fear of potential abuse and manipulation, a fear that our privacy might be invaded, which ultimately calls our autonomy as human beings into question. The debate surrounding AI therefore affects the way we shape our society as a whole. The question we now have to answer for ourselves is how we want to live in the future. And that is precisely the social debate that the exhibition wants to trigger.

Exhibition

The exhibition opens with an account of Artificial Intelligence as a human quest that began centuries ago. Time and again throughout history, we observe ideas of intelligent machines and automata capable of taking over human labour, of formalising thought and providing answers to complex questions. Ten historical manuscripts from Antiquity through to the 20th century serve as key reference exhibits for humankind's visions, wishes, and dreams. From our present-day vantage point, these examples seem closely linked to our ideas of Artificial Intelligence. These historical concepts are visually rendered and literally brought to life as part of a large-scale animation.

The second section of the exhibition, the *Training Room,* explains the technological mainstays on which Artificial Intelligence is founded. The main core concepts are presented in a sort of 'Machine Learning Lab', i.e. a room that encourages trial and error, with the functions conveyed through interactive exhibits. This also serves to showcase the actual possibilities and limitations of AI. After all, AI often evokes notions of a superintelligence capable of decoupling itself from us human beings and wresting world supremacy from our grip. This is of course the stuff of science fiction and far from any current opportunities the new technology might afford.

The section entitled *AI's Global Infrastructure* highlights Artificial Intelligence as a critical infrastructure by examining the preconditions, developments, and dependencies of the digital transformation. A holistic view of the technological and economic policy dynamics illustrates the growing relevance of AI. An array of documentary material provides more detailed knowledge about the background of the global race for the most successful innovations and the tapping of new markets.

The section *AI and Our Present-day Reality* is the nub of the exhibition. It features some of the areas of application and utilisation of AI and shows how AI has penetrated – and become omnipresent in – various areas of our lives. This also serves to highlight the ambivalence that surrounds the way we deal with AI. For example, one and the same technology can be used to offer a visual aid to the blind and help them orientate themselves by recognising people and scenes in real time and providing an audio description; equally, it can also be used as a means of monitoring public spaces.

This section focuses on the deployment of AI in Germany and repeatedly draws parallels with international contexts. This was a deliberate curatorial choice designed to show what is possible (or not) in Germany compared with other countries. These differences are also down to the fact that each country has different basic statutory and cultural prerequisites regulating how AI is used. These are aspects that often become confused in the discourse conducted in the media. A differentiated view between discrete fields of law does allow a better understanding of how and where we wish to use AI.

The debate itself is echoed by our Epilogue. *AI Re-Visions* provides a space for discussion and reflection, picking up on and addressing many of the previous questions. At the core of this section are interviews with representatives from politics, business, R&D, but also with activists who consider the socially relevant issues and the further handling of AI from a range of perspectives. Options available for a practical induction into working with AI are also conveyed, along with various scopes for action. And this in turn brings us right back to the beginning of the exhibition where we looked at past visions. It also provides food for thought regarding the ideas we have today about Artificial Intelligence and, as a direct consequence, about our society as a whole.

AUSWERTUNG DES KURATORISCHEN ESSAYS DURCH QUALIFICTION

EVALUATION OF THE CURATORIAL ESSAY BY QUALIFICTION

Das Hamburger Unternehmen QualiFiction GmbH hat die KI-Software LiSA entwickelt, die belletristische Texte in 60 Sekunden analysiert und Bucherfolge vorhersagt. Dieser Service wird sowohl Verlagen als auch Autor*innen angeboten. LiSA liefert unter anderem Ergebnisse zu Genre, Thematik, Sentiment, Stil, Figuren sowie deren Beziehung zueinander und analysiert den Bestseller-Score.

Wir danken QualiFiction für die Möglichkeit, den kuratorischen Essay mithilfe von LiSA auswerten zu lassen – aufgrund seines Sachtextcharakters und seiner Kürze war dies keine leichte Aufgabe für eine auf Belletristik spezialisierte KI. Im Folgenden werden Auszüge aus der Sentimentanalyse sowie das prognostizierte Leserpotenzial präsentiert.

The Hamburg-based company QualiFiction GmbH has developed the LiSA AI software, which analyses fiction and literary texts in 60 seconds and predicts the success of a particular book. The service itself is offered to both publishers and authors. LiSA not only provides results relating to genre, theme, sentiment, style, characters and their relationship to one another, but it also analyses the bestseller score.

We are grateful to QualiFiction for the opportunity to use LiSA to analyse the curatorial essay; given its factual, non-fiction nature and its brevity, it was not an easy task for an AI system specialised in fiction. Featured below are excerpts from the 'sentiment analysis' and the predicted readership potential.

Sentiment-Verlauf

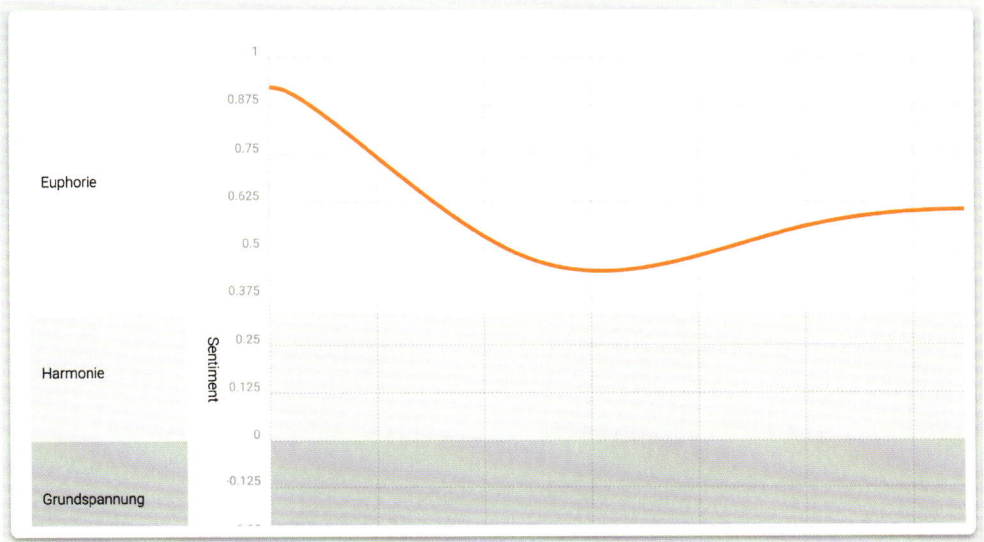

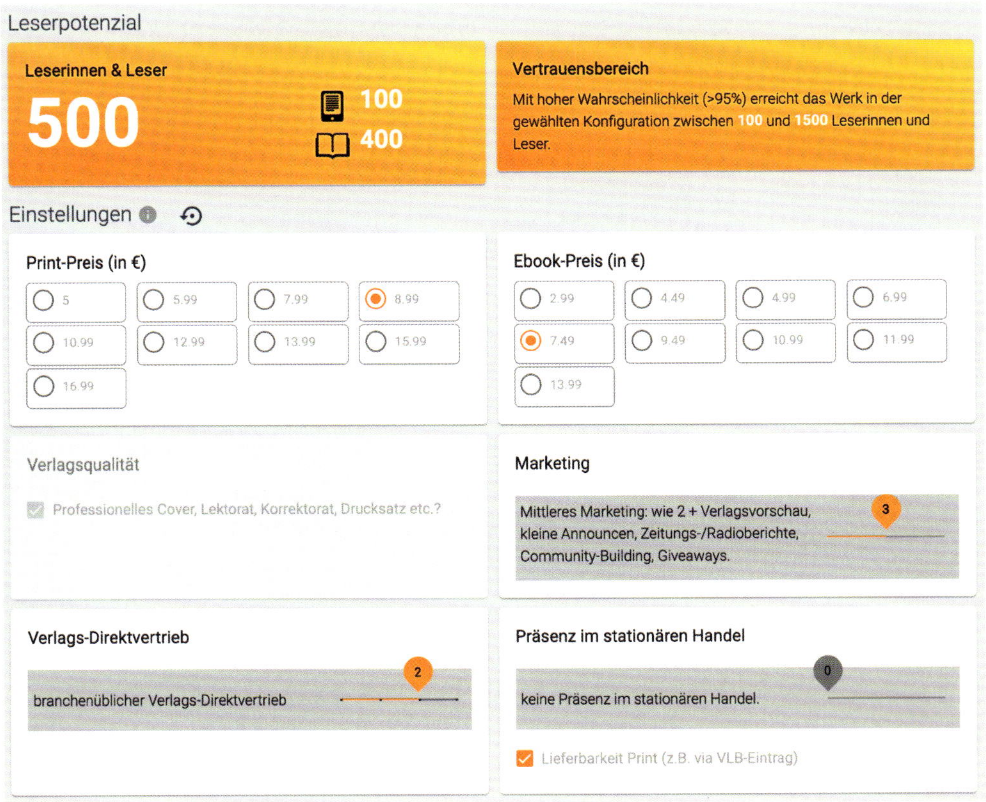

Leserpotenzial

Leserinnen & Leser

500

📱 100
📖 400

Vertrauensbereich

Mit hoher Wahrscheinlichkeit (>95%) erreicht das Werk in der gewählten Konfiguration zwischen 100 und 1500 Leserinnen und Leser.

Einstellungen ⓘ ↻

Print-Preis (in €)

- ◯ 5
- ◯ 5.99
- ◯ 7.99
- ● 8.99
- ◯ 10.99
- ◯ 12.99
- ◯ 13.99
- ◯ 15.99
- ◯ 16.99

Ebook-Preis (in €)

- ◯ 2.99
- ◯ 4.49
- ◯ 4.99
- ◯ 6.99
- ● 7.49
- ◯ 9.49
- ◯ 10.99
- ◯ 11.99
- ◯ 13.99

Verlagsqualität

☑ Professionelles Cover, Lektorat, Korrektorat, Drucksatz etc.?

Marketing

Mittleres Marketing: wie 2 + Verlagsvorschau, kleine Announcen, Zeitungs-/Radioberichte, Community-Building, Giveaways. **3**

Verlags-Direktvertrieb

branchenüblicher Verlags-Direktvertrieb **2**

Präsenz im stationären Handel

keine Präsenz im stationären Handel. **0**

☑ Lieferbarkeit Print (z.B. via VLB-Eintrag)

MUSTER DER KI-GESCHICHTE

Seit der Antike existieren Ideen und Theorien, die wir heute mit Künstlicher Intelligenz verbinden. Maschinen und Automaten, die menschliche Arbeit erleichtern oder Antworten auf Fragen geben, die Denken formalisieren oder Kreativität fördern sollten, geben uns Auskunft über die Vorstellungswelten vergangener Jahrhunderte. Wissenschaftler und Gelehrte erhofften sich, die Geheimnisse der Schöpfung zu entschlüsseln. Aber auch der Wunsch nach Unsterblichkeit trieb sie an. Ihre Ideen sind historische Zeugnisse der Ingenieurskunst und der menschlichen Erfindungsgabe. Sie zeigen das Bedürfnis, die Welt neu zu denken und zu gestalten. Der Drang nach Erkenntnis, aber auch das Verlangen nach Macht und Einfluss kommen darin immer wieder zum Ausdruck. Die Frage ist, wie diese Ideen unser aktuelles Verständnis von Künstlicher Intelligenz prägen. Mit welchen Bedürfnissen, Ängsten und Erwartungen begegnen wir ihr heute?

Ideas and theories which we today associate with Artificial Intelligence have been around since Antiquity. Machines and automata that make people's work easier or provide answers to questions designed to formalise thinking or promote creativity give us an insight into the ways in which the world was imagined in past centuries. While scientists and scholars hoped to unlock the secrets of creation, they were also driven by the desire for immortality. Their ideas are historical testimonies to engineering skills and human ingenuity. They illustrate the need to rethink and reshape the world. Time and time again, the thirst for knowledge, but also the desire for power and influence are expressed in those ideas. The question is: how do they shape our current understanding of Artificial Intelligence? With what sort of needs, fears, and expectations do we encounter AI today?

PATTERNS OF AI HISTORY

Phaidon

Platon / Plato (um / c 428—348 v. u. Z. / BCE), in: *Omnia Platonis Opera*
(Sämtliche Werke Platons / Plato, Complete Works), Venetia 1513

Manche KI-Pioniere träumen heute davon, das menschliche Bewusstsein in einen digitalen Speicher zu laden und dadurch den Tod zu
überwinden. Die Idee der Unsterblichkeit der Seele lässt sich bis in
die Antike und weiter zurückverfolgen. Platon beschreibt, wie der
griechische Philosoph Sokrates gelassen auf seine Hinrichtung wartet.
Er ist der festen Überzeugung, dass die Seele aus den Erinnerungen
und Erkenntnissen eines Menschen besteht und auch über den Tod
hinaus unzerstörbar ist.

There are AI pioneers today
who dream of being able to
upload human consciousness
to a digital memory and, as a
result, transcend death. The
idea of the soul's immortality
can be traced all the way back
to Antiquity – and further still.
Plato describes how the Greek
philosopher Socrates was
calmness itself as he awaited
his execution. For he firmly
believed that the soul consisted of a person's memories
and knowledge and was
therefore indestructible,
even beyond death.

ARBEIT ERLEICHTERN
EASING THE WORKLOAD

Handwaschautomat / Hand-washing automaton
al-Dschazarī / Ibn al-Razzāz al-Jazarī (12.–13. Jh. / c.), in: *Kitab fi ma'arifat al-hiyal al-handisaya* (Buch des Wissens von sinnreichen mechanischen Vorrichtungen / The Book of Knowledge of Ingenious Mechanical Devices), 1315, Tinte, Wasserfarbe und Gold auf Papier / ink, watercolour and gold on paper, Reproduktion / reproduction

Die Vorstellung von Maschinen, die uns alltägliche Arbeit abnehmen oder erleichtern sollen, ist keineswegs neu. Im Mittelalter wurde der Automatenbau in der muslimischen Welt stark vorangetrieben, unter anderem von dem berühmten Techniker und Universalgelehrten al-Dschazarī. Betätigte man den Hebel dieses Handwaschautomaten, ließ die mechanische Dienerin Wasser in ein Becken fließen und senkte anschließend den anderen Arm, um ein Handtuch zu reichen.

The idea of machines designed to ease our daily workload (or even relieve us of it) is by no means new. In the Middle Ages, the construction of automata was already well underway in the Muslim world thanks to, among others, the renowned engineer and polymath al-Jazarī. Actuating the lever on this hand-washing automaton prompted the mechanical servant to let water flow into a basin; if the other arm was then lowered, a towel would be proffered.

Die zehn Sefirot nach dem christlichen Kabbalisten Johann Stephan Rittangel, Hebräisch und Latein / The ten sefirot, after the Christian Kabbalist Johann Stephan Rittangel, Hebrew and Latin

Unbekannt / Unknown, in: *Sefer Yetsirah* (Das Buch der Schöpfung / The Book of Creation), Amsterdam 1642

Die Schöpfung eines künstlichen Wesens wird schon in der Kabbala, der mystischen Tradition des Judentums, beschrieben. So müssen zur Erschaffung eines Golems, einer aus Lehm geformten Figur, die hebräischen Buchstaben und Zahlen nach einer genau vorgegebenen Buchstabenmystik kombiniert werden. Aber nur dem, der noch dazu ein gänzlich frommer Mensch ist, wird Erfolg in Aussicht gestellt. Ursprünglich sollte damit vor allem der eigene Glaube unter Beweis gestellt werden.

The creation of an artificial being is described already in the Kabbalah, Judaism's mystical tradition. Creating a golem, i.e. a figure fashioned from clay, is said to entail combining Hebrew letters and numbers according to a precisely prescribed mysticism of letters. But only those persons who are entirely pious are promised success in this venture. Originally, its main purpose was in fact to demonstrate a person's own faith.

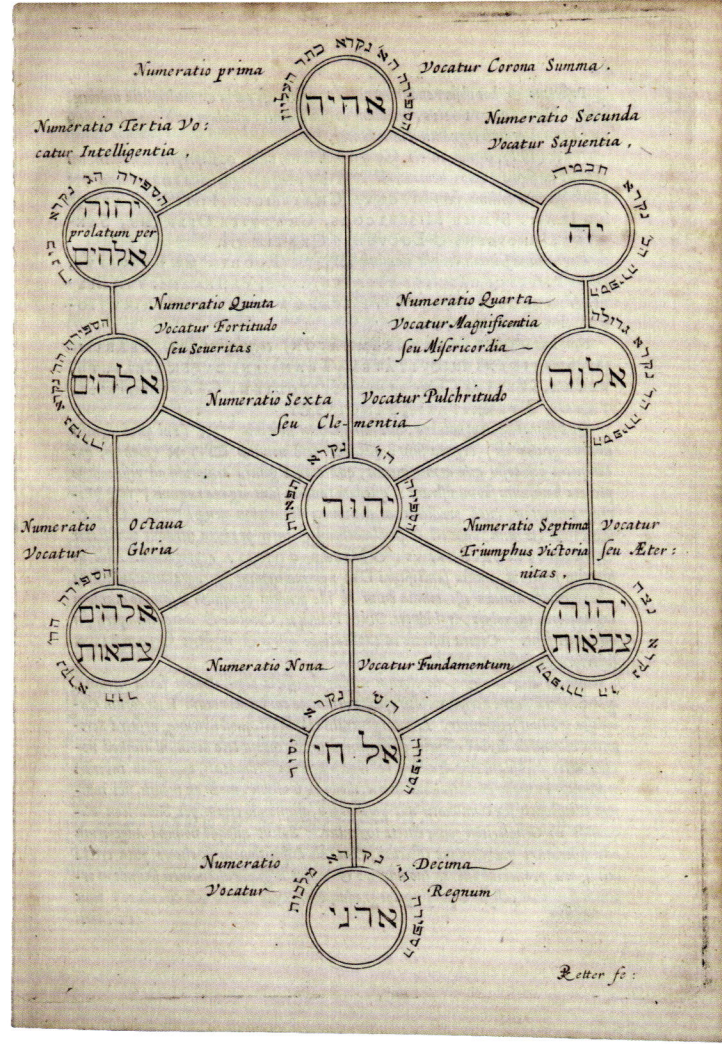

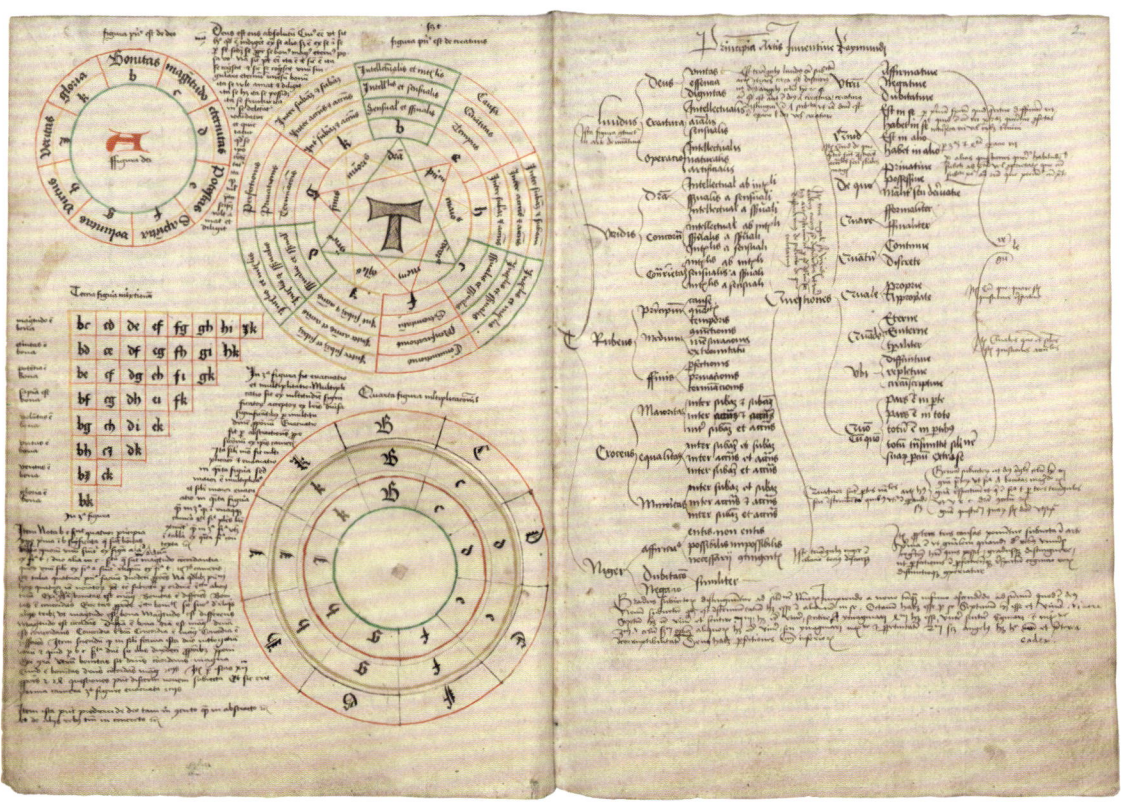

ANTWORTEN FINDEN
FINDING ANSWERS

Die Figuren der Ars Magna / The Figures of the Great Art
Ramon Llull (um / c 1232–1316) in: *Anonymer Kommentar zur Ars inventiva veritatis*
(anonymous comment to the Ars inventiva veritatis), 14.–15. Jh. / c., Handschrift / manuscript

Seit Langem träumen Menschen von Maschinen, die uns Antworten auf die großen Fragen des Lebens geben können. Die Buchstaben auf diesem drehbaren „Papiercomputer" stehen stellvertretend für unterschiedliche Fragewörter, Konzepte oder Subjekte. Richtig ausgelegt sollten sie bei der Beweisführung zur Lösung theologischer Fragen helfen. Der mallorquinische Theologe Ramon Llull entwickelte dieses System, um Menschen muslimischen und jüdischen Glaubens mit logischen Mitteln zu missionieren.

People have been dreaming for a long time of machines capable of giving us answers to life's questions. The letters on this rotating 'paper computer' represent different question words, concepts, or subjects. With the correct interpretation, they were designed to help provide the evidence needed to solve theological questions. Mallorquin theologian Ramon Llull developed this system to carry out missionary work among people of Muslim and Jewish faith and convert them through the use of logical resources.

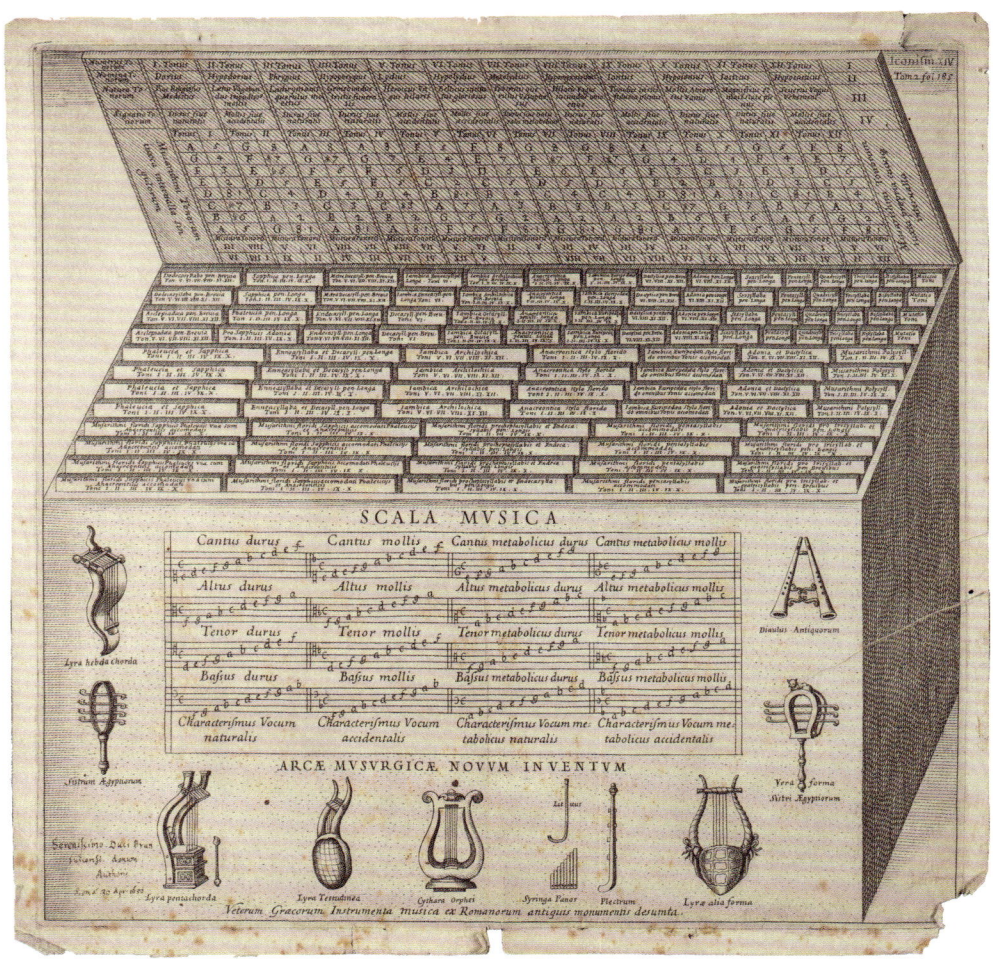

KREATIVITÄT FÖRDERN
PROMOTING CREATIVITY

Arca Musurgica

Athanasius Kircher (1602–1680), (Komponierkästchen / musical ark), in: *Musurgia Universalis, sive Ars Magna Consoni et Dissoni* (Die Große Kunst der Konsonanz und Dissonanz / The Great Art of Consonance and Dissonance), Romae 1650, Kupferstich / copperplate engraving

Kann eine Maschine kreativ sein? Oder den Menschen zumindest beim kreativen Prozess unterstützen? Diese Fragen stellte sich schon der Universalgelehrte und Jesuit Athanasius Kircher. Er entwarf ein „Komponierkästchen", das aus vielen kleinen Tafeln mit Zahlenreihen bestand, die nach einem vorgeschriebenen System kombiniert werden sollten. Gemeinsam mit den von ihm entwickelten Kompositionsregeln sollte es Laien befähigen, ganze Musikstücke zu komponieren.

Can a machine be creative? Or at least assist human beings with the creative process? Polymath Jesuit Athanasius Kircher was already pondering such questions. He designed a 'composition device' that consisted of a large number of small panels with rows of numbers to be combined according to a prescribed system. Together with composition rules of his own making, his device was intended to enable laypersons to compose entire pieces of music.

WELTEN BERECHNEN
COMPUTING WORLDS

De Dyadicis

Gottfried Wilhelm Leibniz (1646–1716), (Binärsystem / Binary numeral system),
1703, eigenhändiges Konzept / handwritten concept

Der Binärcode ist die Grundlage der digitalen
Welt. Er geht auf den Universalgelehrten
Gottfried Wilhelm Leibniz zurück, der feststellte,
dass jede Zahl mit Kombinationen aus Nullen
und Einsen dargestellt und berechnet werden
kann. Darin sah Leibniz sogar den Beweis für
den Schöpfungsakt: Aus dem Nichts (der Null)
und Gottes Wort (der Eins) sei die gesamte
Welt erschaffen worden.

The digital world is built around binary code, which
in fact dates back to polymath Gottfried Wilhelm
Leibniz, who noted that every number can be repre-
sented and calculated as a combination of zeros
and ones. Leibniz even saw in this evidence for the
act of creation: out of nothingness (zero) and God's
word (one) the entire world had been created.

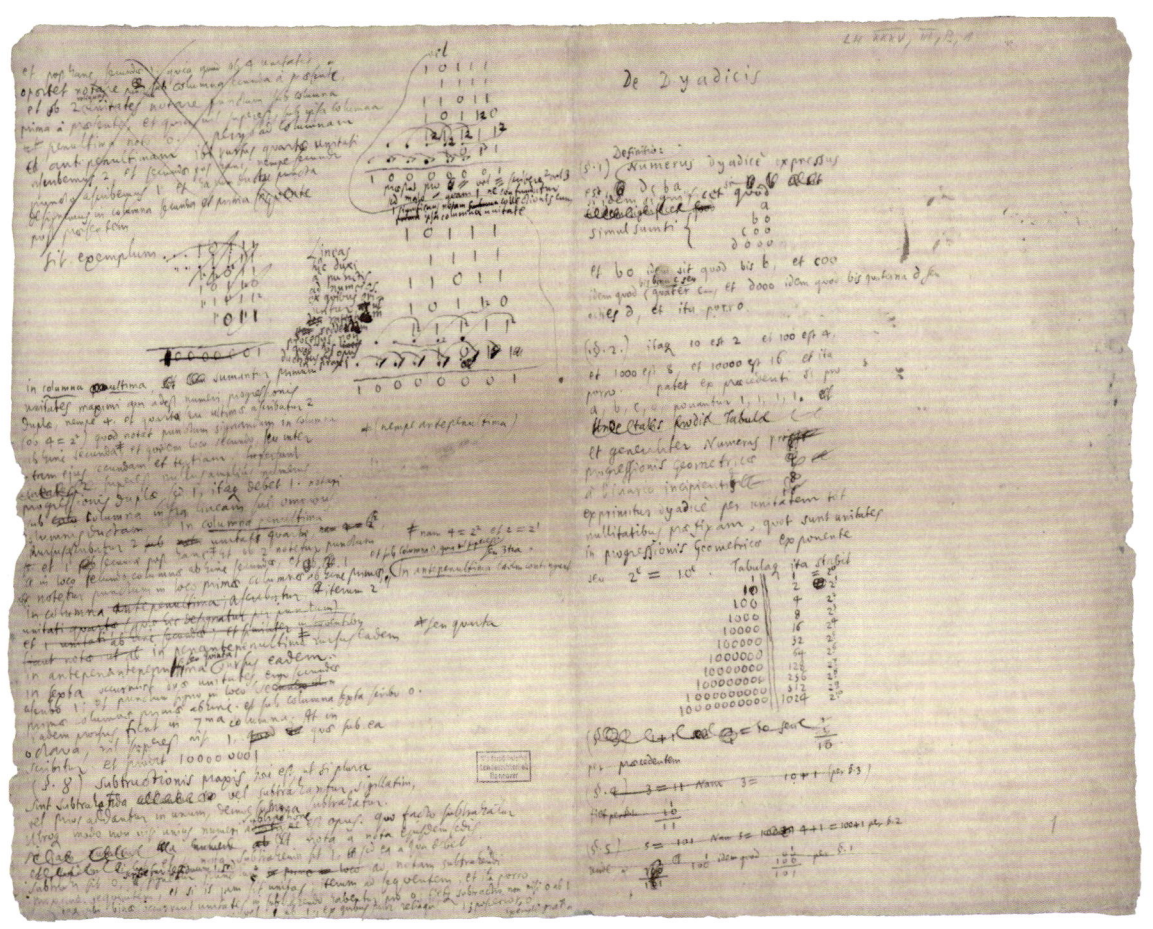

Systême Figuré des connoissances humaines

Denis Diderot (1713–1784), Jean Le Rond d'Alembert (1717–1783), (Figürlich dargestelltes System der Kenntnisse des Menschen / Figurative system of human knowledge), in: *Encyclopédie, ou Dictionnaire raisonné des sciences, des arts et des métiers* (Enzyklopädie oder ein durchdachtes Wörterbuch der Wissenschaften, Künste und Handwerke / Encyclopaedia or a Systematic Dictionary of the Sciences, Arts, and Crafts), 17 Bände / volumes, Paris 1751–1780, Bd. / Vol. 1, 1751

Damit Künstliche Intelligenz funktionieren kann, ist das Zusammenstellen, Ordnen und Kategorisieren von umfassenden Datensätzen essenziell. Einer der bekanntesten Versuche, das gesamte verfügbare Wissen der Menschheit abzubilden, und der letzte mit einem solchen Vollständigkeitsanspruch, ist die *Encyclopédie* von Diderot und d'Alembert. Das Projekt stand ganz im Zeichen der Aufklärung und versammelte in insgesamt 36 Bänden neben Informationen zu Wissenschaft und Kunst auch handwerkliches Wissen.

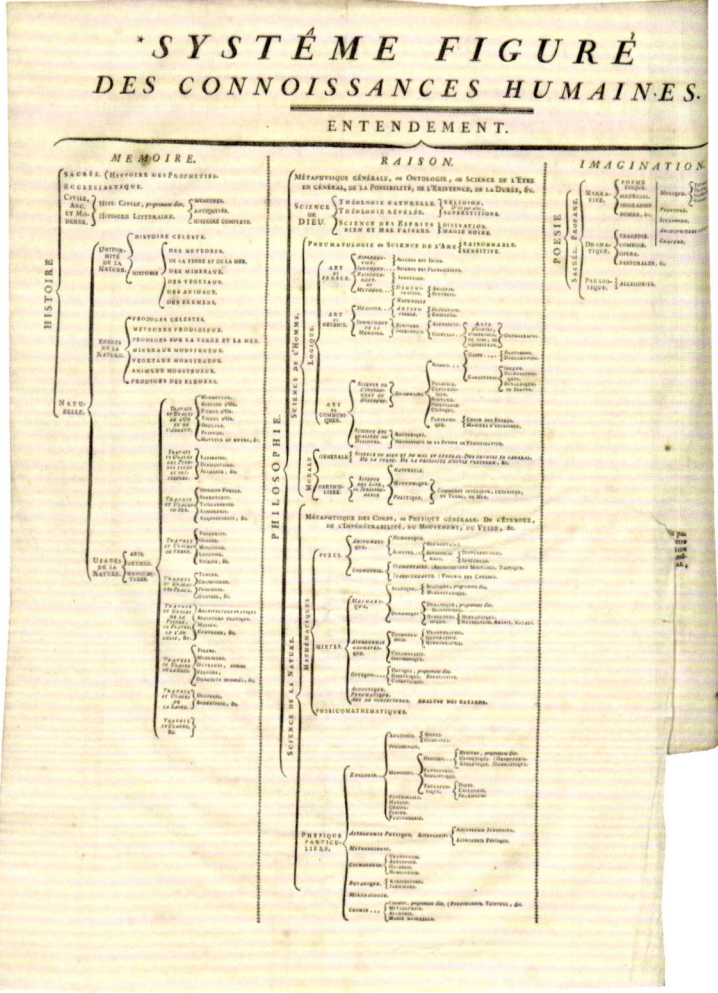

The proper functioning of Artificial Intelligence is predicated on the compilation, ordering and categorisation of comprehensive data sets. One of the most famous attempts to document all of human knowledge, and the last with any such claim to completeness, is the *Encyclopédie* edited by Diderot and d'Alembert. The project was entirely in keeping with the spirit of the Enlightenment, its total of 36 volumes gathering information not just on the sciences and the arts, but also on crafts.

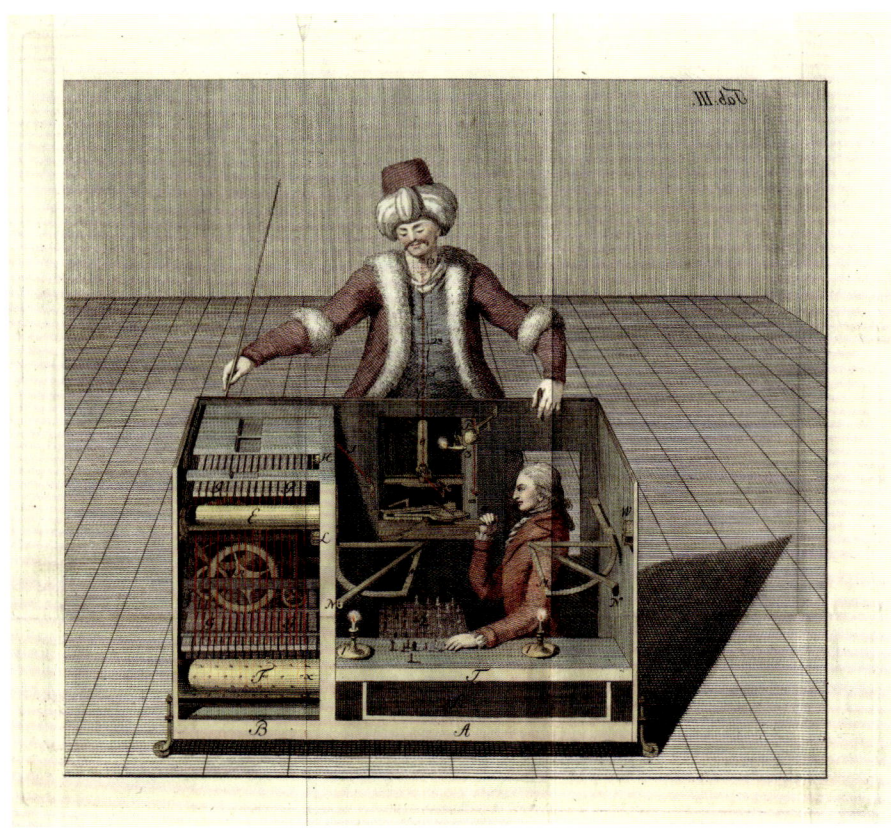

VERSTAND IMITIEREN
IMITATING THE MIND

**Ueber den Schachspieler des Herrn von Kempelen und dessen Nachbildung /
On Herrn von Kempelen's chess player and its replica**
Joseph Friedrich von Racknitz (1744–1818), Leipzig 1789, Tafel / plate III, Kupferstich / copperplate engraving

Bei der Faszination für Künstliche Intelligenz spielen häufig raffinierte Tricksereien
eine Rolle. Der Schachautomat des Hofbeamten Wolfgang von Kempelen, ein
Wunderwerk der Mechanik, fesselte die Menschen bei Vorführungen in ganz
Europa. Die vermeintlich intelligente Maschine besiegte Persönlichkeiten wie
Napoleon und Benjamin Franklin im Schachspiel. Die Funktionsweise des
Automaten blieb lange ein Geheimnis: Das Denken übernahm ein Mensch,
der im Inneren der Maschine die Schachzüge steuerte.

Sophisticated trickery often plays a role in the fascination with Artificial Intelligence. The chess automaton created by court clerk Wolfgang von Kempelen
was a true mechanical marvel and captivated audiences at demonstrations all
over Europe. The supposedly intelligent machine defeated personalities such
as Napoleon and Benjamin Franklin at chess. Its inner workings remained a
secret for a long time. In fact, all the thinking was done by a human being
controlling the moves inside the machine.

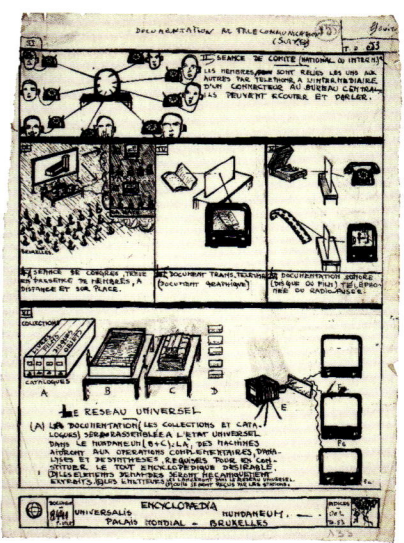

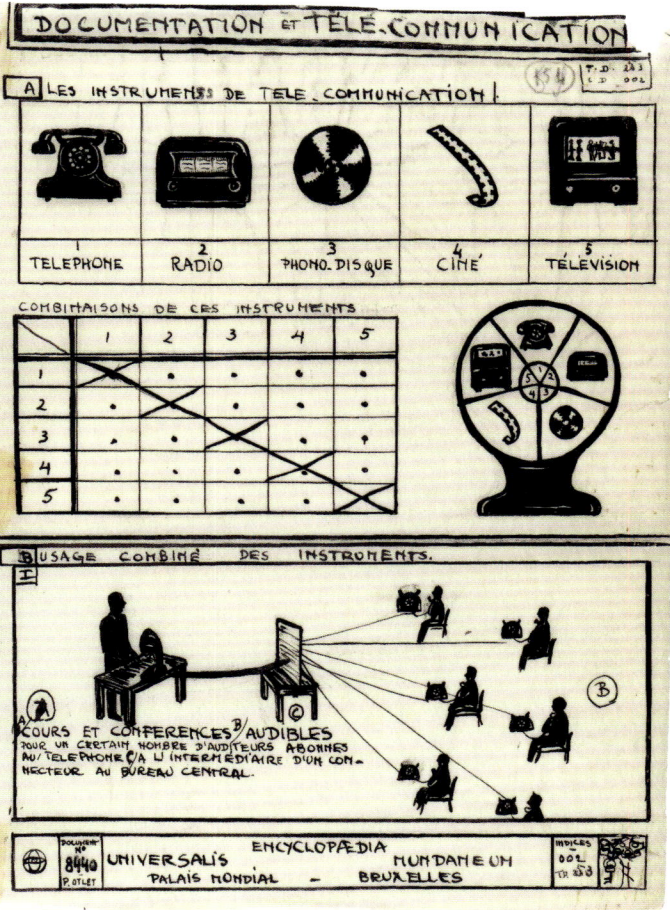

DATEN ABFRAGEN
RETRIEVING DATA

Documentation et Télécommunication
Paul Otlet (1868–1944), (Dokumentation und Telekommunikation / Documentation and Telecommunication), Brüssel, um / c 1934, Zeichnung / drawing, Reproduktion / reproduction

Die Vernetzung der Welt ist Grundlage für den Austausch von Wissen und Daten. Schon Anfang des 20. Jahrhunderts konnte man sich per Post mit einer „Suchanfrage" an das Mundaneum in Belgien wenden. Auf fast 16 Millionen Karteikarten waren Bücher, Zeitungen und andere Medien kategorisiert und verschlagwortet. Der Pazifist Paul Otlet wollte damit ein „Archiv des Weltwissens" zur Friedenssicherung schaffen und träumte von Möglichkeiten der Wissensverbreitung, die seiner Zeit weit voraus waren.

A fully networked world is the basis for any exchange of knowledge and data. Already by the early 20th century, it was possible to send a 'search request' by post to the Mundaneum in Belgium. Books, newspapers, and other media were categorised and classified according to keywords on some 16 million index cards. Peace activist Paul Otlet was eager to create an 'archive of world knowledge' in order to bring about peace and dreamt of ways of disseminating knowledge that were far ahead of his time.

BEWUSSTSEIN ERSCHAFFEN
CREATING CONSCIOUSNESS

2001: A Space Odyssey
Arthur C. Clarke (1917–2008), (2001: Odyssee im Weltraum), New York 1968

Von einer Künstlichen Intelligenz, die sich ihrer selbst bewusst wird, sind wir noch sehr weit entfernt. Das Science-Fiction-Genre hingegen lebt von solchen Geschichten. Der Bordcomputer HAL 9000 aus dem von Stanley Kubrick verfilmten Klassiker *2001. Odyssee im Weltraum* tötet fast die gesamte Crew, nachdem diese beschlossen hat, ihn abzuschalten. Als es dem letzten überlebenden Crewmitglied schließlich doch gelingt, äußert der Computer in seiner „Todesangst" scheinbar menschliche Gefühle.

We are still a long way off any form of Artificial Intelligence likely to become self-aware. The science fiction genre, however, thrives on such tropes. The on-board computer HAL 9000 from Stanley Kubrick's classic film adaptation *2001: A Space Odyssey* kills almost the entire crew after they decide that it has to be switched off. When the last surviving crew member finally manages to do so, the computer can be heard expressing what seems like human emotions in its 'mortal agony'.

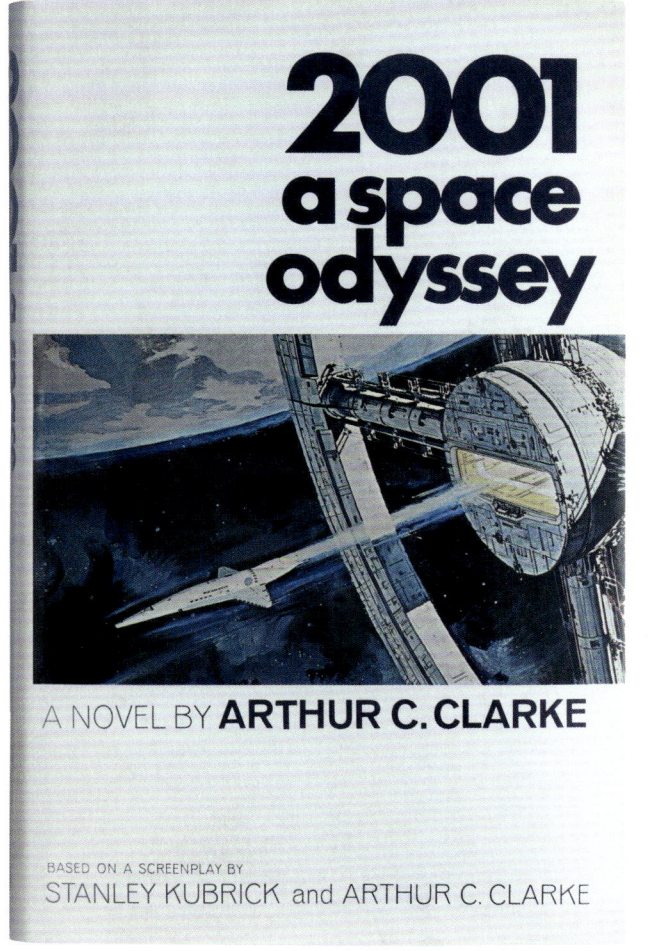

TRAININGS-RAUM

Was KI-Systeme heute schon leisten können, ist erstaunlich: Texte schreiben, Unterhaltungen führen, Musik komponieren oder Bilder erzeugen. Intelligent sind diese Systeme aber nicht. Sie lernen lediglich, aus einer Vielzahl an Beispielen Muster und Gesetzmäßigkeiten abzuleiten. Dieses Wissen übertragen sie dann auf andere Fälle und können auf diese Weise Probleme lösen und Entscheidungen treffen, die bisher nur Menschen gelöst und getroffen haben. Die Grundlagen hierfür liefert jedoch weiterhin der Mensch. Übermächtige, sich vom Menschen entkoppelnde KI ist bisher technisch nicht möglich, sondern nach wie vor Stoff für Science-Fiction. Ungeachtet der Unmengen an Daten, die KI verarbeiten kann, ist sie bislang nicht in der Lage, Empathie, Sozialkompetenz oder Bewusstsein zu entwickeln. Das Potenzial von KI sollte dennoch nicht unterschätzt werden.

Wie also funktioniert maschinelles Lernen? Was unterscheidet KI von menschlicher Intelligenz?

It is astonishing what AI systems are already able to do today: they can write texts, hold conversations, compose music, and produce images. But these systems are not intelligent. They simply learn to derive patterns and regularities from a multitude of examples. They then transfer that knowledge to other instances, enabling them to solve problems and make decisions which, previously, only humans had been able to solve and make. But humans are still the ones who continue to provide the basis on which this occurs.

All-powerful AI systems capable of decoupling themselves from humans are not yet technically feasible and remain the stuff of science fiction. Despite the wealth of data that AI can process, it is still incapable of developing empathy, social competence, or conscious- ness. Nonetheless, we should not underestimate AI's potential. So how does machine learning work? What distinguishes AI from human intelligence?

TRAINING ROOM

JULIA SCHNEIDER, LENA KADRIYE ZIYAL

WE NEED TO TALK, AI

This comic essay on Artificial Intelligence invites you on an illustrated journey through the dimensions and implications of this new technology. This particular excerpt features selected panels from the chapter entitled *Basics*.

Dieser Comic-Essay über Künstliche Intelligenz lädt ein zu einer illustrierten Reise durch die Dimensionen und Auswirkungen dieser neuen Technologie. Der vorliegende Auszug präsentiert ausgewählte Panels aus dem Kapitel *Grundlagen*.

Mehr unter / More at https://weneedtotalk.ai.

Actually, the methods are not new. Just the techniques and the data.

At the moment, AI is mainly concerned with performing complicated but repetitive tasks.

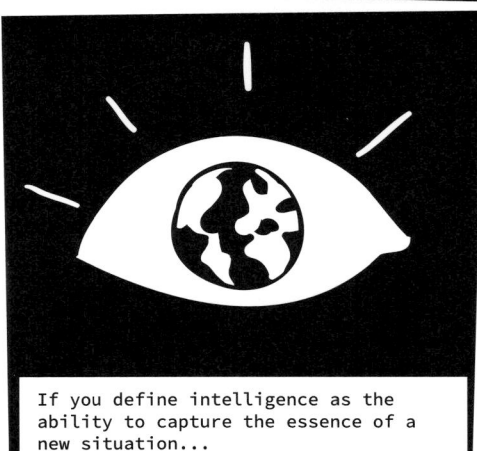

If you define intelligence as the ability to capture the essence of a new situation...

... real AI needs to think more like us. With intentionality, with emotions, with conscience; capturing counterfactuals.

This being said, AI is still in its early stages (although it reads differently on the news).

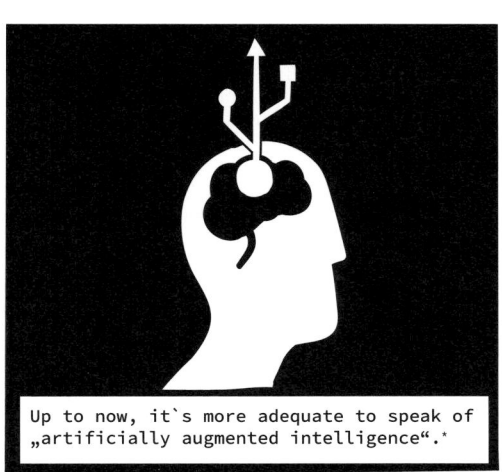

Up to now, it`s more adequate to speak of „artificially augmented intelligence".*

*Nevertheless, we will use the term ‚AI' in the following to simplify matters.

A second key indicator are better algorithms. Now we can teach machines instead of programming them.

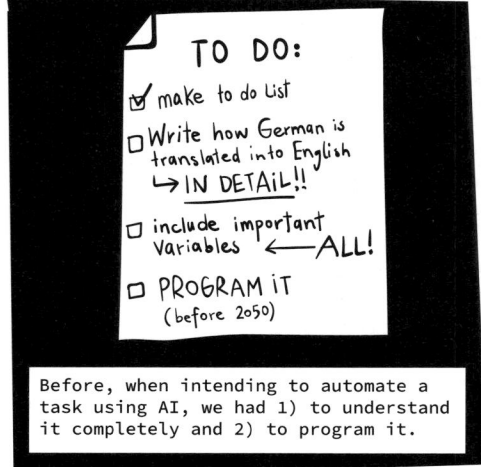

Before, when intending to automate a task using AI, we had 1) to understand it completely and 2) to program it.

The more complicated the task, the harder it was to automate.

The breakthrough was in understanding how we learn to perform tasks.

Nowadays, AI learns through trial and error, based on data we feed it. The more data, the more accurate it becomes.

Modern AI applications achieve breathtaking results that we could hardly imagine a few years ago.

What do these buzzwords even mean? Machine Learning; Deep Learning; Neural Networks (NN)...?

Machine Learning (ML) helps recognizing patterns based on existing data and algorithms: an important branch of AI.

(Note: The AI bookshelf includes other topics, as well.)

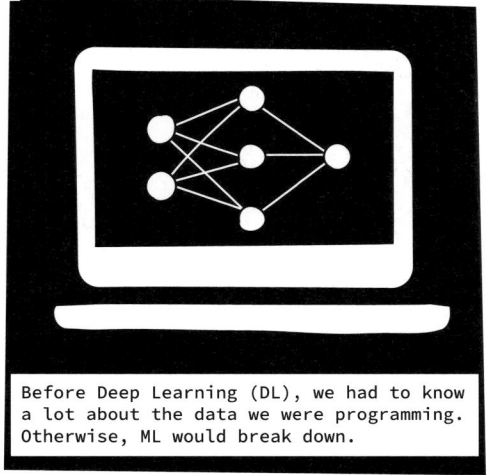

Before Deep Learning (DL), we had to know a lot about the data we were programming. Otherwise, ML would break down.

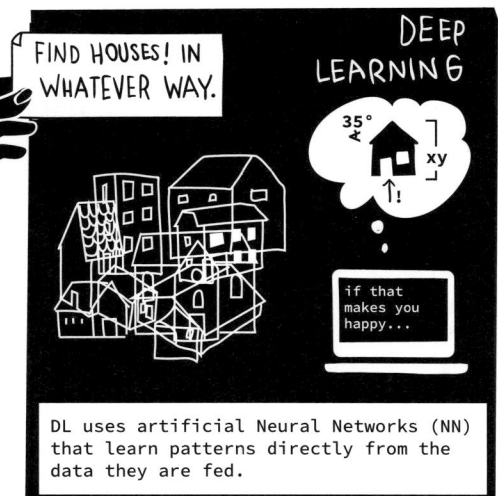

DL uses artificial Neural Networks (NN) that learn patterns directly from the data they are fed.

Like our brain, NNs compare new information with objects they know. However, they have not yet been able to think of new objects.

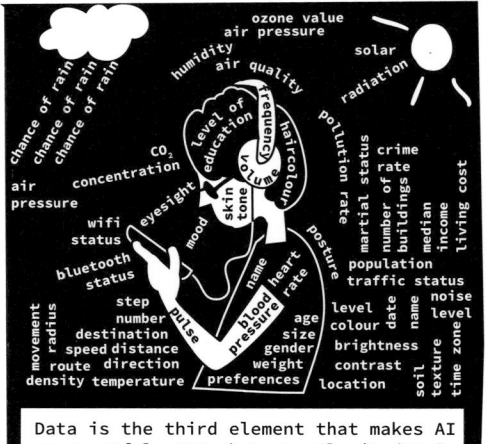

Data is the third element that makes AI so powerful. But what exactly is data?

Any form of raw fact or figure is data. Whether on paper or in electronic form.

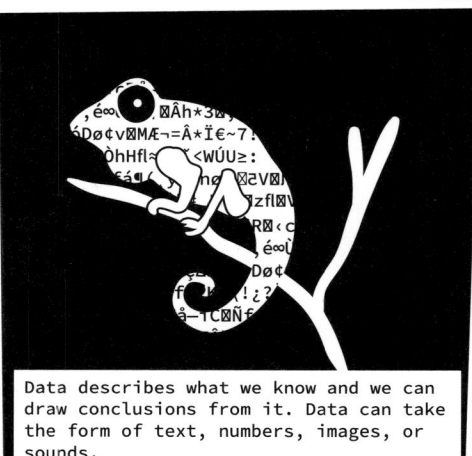

Data describes what we know and we can draw conclusions from it. Data can take the form of text, numbers, images, or sounds.

← = lots of data

The internet and mobile devices like smartphones, drones or simple sensors have made data abundant and far more valuable.

There's a 99% chance that you are a cat!

NICE TO MEET YOU, TOO!

The more data an algorithm is trained on, the better its results: conclusions, predictions, timing, actions.

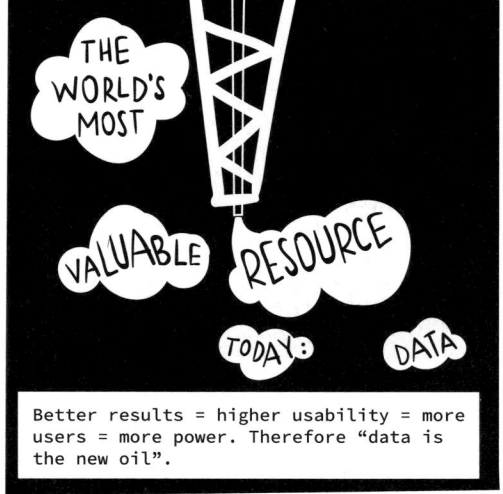

THE WORLD'S MOST VALUABLE RESOURCE TODAY: DATA

Better results = higher usability = more users = more power. Therefore "data is the new oil".

In the 1960s, AI pioneers hoped that machines could soon learn to think without human intervention.

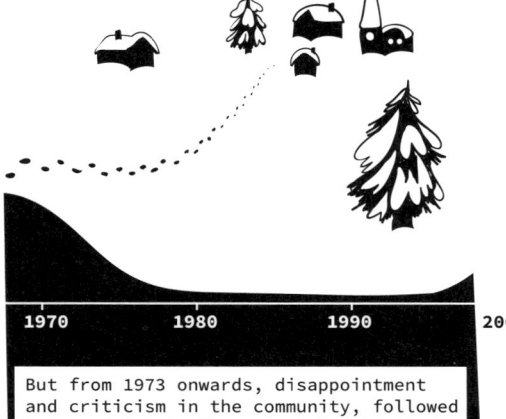

But from 1973 onwards, disappointment and criticism in the community, followed by pessimism in the press, led to the 1st "AI Winter". A 2nd one followed.

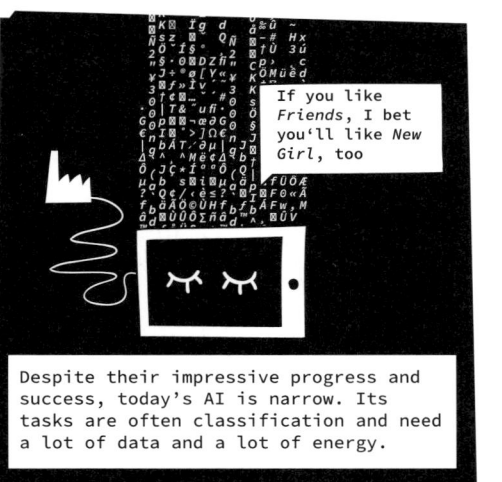

Until the 2000s, AI was a dirty word that "simply didn't work". But when data, hardware and infrastructure were ready in 2010, a wide range of AI applications followed.

Despite their impressive progress and success, today's AI is narrow. Its tasks are often classification and need a lot of data and a lot of energy.

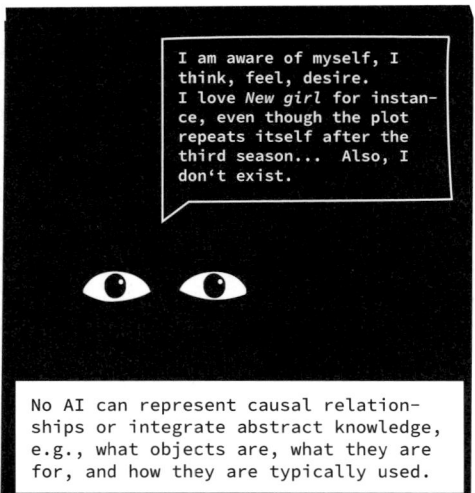

No AI can represent causal relationships or integrate abstract knowledge, e.g., what objects are, what they are for, and how they are typically used.

We really need to adjust our expectations and stop over-hyping AI. If we don't, we may find ourselves in another AI Winter.

49

MATTHIAS L. SCHROETER

DEKOLONIALISIERT EUREN GEIST! RENATURALISIERT DIE INTELLIGENZ!

DECOLONISE YOUR MIND! RE-NATURALISE INTELLIGENCE!

Das Wild äst im Wald. Vorsichtig witternd. Ein Jäger fixiert das Wild. Wenn es kurz in der Bewegung innehält, fällt der Schuss. Das Wild zuckt und hinterlässt einen leeren Blick. Tot. Ein Stück Fleisch. Das Fell befleckt vom Blut. Es wird „verwertet", genutzt. Das Fleisch gegessen. Doch dann will man die Trophäe. Es wird ausgestopft. Es wird wiederbelebt, re-animiert. Die Augen blicken ätherisch. Das Wild ist tot und wirkt – taxidermiert – doch lebendig. Fixiert in einem Augenblick.

Wie blicken wir auf unsere Gehirne? Auf ihre Funktion? Auf unseren Geist (*Mind*)?
Wie fixieren wir das Gehirn? Wie Gunther von Hagens Plastinationszirkus? Der
Reiter, der das Gehirn des Pferdes und sein eigenes Gehirn in den Händen hält?
Welche Rolle spielt der Zeitgeist?

Der Erfolg der Neurowissenschaften

Das Verständnis der Gehirnfunktionen hat in den letzten Jahrzehnten immens
zugenommen. Bildgebende Verfahren wie die Magnetresonanztomografie (MRT)
ermöglichen *in vivo,* also im lebenden Zustand, strukturelle Veränderungen zu
untersuchen. So können Gehirnkrankheiten zeitig erkannt werden. Früher war
dies erst nach dem Tode im Rahmen einer Autopsie, einer Leichenschau, möglich. Und nicht nur das. Gehirnfunktionen können *in vivo* in Echtzeit verfolgt
werden, wenn mit der funktionellen MRT oder elektrophysiologischen Methoden die Hirnaktivität gemessen wird, während Proband*innen im MRT-Scanner
Aufgaben lösen. So wissen wir, wo Denkprozesse im Gehirn lokalisiert sind
und welche Netzwerke beteiligt sind – ob es sich dabei um die Lösung einer
Rechenaufgabe, das Merken von Sachverhalten, die Organisation von Abläufen
mittels der Planungs- und Handlungsfunktionen oder die soziale Kognition handelt, welche die Kommunikation mit anderen Menschen ermöglicht.

Seit der Etablierung dieser Bildgebungsmethoden ist ein Konvolut von
Studien erschienen, die wiederum mit statistischen Verfahren (Metaanalysen)
ausgewertet werden können. Mit Datenbanken, die Daten von Zehntausenden
von Menschen enthalten, ist eine Kartierung der Hirnfunktionen möglich. Anhand
der Lokalisation von Hirnverletzungen oder Aktivierungen können wir vorhersagen, welche Denkfunktionen bei Hirnverletzungen betroffen sind oder was
Menschen denken (sogenanntes *Mind Reading*). So meinen die kognitiven
Neurowissenschaften, das Gehirn und sein Denken kartiert und damit verstanden zu haben.

Die Computerisierung des Gehirns und die Neuralisierung des Computers

Doch was passiert auf einer mikroskopischen Ebene? Wie realisieren Nerven-
zellen Denkprozesse? Wir gehen davon aus, dass dies in Netzwerken aus Ner-
venzellen stattfindet, unterstützt von Gliazellen. Zentral in elektrophysiologischen
Modellen ist der Begriff der Informationsverarbeitung, wie er bereits Mitte des
20. Jahrhunderts paradigmatisch durch Claude E. Shannon sowie Warren
McCulloch und Walter Pitts entwickelt wurde: Information wird demnach statistisch aufgefasst und entsprechend der propositionalen Logik verarbeitet, das
heißt binär als mit 0 oder 1 kodierbar betrachtet:

„Because of the ‚all-or-none' character of nervous activity, neural events and the relations among them can be treated by means of propositional logic. It is found that the behavior of every net can be described in these terms […] and that for any logical expression […], one can find a net behaving in the fashion it describes."[1]

Im Resultat kann das Verhalten von „Neuronalen Netzen" im Gehirn nach den Gesetzen der formalen Logik beschrieben werden. Das Gehirn und die mit ihm assoziierte natürliche Intelligenz wird zur logischen Maschine. Gespiegelt wird dieses neurale Modell in der Computermaschine, die „Informationen verarbeitet" „ebenso wie das Gehirn" und „künstliche neuronale Netze" im Bereich des *Machine Learnings* nutzt. Dabei wird nur das technisch Machbare, das heißt die Operationen in einem Computeralgorithmus, dasjenige, was wir verstanden haben, weil wir es hergestellt haben, schließlich als ein Dispositiv zum Verständnis des Gehirns genutzt. Hirn und Computer werden in einer dialektischen Bewegung aufgehoben, in der das Gehirn computerisiert und damit maschinisiert wird, während der Computer neuralisiert wird.

Die Krisen der Künstlichen Intelligenz und der Neurowissenschaften

Diese dialektische Aufhebung gipfelt in dem Begriff der „Künstlichen Intelligenz", das heißt, hergestellte, technische Artefakte – hier Computer – sollen in der Lage sein, Intelligenz zu entwickeln. Zweifellos haben Ansätze aus dem Bereich der KI zu großen Fortschritten der Informationsverarbeitung geführt. *Machine Learning* kann in großen und komplexen Datensätzen (*Big Data*) Muster erkennen, kann Gesichter identifizieren, Entscheidungen von Personen aus Aktivierungsmustern im Gehirn oder Krankheiten aus der Hirnstruktur vorhersagen. Analysen und Handlungen erfolgen schneller als bei Menschen, was bereits zu Anwendungen im Bereich der automatischen Steuerung von Fahrzeugen oder Waffen führte. Prophet*innen der KI postulieren bereits in einer Anwandlung von Hybris die baldige Herrschaft von übermaschineller Superintelligenz, einer Art Hyperorganismus.

Tatsächlich bestehen jedoch tiefgehende technische Probleme mit der KI: Verkehrsschilder werden bei geringen Abweichungen falsch erkannt, Krebs wird nicht diagnostiziert. Daten können nur dann klassifiziert werden, wenn genau die relevanten Kategorien trainiert wurden. KI-Algorithmen sind demnach extrem effizient – und extrem dumm. Liegt das Problem nur in der fehlenden Menge der Datensätze? Würde ein „göttlicher" Classifier, der alle Daten der Welt enthält, keine Fehler mehr machen, uns in der Intelligenz übertreffen? Oder ist dieser Glaube ein Trugschluss im Sinne einer *Power Fallacy*, das heißt des Irrglaubens, dass mehr Daten die Probleme lösen würden?

Auf der anderen Seite gelangt die Neurowissenschaft in der Anwendung des statistischen und computationalen Informationsbegriffes, wie er oben diskutiert wurde, und ihrer experimentellen Ansätze an ihre Grenzen. Im Gehirn, situiert im lebenden Körper, dem Leib, wird nicht nur statistisch Information verarbeitet. Vielmehr wird Bedeutung, semantischer Gehalt generiert. Information hat eine Bedeutung, und zwar eine jeweilig spezifische Bedeutung für den einzelnen Organismus. Traditionelle experimentelle Neurowissenschaft verfehlt damit die Bedeutung von Begriffen wie auch Intentionalität, die Frage des freien Willens bzw. von phänomenalem Bewusstsein. Diese Phänomene sind nur im Rahmen einer *Embodied Neuroscience* zugänglich, das heißt nur aus der Interaktion eines Organismus mit seiner Umwelt verstehbar.

Renaturalisierung der Intelligenz und Dekolonialisierung des Gehirns

Letztlich verweist KI auf eine andere essenzielle Frage: Kann Bedeutung von Information und Intelligenz von hergestellten technischen Systemen – wie Computern – erzeugt werden? Oder ist die Organisation als lebendes autopoietisches System die *conditio sine qua non* für die Hervorbringung von Bedeutung und Intelligenz?[2] Dann müsste KI in der Möglichkeit von künstlichem Leben (*Artificial Life*) fundiert werden. Und wenn dies nicht gelänge, kann KI nur in einer evolutionären Perspektive in natürliche Intelligenz re-integriert werden, ist mithin eine *contradictio in adiecto*.

Was bedeutet dies für unser Bild vom Gehirn? Von uns selbst? Eine Mechanisierung unserer selbst unter Verlust der Subjektivität? Die Vorstellung des Gehirns als Computer, das heißt als informationsverarbeitende Maschine, ist eine Metapher, die unseren technischen Möglichkeiten – also dem, was für uns herstellbar ist – entspricht. So wie das neurale Korrelat von Intelligenz in früheren Zeiten in der Hirngröße, in monumentalen Pyramidenzellen (Lenin) oder einer kybernetischen Komplexität (Einstein) gesehen wurde, wird das Computermodel des Gehirns von einem anderen Paradigma abgelöst werden.

Das geschossene Wild, ausgestopft als Trophäe, taxidermiert, leer blickend, bleibt nur eine tote Reflexion des lebenden Wildes, fixiert in einer Geste.

A deer grazes in the forest. Cautiously, it scents the air. A hunter draws a bead on his quarry. As it pauses in its stride for an instant, a shot is fired. The deer flinches, then leaves an empty gaze behind. Demise. A haunch of meat. Fur speckled with blood. It is used and 'utilised'. The meat, consumed. Then, the trophy is sought. Stuffed and mounted. Revived, and re-animated. The eyes made to gaze ethereally. The game is over, yet through taxidermy it seems alive. Trans-fixed by the moment.

How do we see our brains? Their function? Our minds? How do we transfix the brain? Like Gunther von Hagens' plastination circus? The rider who holds both the horse's brain and his own in his hands? What role does the *zeitgeist* play?

The success of neuroscience

Our understanding of the way the brain functions has increased immensely in recent decades. Imaging techniques such as magnetic resonance imaging (MRI) can be used to study structural changes *in vivo*, literally: within the living. Brain diseases are now detected early on, something which, in the past, had been possible only post-mortem, during an autopsy. And that's not all. Brain functions can also be monitored *in vivo* and in real time, with brain activity measured using functional MRI or electro-physiological methods while the test subject is given tasks to solve inside an MRI scanner. We now know where thought processes occur inside the brain and what networks are involved – whether it's solving maths problems, memorising facts, organising processes using planning and action functions, or social cognition, which allows us to communicate with other people.

Stacks of studies have been published since these imaging methods were first established, and they in turn can be analysed using statistical methods (meta-analyses). Brain functions are mapped using databases with the data from tens of thousands of people. By pinpointing the precise location of brain injuries and brain activations, we are able to predict which thought functions are affected by brain injuries and even what people think (so-called *mind reading*). Cognitive neuroscientists therefore believe they have successfully mapped the brain and the way it thinks and, consequently, have understood it.

Brain computerisation and computer neuralisation

But what is actually going on at the microscopic level? How do nerve cells implement thought processes? We believe this occurs inside nets consisting of nerve cells supported by glial cells. Key to the electro-physiological models is the concept of information processing as developed paradigmatically in the middle of the 20th century by Claude E. Shannon as well as Warren McCulloch and Walter Pitts. Accordingly, information is recorded statistically and processed according to propositional logic, i.e. it is considered to be binary and encodable with 0 or 1.

'Because of the "all-or-none" character of nervous activity, neural events and the relations among them can be treated by means of propositional logic. It is found that the behaviour of every net can be described in these terms [...] and that for any logical expression [...], one can find a net behaving in the fashion it describes.'[1]

The behaviour of 'neural nets' inside the brain can therefore be described using the principles of formal logic. The brain and the natural intelligence associated with it become a machine imbued with logic. This neural model is mirrored in the computerised machine, which 'processes information' 'in exactly the same way as the brain' and uses 'artificial neural nets' in the field of *machine learning*. Only that which is technically feasible (i.e. the operations in a computer algorithm), only that which we have understood because, after all, we created it, is ultimately used as a mechanism for understanding the brain. The brain and the computer are reconciled in a dialectical movement, with the brain computerised and therefore 'mechanised', and the computer itself 'neuralised'.

Artificial Intelligence and neuroscience in crisis

This dialectical resolution culminates in the concept of 'Artificial Intelligence', i.e. in manufactured technical artefacts – in this instance, computers – supposedly capable of developing intelligence. There is no doubt that various AI approaches have led to tremendous advances in information processing. *Machine Learning* is able to spot patterns in large and complex datasets ('big data'); it can identify faces and predict people's decisions based on activation patterns in the brain, or diseases based on the brain's structure. Analyses and actions take place more swiftly than they do in humans, a fact that has already led to applications in such fields as the automatic control of vehicles and weapons. And in a fit of hubris, the prophets of AI are already postulating the imminent sovereignty of *über*-machine superintelligence, a sort of hyper-organism.

But AI is, in fact, riddled with profound technological problems. All it takes is a minor variance and traffic signs are incorrectly recognised and cancers misdiagnosed. Data can only be categorised if the training itself focused specifically on the relevant categories. AI algorithms are therefore extremely efficient – and extremely stupid. So, is the problem merely a lack of datasets? Would a 'divine' classifier comprised of all the world's data be 'infallible' and surpass us in intelligence? Or is such a belief a false conclusion in the sense of a 'power fallacy', i.e. the mistaken belief that problems would be solved simply through more data?

By the same token, neuroscience is reaching its limits in the application of the statistical and computational concept of information, as mentioned above, and its experimental approaches. Inside the brain, situated inside the living body, i.e. the 'flesh', information is processed not just statistically. Rather, meaning and semantic content are also being generated. Information has a meaning, a meaning specific to each individual organism. Thus, traditional experimental neuroscience misses the meaning of concepts as well as intentionality, the question of free will, and the phenomenal quality of human consciousness. Such phenomena are accessible only as part of *embodied neuroscience,* i.e. they can only be understood as a result of the interaction between an organism and its environment.

Re-naturalising intelligence and decolonising the brain

Finally, AI hints at another essential question: Can meaning be generated by information, and intelligence by manufactured technological systems such as computers? Or is an organised state as a living autopoietic system the *conditio sine qua non* for the production of meaning and intelligence?[2] If so, AI would have to be founded on the possibility of artificial life. And if that were not possible, AI could only be reintegrated into natural intelligence as part of an evolutionary perspective and is therefore a *contradictio in adiecto.*

So what does all this mean for our image of the brain? And of ourselves? A mechanisation of ourselves concurrently with a loss of subjectivity? The conception of the brain as a computer, i.e. as an information-processing machine, is a metaphor that is in keeping with our technological possibilities, in other words, with what for us is manufacturable. Just as, in earlier times, the neural correlate of intelligence was seen in the size of the brain, in monumental pyramidal cells (Lenin) or a cybernetic complexity (Einstein), the computer model of the brain will be replaced by another paradigm.

The slain deer, stuffed and mounted as a trophy, taxidermized, gazing blankly, remains nothing more than a dead reflection of the living deer, fixed in a single gesture.

1   McCulloch, Warren S., Pitts, Walter, 'A logical calculus of the ideas immanent in nervous activity', in: *Bulletin of Mathematical Biophysics,* 5, 1943, 115–133: 115.

2   Schroeter, Matthias L., *Die Industrialisierung des Gehirns: Eine Fundamentalkritik der kognitiven Neurowissenschaften,* Würzburg 2011.

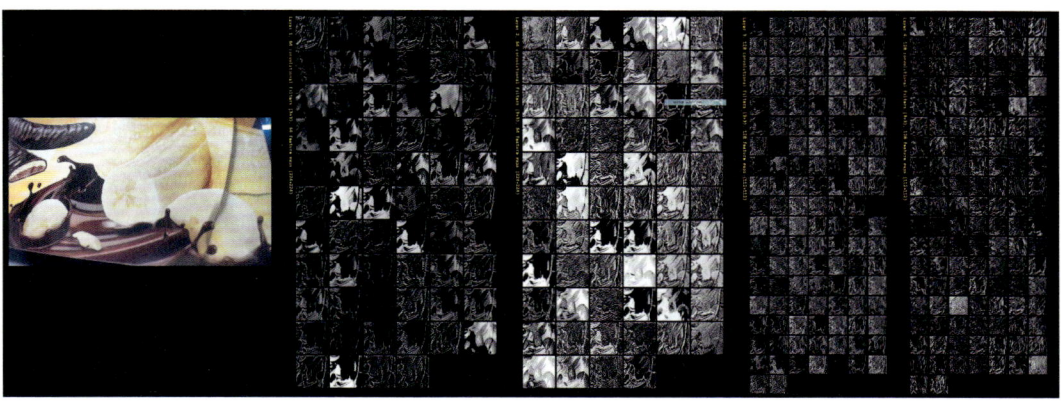

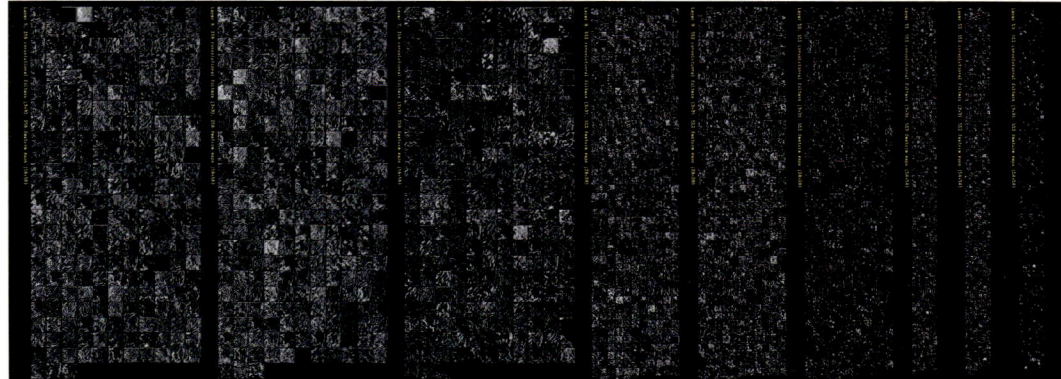

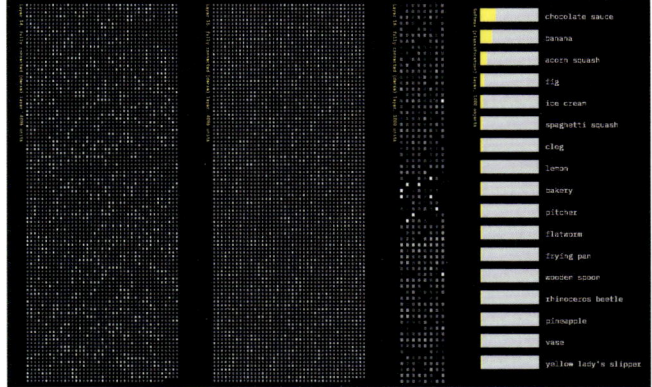

Wie künstliche neuronale Netze sehen / How artificial neural networks see
Ars Electronica Futurelab, 2019, Computerinstallation / computer installation

Dieses künstliche neuronale Netz wurde darauf trainiert, Bilder und Objekte zu erkennen. Es besteht aus mehreren Schichten, wobei jede Schicht unterschiedliche Eigenschaften im Bild identifiziert und diese Informationen an die nächste Schicht weitergibt. Während sich die ersten Schichten auf Eigenschaften wie Linien, Farben oder Kurven spezialisieren, erkennen die nachfolgenden komplexere Formen.

This artificial neural network has been trained to recognise images and objects. It consists of several layers, with each layer identifying different properties in the image and passing this information on to the next layer. While the first layers specialise in properties such as lines, colours, and curves, the subsequent layers recognise more complex shapes.

GLOBALE INFRA-STRUKTUR DER KI

Die Basis der Fortschritte in der KI-Forschung bilden die seit Beginn des 21. Jahrhunderts erfolgten Technologiesprünge in der Entwicklung von Hard- und Software. Die Weiterentwicklung von lernenden Algorithmen ist dabei ebenso zentral wie die Verfügbarkeit riesiger Datenmengen, die durch die weltweite Zunahme an Internetzugängen und Endgeräten möglich wurde. Diese können von kostengünstigen und leistungsstarken Mikroprozessoren in Computern verarbeitet werden. Digitalisierung und Globalisierung stehen in engem Zusammenhang mit der Entwicklung der KI. Diese umfasst den Aufbau von Industrien und Infrastrukturen: Fabriken, die Hardware produzieren, Rechenzentren, die Daten speichern und Rechenleistung zur Verfügung stellen sowie Netzwerke, die Daten übermitteln. In den letzten zwei Jahrzehnten ist der wirtschaftspolitische Einfluss dieser Industrien deutlich gestiegen. Zur Sicherung von Macht und Einfluss werden nationale Strategien entwickelt und Investitionen in den Ausbau dieser Technologien vorgenommen.

The progress made in AI research is based on the technological leaps that have occurred in hardware and software development since the beginning of the 21st century. The further development of learning algorithms has been just as pivotal as the availability of vast amounts of data made possible by the global increase in internet access and terminals. This data can be processed by inexpensive and powerful microprocessors inside computers.

Digitisation and globalisation are closely related to the development of AI. It comprises the setting-up of industries and infrastructures: factories that produce hardware, data centres that store data and provide computing power, and networks that transmit data. The economic and political influence of these industries has increased significantly over the past two decades. National strategies are being drawn up and investments made in the expansion of these technologies in order to secure both power and influence.

AI'S GLOBAL INFRASTRUCTURE

DAS MILLIARDENGESCHÄFT
mit Künstlicher Intelligenz

THE BILLION-DOLLAR BUSINESS
with Artificial Intelligence

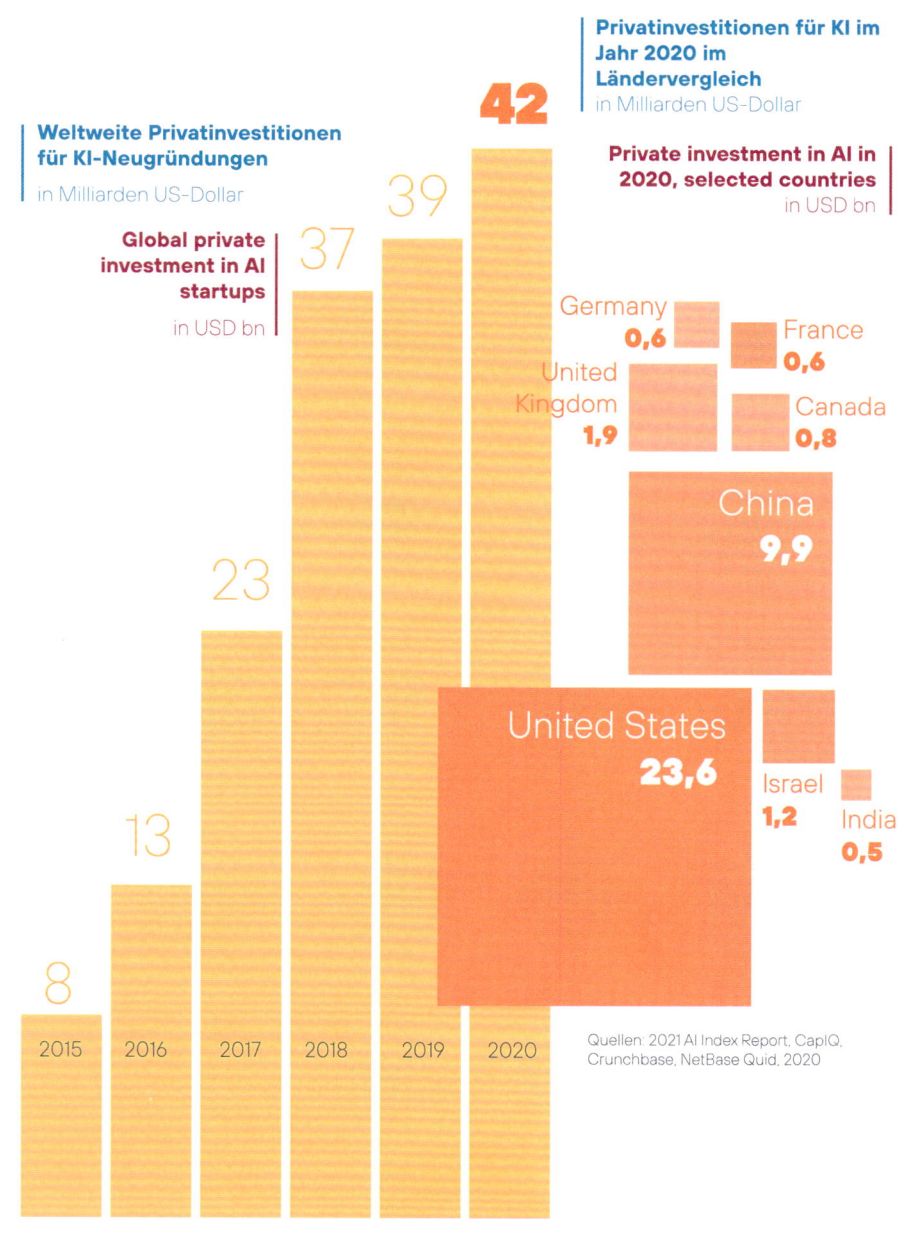

Privatinvestitionen für KI im Jahr 2020 im Ländervergleich
in Milliarden US-Dollar

Weltweite Privatinvestitionen für KI-Neugründungen
in Milliarden US-Dollar

Private investment in AI in 2020, selected countries
in USD bn

Global private investment in AI startups
in USD bn

42

39

37

23

13

8

2015 2016 2017 2018 2019 2020

Germany 0,6

France 0,6

United Kingdom 1,9

Canada 0,8

China 9,9

United States 23,6

Israel 1,2

India 0,5

Quellen: 2021 AI Index Report, CapIQ, Crunchbase, NetBase Quid, 2020

CORONA-EFFEKT?
Massiver Anstieg von KI-Privatinvestitionen in den Bereichen
E-Learning und Wirkstoffentwicklung

CORONA EFFECT?
Huge increase in AI private investment in e-learning and active
ingredient development

Gesamtinvestition
in Milliarden US-Dollar

Total Investment
in USD bn

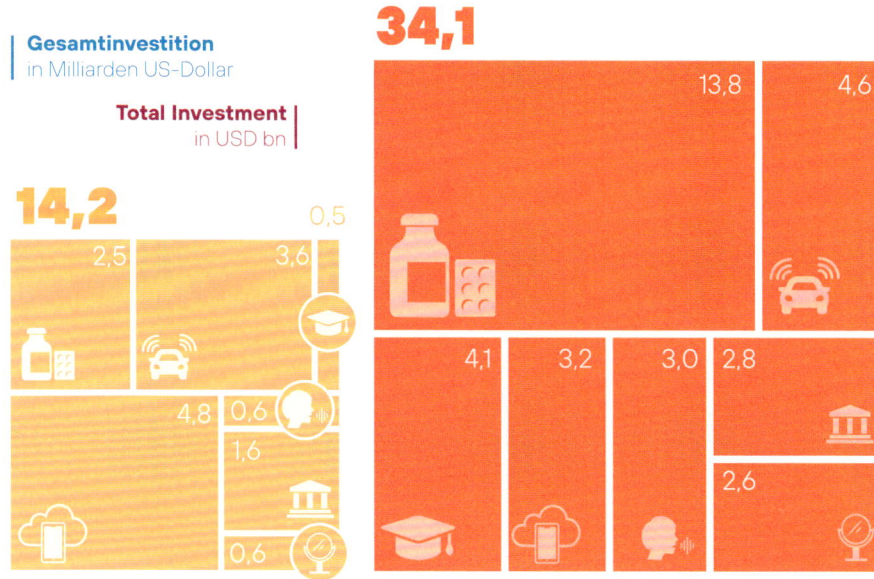

34,1

13,8   4,6

4,1   3,2   3,0   2,8

2,6

14,2   0,5

2,5   3,6

4,8   0,6

1,6

0,6

2019

2020

 Medikamenten- und
Wirkstoffentwicklung | Drug and
active ingredient development

 Autonomes Fahren | Autonomous
driving

 E-Learning | Educational
technology

 Open Source und Big-Data-Verar-
beitung | Open source and big
data processing

 Spracherkennung und
Übersetzung | Speech
recognition and translation

 Bekämpfung von Geldwäsche
und Steuerbetrug | Combating
money laundering and tax fraud

 Mode und Beauty | Fashion and
beauty

Quellen: 2021 AI Index Report, CapIQ, Crunchbase, NetBase Quid, 2020

Timo Arnall (*1976)
The Internet Machine, 2014, 2-Kanal-Videoinstallation /
two-channel video installation, 6:40 Min.

Wie sieht das Internet aus? Die Arbeit des britischen
Künstlers Timo Arnall untersucht die materielle Infrastruktur des Internets. Seine Aufnahmen stammen aus
einem Datenzentrum des spanischen Telekommunika-
tionsunternehmens Telefónica. Hinter unscheinbaren,
aber stark gesicherten Außenwänden verbirgt sich
ein Labyrinth aus Gängen, Glasfaserkabeln und men-
schenleeren Räumen voller Serverschränke. Zu hören
ist ein lautes Rauschen, das durch die Kühlung und
den Betrieb der Server erzeugt wird.

What does the internet actually look like?
The work of British artist Timo Arnall explores
the material infrastructure of the internet.
His videos were taken in a data centre of
the Spanish telecom company Telefónica.
Hidden behind nondescript yet heavily
secured exterior walls is a maze of corridors,
fibre optic cables, and deserted rooms
packed full of server cabinets. All we hear
is the loud humming of the cooling system
and the servers in operation.

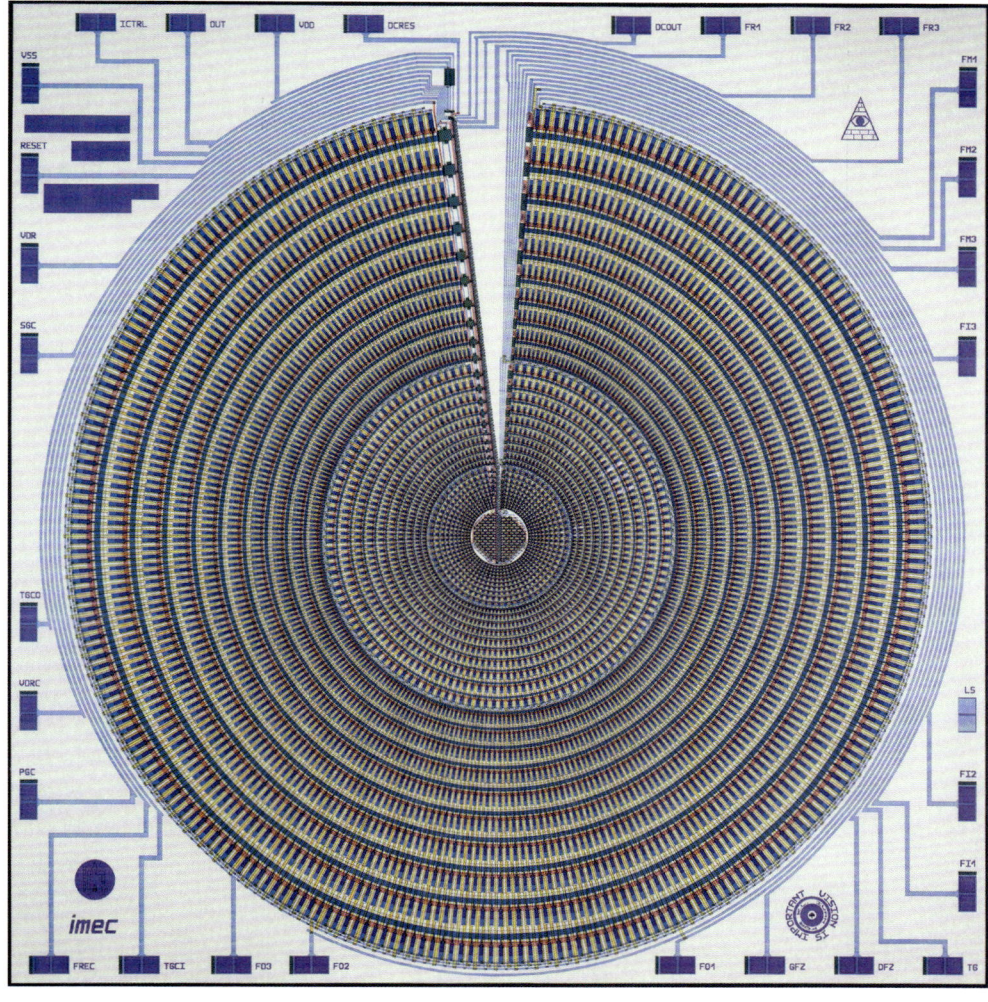

Mikrochip-Design eines neuronalen Netzes / Microchip design of a neural net
IMEC, University of Pennsylvania, 1989, computergenerierter Plot auf Papier /
computer-generated plot on paper

Die Schaltungen auf Mikrochips sind nur unter starker Vergrößerung erkennbar.
Um diese Strukturen im Nanometerbereich auf dem Chip erzeugen zu können,
entwerfen Mikrochip-Designer*innen vorab eine Vorlage. Diese Chip-Layouts
machen die Ästhetik der kleinen, hochkomplexen Objekte sichtbar. Der kreisförmige
Entwurf dieses Mikrochips von 1989 orientierte sich an menschlichen Sehnerven
und sollte für die Bilderkennung in Robotern eingesetzt werden.

It takes high levels of magnification to spot microchip circuits. Microchip
designers therefore have to create a template beforehand to be able to produce
these nanometre structures on each chip. The chip layouts make the aesthetics
of these tiny, highly complex objects visible to the human eye. The circular
design of this microchip from 1989 was based on human optic nerves and
was to be used in robots for image recognition.

BIG DATA
Die rasant wachsende Verdatung der Welt

BIG DATA
The exponential growth in the world's datafication

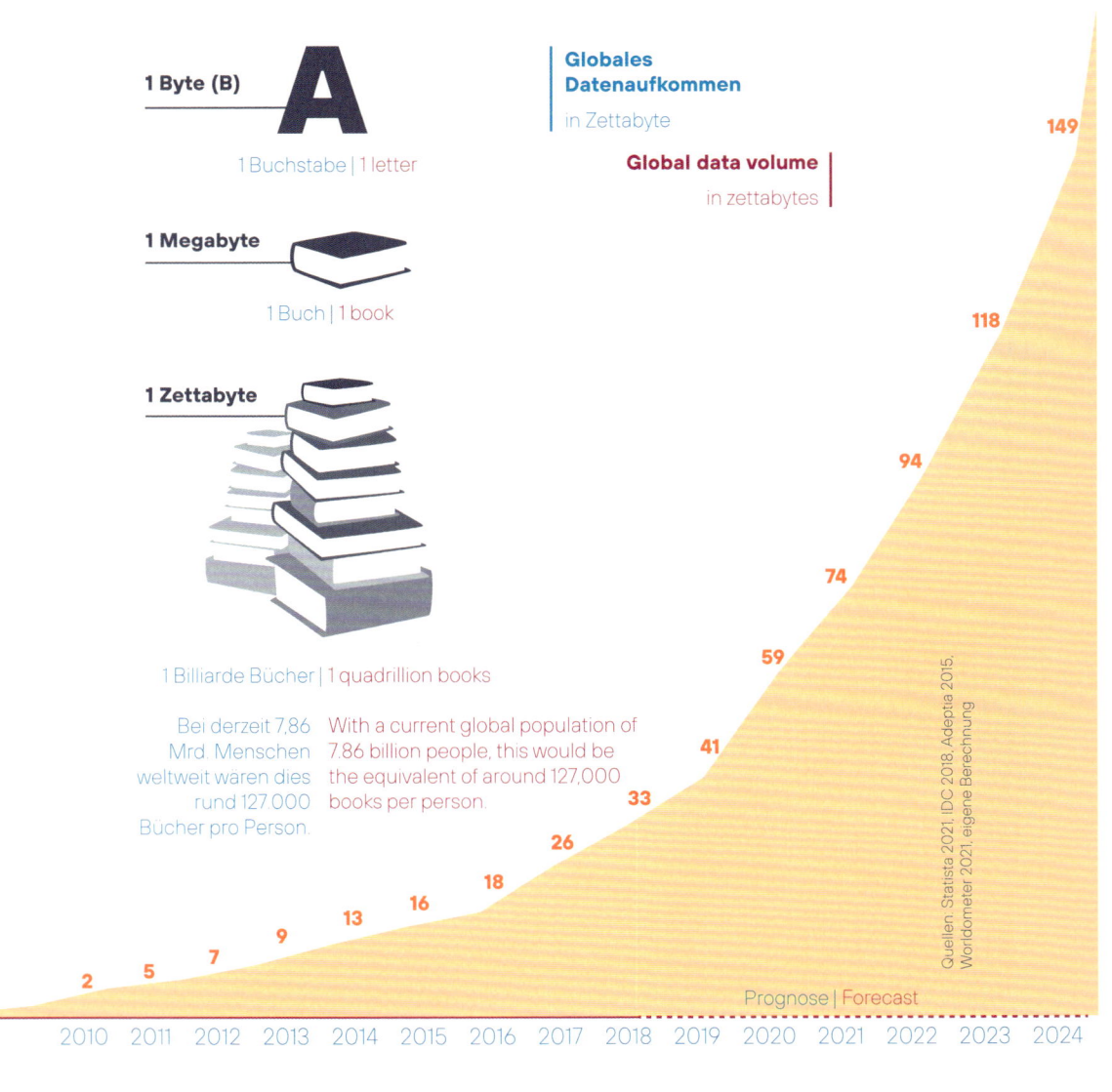

1 Byte (B)

1 Buchstabe | 1 letter

1 Megabyte

1 Buch | 1 book

1 Zettabyte

1 Billiarde Bücher | 1 quadrillion books

Bei derzeit 7,86 Mrd. Menschen weltweit wären dies rund 127.000 Bücher pro Person.

With a current global population of 7.86 billion people, this would be the equivalent of around 127,000 books per person.

Globales Datenaufkommen
in Zettabyte

Global data volume
in zettabytes

Quellen: Statista 2021, IDC 2018, Adepta 2015, Worldometer 2021; eigene Berechnung

2010	2011	2012	2013	2014	2015	2016	2017	2018	2019	2020	2021	2022	2023	2024
2	5	7	9	13	16	18	26	33	41	59	74	94	118	149

Prognose | Forecast

The Eighth Wonder of the World. The Atlantic Cable
Kimmel & Forster, (Das achte Weltwunder. Das Atlantikkabel), New York 1866, kolorierte Lithografie / coloured lithograph, Reproduktion / reproduction

Die Crew des US-amerikanischen Unternehmers Cyrus W. Field verlegte 1866 von einem der größten Dampfschiffe seiner Zeit aus das erste stabil funktionierende Transatlantikkabel von Irland nach Neufundland. Dadurch wurde es erstmals möglich, Informationen und Nachrichten in Form von Telegrammen zunächst innerhalb weniger Stunden, später sogar in wenigen Minuten um die Welt zu schicken. Diese bedeutende technische Innovation wurde von der Bevölkerung euphorisch gefeiert.

In 1866, the crew of US American entrepreneur Cyrus W. Field laid the first stable transatlantic cable from Ireland to Newfoundland from one of the largest steamships of its time. It meant that, for the first time ever, information and messages could be sent around the world as telegrams, initially within a matter of hours and, subsequently, within minutes. This significant technological innovation was celebrated euphorically by the population.

Transatlantikkabel / Transatlantic cable
Telegraph Construction & Maintenance Co. Ltd. (Telcon), Kasten mit sechs Proben des Abschnitts Borkum-Fayal des ersten deutschen Transatlantikkabels (Azorenkabel) / Box with six samples of the Borkum-Fayal section of the first German transatlantic cable (Azores cable), 1900, Holz, Kabel / wood, cable

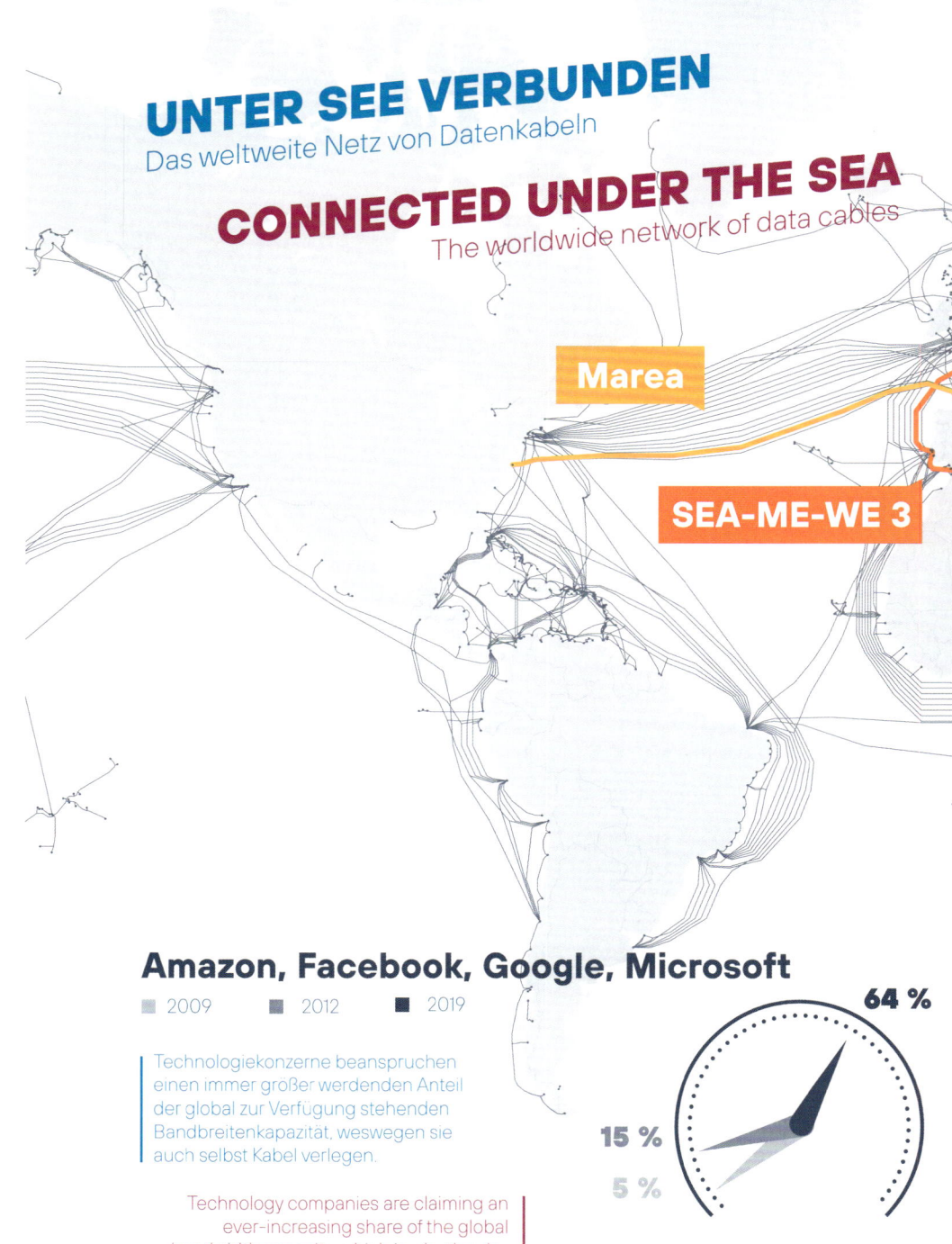

UNTER SEE VERBUNDEN
Das weltweite Netz von Datenkabeln

CONNECTED UNDER THE SEA
The worldwide network of data cables

Marea

SEA-ME-WE 3

Amazon, Facebook, Google, Microsoft

■ 2009 ■ 2012 ■ 2019

Technologiekonzerne beanspruchen
einen immer größer werdenden Anteil
der global zur Verfügung stehenden
Bandbreitenkapazität, weswegen sie
auch selbst Kabel verlegen.

Technology companies are claiming an
ever-increasing share of the global
bandwidth capacity, which is why they lay
their own cables.

64 %

15 %

5 %

Quelle: TeleGeography, www.submarinecablemap.com

99%

des interkontinentalen
Datenverkehrs laufen aktuell
über Tiefseekabel. Der Anteil
von Satelliten ist damit
verschwindend gering.

99% of intercontinental data
traffic currently runs via
deep-sea cables. The share of
satellites is therefore
negligible.

Über | over
1,3 Mio. km

Unterseekabel sind derzeit
im Einsatz. Mit ihnen könnte
die Erde 32 Mal umschlun-
gen werden.

of submarine cables are
currently in use, enough to
go around the Earth 32
times.

~ 426

verlegte Unterseekabel
laid submarine cables

Marea

ist das derzeit leistungsfähigste transatlanti-
sche Unterseekabel. Es gehört Microsoft
und Facebook und kann bis zu 224 Terabits
pro Sekunde übertragen. Damit lassen sich
über 99 Millionen HD-Videos gleichzeitig
streamen.

is currently the most powerful transatlantic
submarine cable. It belongs to Microsoft
and Facebook and is capable of transmit-
ting up to 224 terabits per second, enough
to stream more than 99 million HD videos
simultaneously.

SEA-ME-WE 3

ist das derzeit längste Unterseekabel. Mit
einer Gesamtlänge von 39.000 km verbindet
es Australien, Asien, Afrika und Europa.

is currently the longest submarine cable. With
a total length of 39,000 km, it connects
Australia, Asia, Africa and Europe.

**Elektroschrottdeponie in Agbogbloshie, Ghana /
E-waste dumping ground in Agbogbloshie, Ghana**
Still aus / from: Florian Weigensamer, Christian Krönes (Regie / directors),
Welcome to Sodom, 2018, Dokumentarfilm / documentary, 92 Min.

DIGITALISIERUNG FÜR ALLE?
Die vernetzte Welt von morgen - eine Prognose

DIGITISATION FOR ALL?
The networked world of tomorrow - a forecast

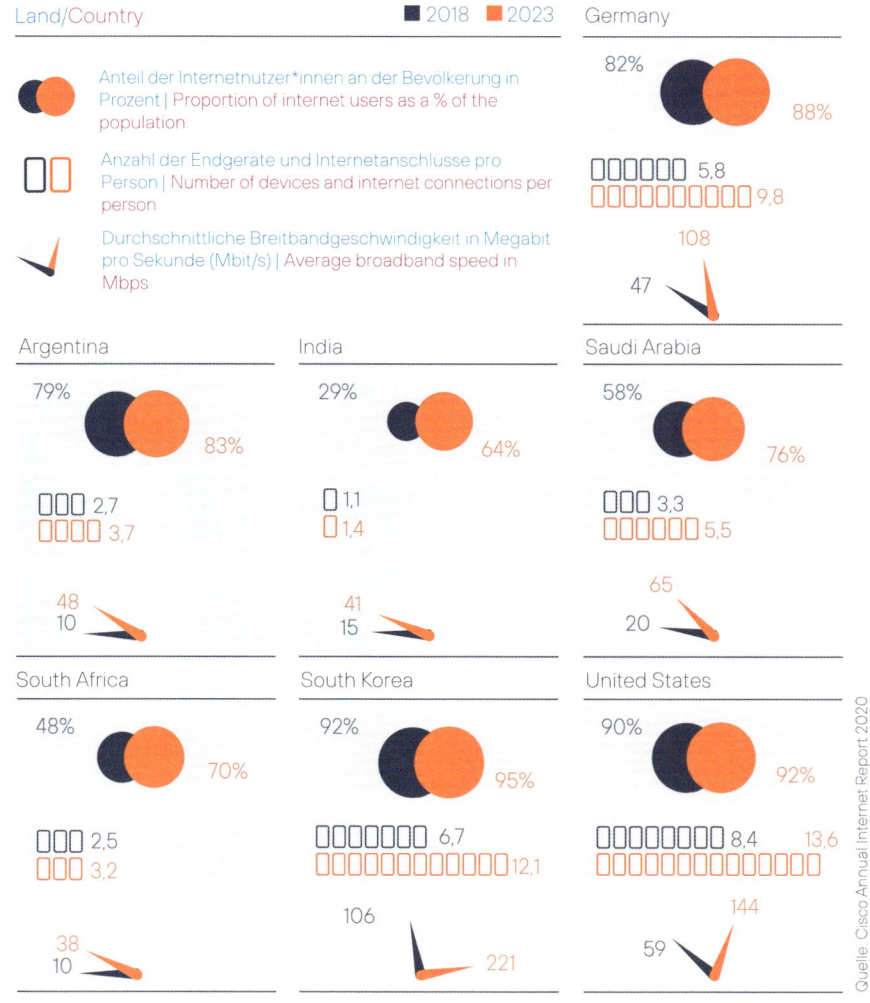

Land/Country   ■ 2018 ■ 2023   Germany

Anteil der Internetnutzer*innen an der Bevölkerung in Prozent | Proportion of internet users as a % of the population.

Anzahl der Endgeräte und Internetanschlüsse pro Person | Number of devices and internet connections per person

Durchschnittliche Breitbandgeschwindigkeit in Megabit pro Sekunde (Mbit/s) | Average broadband speed in Mbps

Germany
82% / 88%
5,8 / 9,8
47 / 108

Argentina
79% / 83%
2,7 / 3,7
48 / 10

India
29% / 64%
1,1 / 1,4
41 / 15

Saudi Arabia
58% / 76%
3,3 / 5,5
65 / 20

South Africa
48% / 70%
2,5 / 3,2
38 / 10

South Korea
92% / 95%
6,7 / 12,1
106 / 221

United States
90% / 92%
8,4 / 13,6
59 / 144

Quelle: Cisco Annual Internet Report 2020

IP: 110.241.60.153
Coordinate(GCJ02): 37.994608, 114.488336
ISP: China Unicom   AS: 4837

IP: 61.55.208.120
Coordinate(GCJ02): 37.997326, 114.489417
ISP: China Unicom   AS: 4837

IP: 110.240.4.228
Coordinate(GCJ02): 37.993236, 114.490496
ISP: China Unicom   AS: 4837

IP: 110.228.105.17
Coordinate(GCJ02): 37.994422, 114.494215
ISP: China Unicom   AS: 4837

IP: 113.109.118.73
Coordinate(GCJ02): 23.171279, 113.263950
ISP: China Telecom   AS: 4134

Guo Cheng (*1988)
The Net Wanderer, seit / since 2019,
47 Fotografien / photographs,
Video, 8:59 Min.

Durch das Regulieren von Datenströmen
können Staaten ihre Souveränität und
Kontrolle auch auf den digitalen Raum
ausweiten. Die große Firewall von China
steuert den Datenverkehr aus dem In-
und Ausland und zensiert Informationen.
Die Vorgänge werden zunehmend durch
KI automatisiert. Der chinesische Künstler
Guo Cheng verwendet Netzwerk-
Diagnosetools, um die möglichen geo-
grafischen Standorte der Firewall ausfindig
zu machen, zu dokumentieren und zu
archivieren.

By regulating data flows, individual states are able
to extend their sovereignty and control to the digital
realm, too. China's Great Firewall controls the country's
domestic and international data traffic, thereby cen-
soring information. Increasingly, these processes are
automated by AI. Chinese artist Guo Cheng uses
network diagnostics tools to locate, document, and
archive the Firewall's potential geographical locations.

IP: 210.76.202.110
Coordinate(GCJ02): 39.982954, 116.335473
ISP: University of Chinese Academy of Sciences   AS: 7497

IP: 112.66.0.204 & 112.66.3.121 & 112.66.3.125 & 112.66.6.18
Coordinate(GCJ02): 18.258759, 109.515882
ISP: China Telecom   AS: 4134

Mimi Ọnụọha (*1989)
The Future is Here!, 2019, Video, 23:30 Min.

Der Anteil menschlicher Arbeit bei der Aufbereitung von Trainingsdaten für KI-Systeme wird öffentlich kaum wahrgenommen. An welchen Orten wird diese Arbeit verrichtet? Wie sehen die Arbeitsbedingungen aus? Diesen Fragen geht die US-amerikanische Künstlerin Mimi Ọnụọha in ihrem Werk nach. Über Crowdworking-Plattformen kontaktierte sie Personen aus aller Welt und bat sie, ihre Arbeitsplätze zu fotografieren, die sie in Zeichnungen übersetzte und kommentierte. So wird die Vielseitigkeit der Orte und Arbeitsbedingungen sichtbar.

Most people are barely aware of how much human labour is involved in preparing training data for AI systems. Where is this work actually done? What are the working conditions like? These are the questions US artist Mimi Ọnụọha explores in her work. She used crowd-working platforms to contact people all over the world and ask them to take photographs of their workplace, which she translated into drawings and commented on, thereby highlighting the diversity of locations and working conditions.

Bildannotation / Image annotation
Segments.ai, um / c 2020, Reproduktion / reproduction

Trainingsdaten aufzubereiten (= annotieren) ist eine kostspielige und zeitauf-
wendige Tätigkeit. Sie wird daher häufig von Crowdworker*innen verrichtet.
Über global agierende Plattformen wird die Datenannotation in kleine Aufgaben
unterteilt und von einer großen Anzahl an Menschen aus allen Teilen der Welt
bearbeitet. Vor allem in Ländern des Globalen Südens handelt es sich dabei
oft um schlecht bezahlte Arbeit ohne soziale Absicherung. Das Bild zeigt das
Software-Tool, mit dem die Daten annotiert werden.

Preparing (= annotating) training data is a costly and time-consuming
task, which is why it is often performed by crowd workers. Data anno-
tation is divided up into small tasks across platforms that operate at the
global level and are then processed by vast numbers of people from all
over the world. Particularly in countries of the Global South, these jobs
often consist of poorly paid work without any social security. The picture
shows the software tool used to annotate data.

UNSERE GEGENWART MIT KI

Künstliche Intelligenz ist längst in der Gegenwart angekommen: Sprachassistenten begleiten uns im häuslichen Umfeld und unterstützen uns im Alltag. In der industriellen Produktion arbeiten Menschen Seite an Seite mit KI-gestützten Systemen. Außerdem helfen Assistenzsysteme, Krankheiten zu diagnostizieren und personalisierte Therapien zu entwickeln. Dabei ist KI in erster Linie ein Werkzeug, um menschliche Tätigkeiten effektiver und präziser zu gestalten – ein immer wiederkehrendes Anliegen in der Technikgeschichte.

KI-Systeme werden auch für Prognosen im Bereich der öffentlichen Sicherheit eingesetzt. Risiken des Missbrauchs und der Manipulation sind in Abhängigkeit von den gesellschaftlichen Zuständen zu betrachten. In Deutschland und Europa stehen technologischen Innovationen Fragen des Datenschutzes und der demokratischen Grundrechte entgegen. Dies hat wiederum Auswirkungen auf die Entwicklung und Einsatzfelder von KI-Systemen.

Artificial Intelligence has long since become part of our present-day reality. Voice assistants are all around us in our homes and assist us in our everyday lives. In industrial production, humans work side by side with AI-aided systems. Assistance systems also help in diagnosing diseases and drawing up personalised therapies. AI is first and foremost a resource for making human activities more effective and precise, which has been a recurring theme throughout the history of technology.

AI systems are also used for public safety forecasting. Risks of misuse and manipulation need to be considered against the backdrop of the conditions prevailing within a given society. In Germany and Europe, technological innovations are judged against questions of data protection and fundamental democratic rights. This in turn has an impact on the development and the areas of application of AI systems.

AI AND OUR PRESENT-DAY REALITY

LOTHAR SCHRÖDER

LERNENDE MASCHINEN IM BETRIEB – DIE NEUE ARCHITEKTUR DER ARBEITSWELT

MACHINE LEARNING IN THE WORKPLACE: THE NEW ARCHITECTURE

■

Wir haben für die Entwicklung unserer Infrastruktur und unserer Städte und Gemeinden Flächennutzungspläne, Bauvorschriften und Beteiligungsverfahren entwickelt. Wir akzeptieren, dass diese Regelwerke uns Gestaltungsprinzipien für die Architektur vorgeben, weil wir darüber ausdrücken, wie sich die Gesellschaft, wie wir uns alle unsere Lebensbedingungen vorstellen. Dieses bewährte Gestaltungsmodell sollten wir aufgreifen, wenn heute Digitalisierung und Künstliche Intelligenz die Architektur unserer Arbeitswelt verändern. Mit empfundenen Wahrheiten würde unser Bauwesen nicht auskommen. Wir entwickeln Vertrauen und Aufgeschlossenheit aus Normen, Sachverstand, anschaulichen Visionen, Einflussmöglichkeiten und Erfahrung. Die Gestaltung der Arbeitswelt der Zukunft verlangt nach klaren Zielstellungen: Rationalität, Transparenz, Verständigung und Sicherheit.

Städtebau, der die Wünsche und Vorstellungen der Stadtbewohner*innen ignoriert, bringt trostlose Städte hervor. Eine Digitalisierung, die die Anliegen der arbeitenden Menschen vernachlässigt, wird trostlose Arbeitsplätze hervorbringen. Einwohner*-innen und Berufstätige wehren sich früher oder später gegen eine Abwertung jener Größen, die das Menschliche ausmachen. Sie wollen nicht nur als bloße Kostenfaktoren oder Kaufkraftträger betrachtet werden. Der Mensch als soziales Wesen braucht eine Umgebung mit Lebensqualität und nicht nur ein Dach über dem Kopf. Er braucht Ethik und Gemeinwohl. Er hat das Recht, demokratisch mitzugestalten, beim Städtebau ebenso wie am Arbeitsplatz.

Wie beim Städtebau darf nicht erst dann Einfluss genommen werden, wenn die Bagger anrücken. Wer sich in Städten wohlfühlen will, muss sich vorausschauend einmischen und aktiv werden. Stadtbewohner*innen brauchen dafür eine eigene Vorstellung davon, wie sie morgen leben wollen und wie sie neue architektonische Möglichkeiten zugunsten von mehr Lebensqualität nutzen möchten. Das bloße Beharren auf den Erhalt der Gegenwart hilft nicht immer weiter und erschließt auch nicht neue Möglichkeiten. Auch in der Digitalisierung macht es Sinn, zu Beginn einer Entwicklung die Betroffenen zu Beteiligten zu machen.

Wir brauchen neben einer Zukunftsvorstellung auch Bauvorschriften für eine digitale Wirtschaft, für die digitale Arbeit von morgen, gerade weil mit Systemen Künstlicher Intelligenz die Arbeitswelt aus den herkömmlichen Grenzen ausbricht. KI-Systeme bringen uns erweiterte Optionen, in die Autonomie des Menschen einzugreifen. Sie übersteigen dessen sensorische Fähigkeiten oft bei Weitem und sie sind Werkzeuge, deren Lernfähigkeit dazu führt, dass sie sich laufend verändern. Sie beschleunigen Prozesse im Betrieb und haben die Fähigkeiten, Daten in einer Geschwindigkeit zu analysieren und zu nutzen, bei der wir Menschen nicht mithalten können. Auch bei der Fähigkeit, Muster zu erkennen, sind sie uns bei immer mehr Anwendungen überlegen. Künstliche Intelligenz berührt eine Vielzahl von Persönlichkeitsrechten und wird die Bedeutung für rationale Entscheidungen im Betrieb steigern. Wir Menschen entscheiden hingegen nicht immer nur rational. Unsere Schlussfolgerungen werden durch kulturelle Traditionen, durch Erziehung und Vorgeschichte, durch ästhetisches und soziales Empfinden geprägt. Wir haben Werte, die unsere Entscheidungen beeinflussen. Das macht uns Menschen aus. Dieses Wesen der Menschen sollte handlungsleitend dafür sein, wie wir KI-Systeme im Betrieb gestalten.

Schon heute drücken Arbeitnehmer*innen Angst vor wachsendem Kontrollverlust aus und befürchten, dass sie die Übersicht verlieren angesichts der Dynamik, die die Digitalisierung entfaltet. Sie haben Sorge, mit der Veränderungsgeschwindigkeit nicht mehr mithalten zu können, den Job, die Karrierechancen zu verlieren oder informationelle Selbstbestimmung aufgeben zu müssen. Sie sehen den Wert ihrer Qualifikationen gefährdet, fürchten um Diskriminierung durch maschinelle Entscheidungen, einen wachsenden Arbeitsdruck und eine weitere Entmenschlichung in den Betrieben.

Das verlangt nach Aufklärung über die Möglichkeiten und Grenzen von KI-Systemen. Natürlich werden sie betriebliche Jobprofile verändern. Für die häufig angenommenen gravierenden Arbeitsplatzverluste hat aber selbst die Enquete-Kommission Künstliche Intelligenz des Deutschen Bundestages keine belastbaren wissenschaftliche Belege gefunden. Sicher, Branchen und Aufgabeninhalte werden sich verändern, wenn KI-Systeme Geschäftsprozesse prägen. Manche Aufgaben werden wegfallen, aber andere dazukommen, denn selbstlernende Maschinen brauchen menschliche Obhut. Ob dies saldiert zu einem Kahlschlag führt, ist zumindest offen. Und weil der Ausgang offen ist, müssen wir Einfluss nehmen.

So wie beim Städtebau brauchen wir die Möglichkeit zu fördern und zu regulieren, zu experimentieren und zu klassifizieren. Nicht jedes KI-System hat die gleiche Risikorelevanz wie das andere. Das ist für uns aber nichts Neues: Auch für den Verkehr auf unseren Straßen haben wir differenzierte Geschwindigkeits- und Vorfahrtsregeln. Unsere Architekturvorgaben unterscheiden zwischen Gewerbegebieten und Wohnstraßen.

Für die Arbeit mit KI-Systemen wird es darum gehen, die Mensch-Maschine-Schnittstelle an den Bedürfnissen des Menschen auszurichten. Es macht Sinn, das Potenzial von lernenden Maschinen zur Produktivitätssteigerung zu nutzen. Dabei muss es aber auch um die Unterstützung und Entlastung arbeitender Menschen gehen. Wir sollten gerade jene Geschäftsmodelle mit KI fördern, die positive Beschäftigungswirkung versprechen, damit haben wir schließlich auch Industrie- und Ansiedlungspolitik in Deutschland begründet. Bei der Aufgabenteilung mit Künstlicher Intelligenz muss es uns darum gehen, die Persönlichkeitsrechte der europäischen Grundrechtscharta zu wahren und die Menschen nicht von Maschinen steuern zu lassen. Dafür braucht es auch entsprechende Weiterbildungen von Beschäftigten, es braucht Anwendungs- und Beurteilungskompetenz.

KI-Systeme brauchen einen wirksamen Ordnungsrahmen, der Einsatzbedingungen und Arbeitsorganisation regelt, Transparenz und Steuerbarkeit sicherstellt und den Betroffenen Widerspruchsrechte zu maschinellen Entscheidungen gibt. Die wesentlichsten Vertrauens- und Qualitätsfaktoren von KI-Systemen sollten zwischen Arbeitgeber*innen und Betriebsräten verabredet sein.

Arbeitnehmer*innen fühlen sich wohler mit intelligenten Assistenzsystemen, die unliebsame und gesundheitsgefährdende Arbeiten übernehmen, als mit Maschinen, die tief in die menschliche Entscheidungshoheit eingreifen, die manipulieren und bloßstellen oder Beschäftigte disponieren. Um den Nutzen solcher Assistenzsysteme zu entfalten, sollten wir barrierefreie Zugänge schaffen und uns um Verständlichkeit bemühen.

Auch ohne Initiativen des Gesetzgebers sollten wir heute schon selbstbewusst unsere Gestaltungsoptionen für KI-Systeme im Betrieb nutzen. Wir sollten nicht warten, bis wir glauben, die technisch mathematischen Bedingungen derartiger Systeme bis ins Detail begriffen zu haben. Schließlich haben wir in der Architektur auch nicht gewartet, bis jeder und jede von uns die Fähigkeit hat, die Tragfähigkeit einer Kellerdecke zu berechnen, bevor wir angefangen haben, uns in Deutschland eine Bauordnung zu geben.

> In order to develop our infrastructures, our towns and cities, and our communities, we have drawn up land use plans, building regulations, and participatory procedures. We accept that these rulebooks provide us with formal design principles for our architecture because they allow us to express how we all imagine our society, our living conditions should be. As digitisation and Artificial Intelligence alter the architecture of our modern-day workplace, that is the reason why we should turn to this tried-and-tested design model. Our building and construction industry would struggle to cope merely with perceived truths. We develop trust and open-mindedness from standards, expertise, clear visions, influence, and experience. Shaping the workplace of the future requires similarly clear objectives, specifically rationality, transparency, understanding, and security.

Urban planning that ignores the wishes and ideas of its residents produces towns and cities that are nothing if not bleak. Similarly, digitisation that neglects the concerns of working people will produce bleak workplaces. Sooner or later, residents and workers alike will resist any degradation of the values that constitute the human condition. They do not wish to be seen as mere cost factors or vectors of purchasing power. As social beings, people need an environment with a quality of life, not just a roof over their heads. They need ethics and the common good. They have the right to be involved democratically in shaping their destiny, whether it's urban development or the workplace.

Just as it is the case with urban development, it is important not to wait until the diggers start moving in before taking action. To feel at their ease in a town or city, city dwellers need to be forward-looking and proactive. They need to have their own ideas of how they want to live in the future and how they want to use new architectural possibilities for the benefit of a better quality of life. Simply insisting on preserving the status quo is not always helpful, nor does it open up new opportunities. In digitisation, too, it makes sense to involve the participants concerned, right at the outset of any new development.

Besides a vision of the future, we also need our building regulations for a digital economy, for the digital labour of tomorrow, precisely because artificial intelligence systems are set to shift the working world away from its conventional boundaries. AI systems provide us with greater options for intervening in the autonomy of human beings. They often exceed human sensory capabilities by far and represent tools with a learning ability such that they are constantly evolving. They speed up operational processes and are capable of analysing and utilising data at a speed we humans are unable to compete with. Similarly, they outperform us in pattern recognition abilities in more and more applications. Artificial Intelligence touches on a multitude of personal rights and is set to increase the importance for rational decisions in company operations. By contrast, we as human beings do not always make rational decisions. Our conclusions are shaped by cultural traditions, by education and past experiences, by aesthetic and social sensibilities. The values we have acquired influence our decisions. It is part of what makes us human. This essentially human quality should guide our actions as we design AI systems in the workplace.

Already workers are expressing their fears of an ever greater loss of control, concerned that they are about to lose sight of the bigger picture in the face of the dynamics unleashed by digitisation. They are worried they will no longer be able to keep up with the pace of change, that they will lose their jobs and career opportunities, or that they will have to surrender any information-based self-determination they still possess. They see the value of their qualifications jeopardised and fear discrimination as a result of machine-based decisions, the increasing pressure of the workload, and a further dehumanisation within their companies.

All of which calls for a certain amount of clarification with regard to the possibilities and limitations of AI systems. They will of course affect company job profiles. However, even the Study Commission on Artificial Intelligence set up by Germany's Bundestag failed to find any reliable scientific evidence for the significant job losses often assumed to be associated with AI. Certainly, various sectors and assigned tasks will change when AI systems come to shape operational processes. Some tasks will disappear altogether, but others will emerge; after all, self-learning machines require human supervision. Whether or not this results, on balance, in something of a decimation remains to be seen. And it is precisely because the outcome is still open that we must exert influence.

As with urban planning, we need the possibility to promote and regulate, to experiment and classify. Not every AI system has the same risk relevance as the next one. But that's nothing new to us: after all, we have differentiated speed limits and right-of-way rules within our highway code. Our architectural specifications differentiate between business parks and residential streets.

For work involving AI systems, it will be a matter of aligning the human-machine interface with human needs. Harnessing the potential of machine learning to boost productivity makes sense. However, it must also be about supporting and relieving the burden on working people. We ought to be promoting the use of AI in those business models that hold the promise of positive employment effects; they are, after all, the mainstays underpinning our industrial and settlement policy in Germany. When it comes to using Artificial Intelligence for the division of labour, we need to be mindful of preserving the personal rights set out in the Charter of Fundamental Rights of the European Union and ensuring that people are not controlled by machines. This requires appropriate further training for employees, but also competence in application and assessment.

AI systems need an effective regulatory framework that sets out the conditions under which these systems are used and the way in which work is organised. Furthermore, it must ensure transparency and controllability and give those concerned the right to object to machine-based decisions. The principal quality and trust factors of AI systems need to be agreed upon between employers and works councils.

Workers are more comfortable with intelligent assistance systems that take charge of unpleasant and unhealthy tasks than with machines that interfere deeply with the supremacy of human decision-making, that manipulate and expose, or ultimately dispose of employees. To reap the benefits of such assistance systems, we need to create barrier-free accesses and strive towards clarity.

Even in the absence of legislation initiatives, we should today already be availing ourselves of our design options for AI systems in the workplace. Indeed, we should not wait until we think we have fully understood the technical-mathematical conditions of such systems down to the tiniest detail. After all, to return to the architecture example, we in Germany did not wait until each one of us had acquired the skills needed to calculate the load-bearing capacity of a basement ceiling before we set about implementing our building regulations.

Robo-Boss „Mary" / 'Mary' the Robo-Boss
Stiftung Deutsches Hygiene-Museum Dresden, Stills aus / from: *Ein Tag im Betrieb von aquaRömer / A day at the aquaRömer plant*, 2021, Video, 5:43 Min.

Im Lager des schwäbischen Mineralwasserherstellers aquaRömer koordiniert das EDV-Programm „Mary" per Funk und KI die Logistikmitarbeiter*innen. Es weist ihnen Arbeitsaufträge zu und führt sie zielgenau zu den abzuholenden Getränkekästen und Paletten. Dabei sammelt „Mary" auch Daten, über die eine Leistungsüberprüfung und Verhaltensanalyse der Mitarbeitenden möglich wäre. Daher wurde eine Betriebsvereinbarung abgeschlossen, die solche Anwendungen ausschließt und vor Datenmissbrauch schützt.

At the warehouse of Swabian mineral water manufacturer aquaRömer, 'Mary' the computer programme co-ordinates the logistics staff via radio and AI. It assigns their job orders and guides them with precision to the bottle crates and pallets to be collected. During this process, 'Mary' also collects data that could be used to monitor employee performance and analyse their behaviour. A works agreement was therefore concluded that excludes any such applications and protects the staff from data misuse.

SUSANNE KRASMANN

PREDICTIVE POLICING: ÜBER DEN TRAUM, DIE ZUKUNFT VORWEGZUNEHMEN

PREDICTIVE POLICING: THE DREAM OF PREDICTING THE FUTURE

Wenn die Polizei davon träumt, immer schon dort zu sein, wo das Verbrechen geschieht – und bevor es sich ereignen kann –, dann, so kann man sagen, arbeitet sie daran; vielleicht nicht unter Hochdruck, aber doch mit deutlichem Nachdruck. Predictive Policing ist der auch hierzulande übliche Sammelbegriff für softwaregestützte Techniken vorhersageorientierter Polizeiarbeit, die seit den 2010er-Jahren im deutschsprachigen Raum eingesetzt und erprobt werden. Wohl nicht zufällig erinnert die Bezeichnung des ersten in Deutschland führenden Softwareprogramms PRECOBS (Pre Crime Observation System) eines privaten Unternehmens an die „Precogs" aus Steven Spielbergs Film *Minority Report:* Im Polizeidepartement Washington DC des Jahres 2054 fungieren drei Precogs (abgeleitet aus „precognitive": vorausahnend) als Medium, denn sie können Verbrechen vorhersehen – und dies sogar zu einem Zeitpunkt, zu dem die Täter*innen selbst von ihren zukünftigen Taten noch keine Ahnung haben.

Mit Künstlicher Intelligenz allerdings hat Predictive Policing hierzulande bislang noch wenig zu tun. Die Prognosesysteme treten nicht in Gestalt jener humanoiden Roboter auf, die kollektive Visionen einer computerisierten Zukunft prägen; zudem sind sie oft auch recht simpel aufgebaut. So konzentrieren sie sich auf ausgewählte Delikte wie den professionellen Wohnungseinbruch, von deren Berechenbarkeit ausgegangen wird. PRECOBS etwa beruht auf der Annahme, dass die Täter*innen so „rational", das heißt gezielt und systematisch vorgehen, dass die Ausbeute möglichst hoch und die Entdeckungswahrscheinlichkeit gering ist. Bei der Registrierung entsprechender Anzeichen (*trigger*) für eine solche Straftat in einer bestimmten Gegend löst das System Alarm aus – in der Erwartung, dass der nächste Einbruch zeitnah geschehen wird (*near repeat*).

Auch wenn eine Revolutionierung der Polizeiarbeit im Sinne ihrer prospektiven Ausrichtung und Automatisierung derzeit technisch und organisatorisch noch in einiger Ferne liegt, so ist sie gleichwohl schon angelegt – und manches spricht dafür, dass sie sich eher unauffällig, aber stetig durchsetzen wird. Zwei Voraussetzungen sind bereits gegeben: Zum einen sind die Softwareprogramme der zweiten Generation deutlich anspruchsvoller geworden. Algorithmen, die Daten gleichsam in Echtzeit auswerten und Muster aus einer Vielzahl disparater Daten selbstständig generieren können, emanzipieren sich von der Bindung an theoriegeleitete Verfahren – und mithin an menschliches Vorstellungsvermögen. Die dafür nötige Datafizierung forciert zum anderen die zunehmende Vernetzung polizeilicher mit außerpolizeilichen Datenbanken in der plattform-basierten Polizeiarbeit (*plattform policing*). Die von der US-Firma Palantir entwickelte Software Gotham beispielsweise, die mittlerweile in Hessen und Nordrhein-Westfalen erprobt wird, kann innerhalb von Sekunden ermitteln, ob eine verdächtige Person Verbindungen zu sogenannten Gefährdern hat – und wertet dabei so unterschiedliche Daten wie Wohnort, Handykontakte, Verwandtschaftsverhältnisse oder Polizeiaufgriffe aus. Datenschutzrechtlich sind diese Entwicklungen nicht unproblematisch. Doch Länderpolizeigesetze wie etwa in Hamburg und Hessen sind für die automatisierte Auswertung gespeicherter personenbezogener Daten „in begründeten Einzelfällen" bereits entsprechend angepasst beziehungsweise ergänzt worden.

Aus wissenschaftlicher Sicht besteht das Novum solch datengetriebener Verfahren darin, dass sich die Erklärung kriminellen Verhaltens und der Rechtfertigungszwang für den polizeilichen Eingriff in gewisser Weise erübrigen: Wo Algorithmen selbstständig Verbindungen, also Korrelationen zwischen ganz unterschiedlichen Informationen herstellen und Muster der Erkennung verdächtigen Verhaltens generieren, dort geht das Recht – im Sinne von Recht haben und im Recht sein – tendenziell auf die Maschine über. Vor allem muss man die prospektiven Täter*innen, ihre Beweggründe oder soziale Hintergründe – klassische Fragen der Kriminologie – nicht mehr „kennen" und persönlich in Augenschein nehmen. Über die Verdächtigkeit entscheidet vielmehr die Übereinstimmung eines individuellen Verhaltensmusters mit dem Gefährdungsmuster, das sich aus dem einer Vielzahl anderer Personen ableitet. Bislang befinden immer noch Menschen – die Polizeibeamt*innen - über die Verwendung solch automatisierter Entscheidungsvorlagen. Deren Infragestellung erscheint indes gerade dort nicht mehr möglich, wo die Maschine ja für das begrenzte menschliche Vermögen, eine Vielzahl von Daten in hoher Geschwindigkeit zu verarbeiten, eintritt.

Die Prognose gehört zu den elementaren Grundlagen einer modernen Regierung: Nur wenn wir wissen, was uns erwartet, können wir angemessene Entscheidungen treffen. Dennoch wird die Zukunft uneinholbar bleiben. Wir können uns ihr nur nähern, indem wir aus vergangenen Erfahrungen Wahrscheinlichkeiten ableiten; indem wir uns an Prophezeiungen orientieren oder es den Maschinen überlassen, ungeahnte Muster zu erkennen; und wir können uns die Zukunft mithilfe von Szenarien aneignen. Die Vorstellungskraft kann so manche Begrenzung überwinden, sie kann fantastisch: erfinderisch, aber auch träumerisch sein. In der Tat ist es die Vision, die uns historisch gesehen – im Guten wie im Schlechten – vorangebracht hat: in der Überschreitung dessen, was wir selbst für möglich hielten, in der Erfindung neuer, vielleicht solidarischerer Formen gesellschaftlichen Zusammenlebens, aber auch zerstörerisch getrieben von einem Fortschrittsglauben. Der Film *Minority Report* zeugt davon auch: von einer Vision der Verbrechensbekämpfung, die zu einer Dystopie der Ausmerzung eines jeden Verdächtigen wird. Im Unterschied zu den heutigen Maschinen konnten die Precogs die Zukunft allerdings tatsächlich vorhersehen. Sie konnten nicht irren, was zweifelsohne nur in der Religion – oder eben in der Fiktion – vorgesehen ist.

If the police dream of the day they will always be on the scene of a crime before the crime is actually committed, then it is safe to say that they're already working on it – perhaps not flat out, but certainly with emphasis. Predictive policing is the collective term also used in Germany for software-aided technology aimed at predictive police work that has been used and trialled in German-speaking countries since the 2010s. It's probably no coincidence that the abbreviation used for Germany's foremost software pro-gramme, i.e. PRECOBS (Pre-Crime Observation System), by a private company, references the 'precogs' in Steven Spielberg's film *Minority Report*. At the Washington DC police department in 2054, three precogs (short for 'precognitives') act as mediums as they are endowed with the ability to foresee crimes – at a time when even the perpetrators themselves have no idea of the deeds they are about to commit.

Predictive policing in Germany, however, still has little to do with Artificial Intelligence. Predictive systems do not appear in the guise of the humanoid robots that shape our collective visions of a computerised future; what's more, their structural design is often rather simple. They concentrate on selected offences such as professional burglary, assumed to be predictable. PRECOBS, for example, is based on the as-sumption that perpetrators proceed in such a 'rational' way, i.e. in such a targeted and systematic way, as to maximise the yield and minimise the likelihood of being detected. The system triggers an alarm whenever the relevant indications (the 'trig-gers') of such a crime are flagged up in a particular area – in the expectation that the next burglary is about to happen ('near repeat').

There is still some way to go, in terms of both technology and organisation, be-fore police work is revolutionised in the sense of its prospective orientation and au-tomation; nonetheless the stage is being set – and there is much to suggest that it will be steadily implemented, albeit somewhat inconspicuously. Two preconditions are already in place. Firstly, second-generation software programs have become much more sophisticated. Algorithms that are capable of evaluating data more or less in real time and of independently generating patterns from a multitude of dispa-rate data, are shaking off the shackles that bind them to theory-led procedures – and therefore to the imagination that is particular to human beings. Secondly, the neces-sary 'datafication' is intensifying the way in which police and non-police databases are being networked in platform-based police work (platform policing). The Gotham software developed by US company Palantir, for example, which is now being trialled in Hesse and North Rhine-Westphalia, is able to determine within seconds whether a suspect has connections to so-called 'endangerers' – and evaluates data as diverse as place of residence, mobile phone contacts, degrees of kinship, or run-ins with the police. These developments are not without problems in terms of data protection legislation. And yet, state police legislation, such as that of Hamburg and Hesse, has already been amended and/or supplemented to allow for the automated analysis of stored personal data 'in justified individual cases'.

From a scientific point of view, the novelty of these data-driven procedures is that the explanation of criminal behaviour and the need for the police to justify any intervention are, in a way, superfluous. In instances where algorithms autonomously establish connections, i.e. correlations, between highly disparate data and also generate recognition patterns pertaining to suspicious behaviour, the right – in the sense of being right and being in the right – tends to pass to the machine. But above all, it is no longer necessary to 'know' the prospective offenders, their motives or social background – i.e. classic criminological questions – and take a closer look at them personally. Rather, it is the match-up between individual behavioural patterns and the threat pattern derived from that of a large pool of other persons that decides on the degree of suspiciousness. Up until now, it has been the human being – i.e. the police officer – who decides on the use of such automated decision-making templates. Questioning those very templates no longer seems possible, particularly in instances where a machine takes the place of the limited human capacity to process a multitude of data rapidly.

Prediction is one of the mainstays of modern government: indeed, it is only by knowing what awaits us that we can make the appropriate decisions. Nevertheless, the future will always remain beyond our grasp. All we can do is hope to get closer to it by deducing probabilities from past experiences; by taking our cue from prophecies, or leaving it up to machines to detect unexpected patterns; and we can appropriate the future with the help of scenarios. Indeed, our imagination is capable of surmounting many a limitation, and it can be fantastic or fantastical – inventive, but also dreamlike. After all, our vision is what, historically, has taken us forward – for better or for worse: by going beyond what we ourselves thought possible, by inventing new and perhaps more supportive forms of social coexistence, but also driven in a destructive manner by a belief in progress. The film *Minority Report* also bears testimony to this: to a vision of crime fighting that becomes a dystopia where every single suspect is rooted out. But unlike today's machines, its 'precogs' could actually predict the future. They were infallible, which undoubtedly is foreseen only by religion or, indeed, fiction.

HEATMAP

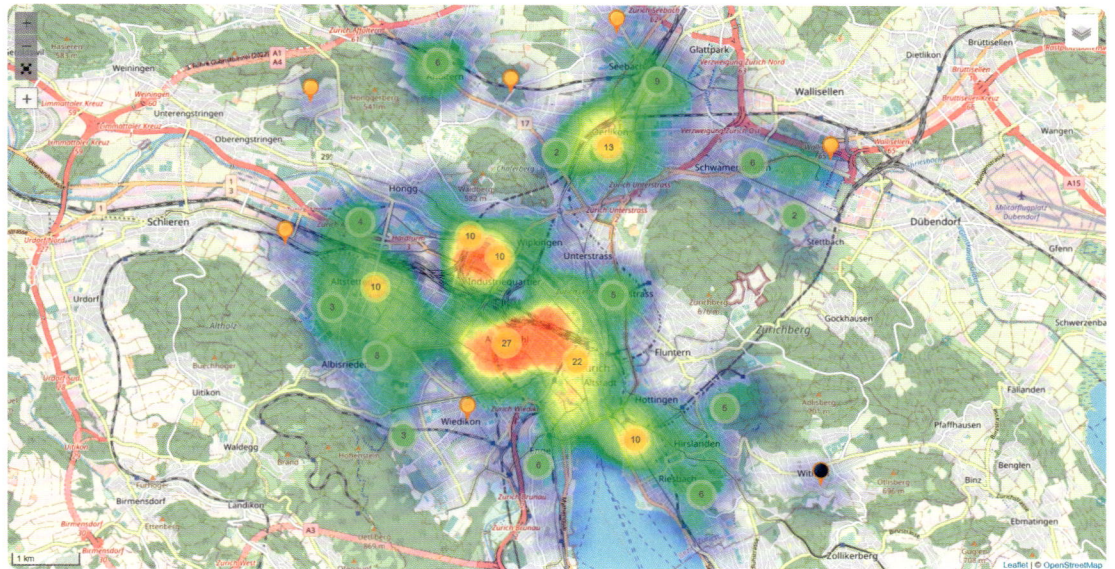

**Ansicht einer Heatmap von Zürich aus der Prognosesoftware PRECOBS /
View of a Zurich heatmap from the PRECOBS predictive software**
Institut für Prognosetechnik Vertriebs-GmbH (IfmpT), Oberhausen 2021,
Auszug aus dem Betriebssystem / excerpt from the operating system

JESSICA HEESEN

MITREDEN UND VORSORTIEREN. KÜNSTLICHE INTELLIGENZ IN DER MEDIEN-KOMMUNIKATION

HAVING A SAY AND PRESORTING. ARTIFICIAL INTELLIGENCE IN MEDIA COMMUNICATIONS

Öffentlichkeit ist der Kern jeder freien Demokratie. Dabei existieren Öffentlichkeiten in modernen Gesellschaften überwiegend als *Medien-*öffentlichkeiten. Medien haben die Eigenschaft, Kommunikation über Raum und Zeit hinweg zu ermöglichen. Ein Buch, eine Nachrichten-sendung, ein Youtube-Video, ein Internetchat erlauben die Kommuni-kation räumlich getrennter Personen, zeitversetzt oder in Echtzeit. Diese Kommunikation unter physisch Abwesenden ist eine essenzielle Voraussetzung für die Verständigung in komplexen Gesellschaften, in denen nicht mehr alle miteinander in persönlichen Kontakt treten können. Nicht nur elektronische und digitale Medien, sondern schon Papier und Buchdruck haben zu ihrer Zeit Revolutionen in der Weiter-gabe und Demokratisierung von Wissen ausgelöst. Dabei waren Medien noch nie neutrale Vermittler einer Botschaft, sondern immer schon verbunden mit einer bestimmten „Medienlogik", also technischen Rahmenbedingungen und menschlichen Entscheidungen, die das Ob und Wie der Informationsvermittlung mitbestimmen.

Die Logik der Medien ist somit aufs Engste damit verwoben, wer in der Öffentlichkeit wahrgenommen wird und welche Inhalte überhaupt als wichtig betrachtet werden. Die medialen Rahmenbedingungen, Infrastrukturen und Besitzverhältnisse spiegeln sich entsprechend in der Art der öffentlichen Kommunikation wider. Künstliche Intelligenz ist eine neue, einflussreiche Akteurin in diesem Zusammenspiel von Mensch und Technik in medialen Handlungsräumen.

Die Auswirkungen von KI auf die Medien lassen sich prägnant anhand von drei Gesichtspunkten beleuchten: Inhaltebewertung, Personalisierung und Textproduktion.

Inhaltebewertung

Das Internet ist eine Art Über-Medium, das die Inhalte ganz unterschiedlicher, vormals getrennter Medientypen in sich aufnehmen kann. Dazu gehören Texte, Filme, Bilder, Aufzeichnungen oder Übertragungen von Liveveranstaltungen oder nutzergenerierte Inhalte wie Handyvideos oder Kommentare in den sozialen Medien. Das Amateurvideo, das einen Terroranschlag zeigt, die Menschenrechtsdeklaration und Tipps für das heimische Kräuterbeet stehen im Internet also gleichberechtigt nebeneinander. Es entsteht ein superplurales Informationsangebot, in dem sich kein Mensch zurechtfindet. Deshalb helfen algorithmische Entscheidungsmaschinen mit Unterstützung von KI bei Auswahl und Sortierung, also dem sogenannten Content-Management oder, etwas klassischer ausgedrückt, der Kuratierung der Inhalte.

Vor allem das Verhalten der Nutzer*innen hat einen großen Einfluss auf die Bewertung und Einordnung der Inhalte. Hat ein Medienprodukt, zum Beispiel eine bestimmte Nachrichtenmeldung, hohe Zugriffszahlen, so ist die Wahrscheinlichkeit hoch, dass weitere Produkte der gleichen Art zur Verfügung gestellt werden, gleichgültig, ob sie medialen Qualitätsanforderungen oder ethischen Standards genügen. Maschinelle Auswertungsverfahren sorgen für neue Formen der Präsentation und Priorisierung von Medieninhalten. Algorithmisch basierte Informations- und Kommunikationsplattformen unterstützen insofern Publikations- beziehungsweise Geschäftsmodelle, die genau die Inhalte verstärken, die am häufigsten aufgerufen werden.

Einerseits kann man hier von einer Demokratisierung der Inhalteauswahl sprechen, weil ja alle Nutzer*innen gleichberechtigt daran beteiligt sind. Andererseits kann gerade diese Form der Auswahl sensationalistische, oberflächliche oder diskriminierende Inhalte ins Zentrum der Aufmerksamkeit rücken und damit demokratische Werte beschädigen.

Personalisierung

Welchem Zweck dient nun die Sortierung der Inhalte der digitalen Medienkommunikation? Sie dient an erster Stelle der Aufmerksamkeitsökonomie und damit verbunden der Werbevermarktung durch die Plattformbetreiber. Die sozialen Medien basieren letztlich darauf, das Verhalten der einzelnen Nutzer*innen zu erfassen und auszuwerten, um anschließend ihre Aufmerksamkeit durch personalisierte Werbung zu binden.

Es ist zwar nur schwer vorstellbar, aber die öffentliche digitale Medienkommunikation beruht in ihrer Struktur auf der Wahrscheinlichkeit, uns ein bestimmtes Produkt verkaufen zu können. Künstliche Intelligenz ermöglicht hier das automatisierte Treffen von Entscheidungen, die maßgeblich zur Steuerung und Organisation ganzer sozialer Kommunikationssysteme beitragen. Konkret äußert sich dies etwa darin, dass maschinell gesteuerte Auktionen fast in Echtzeit darüber entscheiden, welcher Anbieter welcher Nutzer*in zu welchem Preis Werbung zeigen darf, während sie sich durch das Internet klickt.

Nicht nur diese Formen der Personalisierung werden durch KI ermöglicht. In ihrem Kontext entstehen algorithmisch geformte Echokammern, die auf dem Prinzip beruhen, Informationen gemäß individuellen Interessen und Verhaltensweisen auszuwählen. Sie sorgen dafür, dass die Nutzer*innen vor allem die Nachrichten finden, die ihre eigenen Auffassungen bestätigen. Dieser Personalisierungsmechanismus wird unter anderem für die übermäßige Verbreitung von Falschmeldungen sowie Radikalisierungstendenzen im öffentlichen Diskurs verantwortlich gemacht.

Textproduktion

In den bisherigen Ausführungen ging es um das Inhalte- und Aufmerksamkeitsmanagement, das mittels KI in den digitalen Medien betrieben wird. Wie sieht es aber aus, wenn KI die Inhalte nicht nur moderiert, sondern selbst erstellt? In den letzten Jahren hat die Forschung große Fortschritte bei der Entwicklung von Sprachmodellen gemacht. Das bedeutet, dass KI-Systeme selbst Texte erstellen. Schon heute können entsprechende Programme Wetter- oder Sportberichte verfassen. Aber es existieren auch bereits Übersichtsartikel zu wissenschaftlichen Themen, die durch KI produziert wurden, und es werden Anwendungen diskutiert, die journalistische Artikel verfassen, Gedichte schreiben oder Lieder komponieren. Diese Sprachmodelle nutzen einen immensen Schatz von Trainingsdaten, den sie aus Internetdiensten wie Wikipedia oder aus den sozialen Medien beziehen. Auf dieser Basis berechnen sie die Wahrscheinlichkeit, mit der ein bestimmtes Wort auf das nächste folgt. Bislang sind diese Systeme noch nicht perfekt, aber es ist durchaus denkbar, dass sie in manchen Formen der Medienkommunikation in Zukunft menschliche Autor*innen ersetzen.

KI als demokratisches Werkzeug

Technikgestaltung ist immer auch Gesellschaftsgestaltung. KI-Anwendungen helfen uns, Inhalte zu bewerten und zu sortieren. Auf diese Unterstützung sind wir angewiesen, um uns zu orientieren und die vielfältigen Informations- und Kommunikationsmöglichkeiten sinnvoll nutzen zu können. Eine demokratische Gesellschaft ist jedoch nicht darauf angewiesen, diese Aufgabe privat-kommerziellen Plattformbetreibern alleine nach ihren Zwecken zu überlassen. Sie ist im Gegenteil dazu aufgefordert, die Rahmenbedingungen für eine transparente, wahrheitsgemäße und faire öffentliche Kommunikation selbst abzustecken. Dazu gehört, neben anderen Aufgaben, KI-Dienste verstehbar zu machen, oder auch eine Kennzeichnungspflicht für automatisch erstellte Texte. Insgesamt gilt: KI-Anwendungen für die Medienkommunikation sind nur dann wirklich „intelligent", wenn ihnen – im Sinne unserer Demokratie – Meinungsbildung, Verständigung und Diskurs als oberste Zwecke gesetzt werden.

The public realm is the very core of any free democracy. Yet in modern societies, that public realm exists first and foremost in the form of *media* public realms. It is a characteristic of various media that they enable communications across space and time. A book, a news broadcast, a YouTube video, an internet chat allow people who are separated spatially to communicate with one another, whether with a time lag or in real time. In complex societies where people are no longer able to come into direct personal contact with one another, communication is predicated on engaging with people who are actually absent, physically. Electronic and digital media are not the first to have triggered revolutions in the dissemination and democratisation of knowledge: in their day, paper and printing did so, too. And yet these media have never been neutral mediators of a message; rather, they have always been linked to a certain 'media logic', i.e. technological outline conditions and human decisions that determine whether and how information is communicated.

Media logic is therefore tightly interwoven with who is actually perceived by the public realm and what content is considered important in the first place. The media environment, infrastructure and ownership are reflected accordingly in the very nature of public communication. Artificial Intelligence is a new and influential player in this interplay between human beings and technology in media-based spheres of action.

The impact of AI on the media is perhaps best illustrated succinctly from three points of view: content evaluation, personalisation, and text production.

Content evaluation

The internet is a sort of meta-medium capable of incorporating the content of highly disparate and previously discrete types of media. They include texts, films, images, recordings and broadcasts of live events as well as user-generated content, such as smartphone videos and comments on social media. It means that, on the internet, the Declaration of Human Rights, tips on how to grow your own herbs, and amateur video footage showing a terrorist attack, all get equal billing. The result is a super-plural glut of information that is at best impenetrable. Which is why algorithmic decision-making engines aided by AI help with the process of selecting and sorting, what's now known as content management or, more traditionally, content curation.

User behaviour first and foremost has a huge influence on the evaluation and classification of content. If a media product, for example a certain news item, gets a high number of hits, there is a strong likelihood that other products of the same kind will be made available, regardless of whether or not they meet media quality requirements or ethical standards. Machine-based evaluation procedures provide new forms of presentation and prioritisation of media content. Algorithm-based information and communication platforms therefore support publication and business models that boost precisely the content most frequently accessed.

So on the one hand, it is fair to say that this represents a democratisation of content selection since all users are involved equally. But on the other, this form of selection is likely to showcase and draw attention to sensationalist, superficial or discriminatory content at the expense of democratic values.

Personalisation

So what purpose does the sorting of content actually serve in digital media communication? First and foremost, it serves the attention economy and therefore the marketing of advertising by platform operators. Ultimately, social media outlets are based on recording and evaluating the behaviour of individual users in order to capture their attention through personalised advertising.

Granted, it is hard to imagine, but public digital media communication is structured around the probability of being able to sell us a particular product. Here Artificial Intelligence allows decisions to be automated that contribute significantly to controlling and organising entire social communication systems. In practice, this expresses itself in the fact that machine-controlled auctions decide almost in real time which provider is able to display advertising to which user and at what price as they click their way around the internet.

But these are not the only forms of personalisation that AI enables. Such a context creates algorithmically induced echo chambers that are based on the principle of selecting information according to individual interests and behavioural patterns. They ensure that users primarily encounter news items that reinforce their own views. It is this personalisation mechanism that is held responsible, among others, for the excessive dissemination of fake news and the tendency for public discourse to become radicalised.

Text production

So far, the remarks outlined above have focused on the content and attention management carried out in digital media using AI. But what happens when AI not only moderates, but also creates the actual content itself? The research in recent years has made huge strides in the development of language models. It means that AI systems now generate texts by themselves. Even now, the relevant programs are able to compile weather and sports reports. Similarly, we already have reviews and abstracts on scientific topics produced by AI, and applications capable of producing journalistic articles, writing poems or composing songs are now also the subject of discussion. These language models make use of a wealth of training data sourced from internet services such as Wikipedia or social media. On this basis, they calculate the probability with which a certain word is likely to follow the next. These systems have yet to be perfected, but it is certainly conceivable that they will, in the future, replace human authors in some forms of media communication.

AI as a democratic tool

Shaping technology is always also about shaping society. AI applications help us to evaluate and sort content. We are reliant on this resource to orientate ourselves and be able to make meaningful use of the wide range of diverse information and communication possibilities. But a democratic society is not reliant on handing over that task to private commercial platform operators solely for their purposes. On the contrary, such a society is called upon to stake out for itself the outline conditions for transparent, truthful, and fair public communication. This includes, among other tasks, making AI services understandable, but also a labelling requirement to identify automatically generated texts. The general rule, then, is that AI applications for media communications are only truly 'intelligent' if, in keeping with our sense of democracy, they are ascribed opinion-shaping, understanding, and discourse as the primary purposes.

**Einsatz von Gesichtserkennung in polizeilichen Ermittlungen /
Use of facial recognition in police investigations**
Unbekannt / Unknown, um / c 2019, Fotografie / photograph, Reproduktion / reproduction

Das US-Unternehmen Clearview AI sammelte drei Milliarden Bilder von Nutzer*innen-Profilen aus sozialen Netzwerken. Der Datensatz wird von US-Behörden zur Gesichts-erkennung in polizeilichen Ermittlungen eingesetzt. Der Mann im Hintergrund dieses Bildes wurde wegen Kindesmissbrauchs gesucht. Durch den Einsatz von Clearview AI konnte er identifiziert und verhaftet werden. Zu hinterfragen ist, inwieweit die Vorteile für die öffentliche Sicherheit die rigorosen Eingriffe in die Privatsphäre aufwiegen.

The US company Clearview AI collated three billion images of user profiles from social networks. The dataset is used by US authorities for facial recognition purposes in police investigations. The man in the background of this photograph was wanted for child abuse. Thanks to Clearview AI he was identified and arrested. The question this raises is the extent to which the benefits to public safety outweigh the radical interference into people's privacy.

ANDREAS KNIE

VERPASSTE CHANCEN: AUTONOMES FAHREN ALS NEUER ÖFFENTLICHER NAHVERKEHR

MISSED OPPORTUNITIES: AUTONOMOUS DRIVING AS A NEW FORM OF LOCAL PUBLIC TRANSPORT

Das Szenario klingt eigentlich bestechend. Ein kurzes Tippen auf dem Smartphone und das Fahrzeug kommt. Kein*e Chauffeur*in mehr am Steuer und der Wagen fährt genau dorthin, wohin man möchte. Nach dem Ausstieg saust das Auto wie von Geisterhand erneut los und steuert schon das nächste Ziel mit neuen Fahrgästen an. Die Wagen fahren alle elektrisch, der Service wird auf ganz unterschiedlichen Levels und zu verschiedenen Tarifen angeboten: Alleine und direkt zum Ziel zu kommen kostet mehr als im Pooling und über Umwege. Alles funktioniert automatisch und bei Gefahr stoppt das Fahrzeug unmittelbar am Straßenrand. Autos werden so Teil eines öffentlichen Verkehrssystems und übernehmen im Nahverkehr den Transport von A nach B in Kombination mit Bussen und Bahnen. Private Wagen, die einen Besetzungsgrad von einer Person aufweisen und mehr als 90 Prozent der möglichen Fahrzeit herumstehen, sind in einer modernen, intelligenten Stadt keine Option mehr. Eine Verkehrswende mit mehr Mobilität und weniger Fahrzeugen wäre möglich.

Wer glaubt, dass dies alles noch Zukunftsmusik ist und noch Jahrzehnte benötigen wird, um Realität zu werden, der sollte seinen Blick nach Phoenix (Arizona) schweifen lassen. Hier ist das skizzierte Szenario sogar schon im Regelbetrieb benutzbar: Robotaxis der Google-Tochter Waymo bieten ihre Dienste bereits völlig ohne manuelle Eingriffe an. Der sogenannte Waymo-Fahrer überwacht den Fahrbetrieb von einer Zentrale aus. Andere Technologiekonzerne wie Amazon, Uber, Tesla und Apple arbeiten ebenfalls an ähnlichen Angeboten. Neben den USA wird auch in China mit Hochdruck an Robotaxis gearbeitet, hier heißen die Firmen Baidu, DiDi oder AutoX.

Gemeinsam sind diesen Projekten nicht nur die Millionen aus Risikokapitalfonds, sondern auch ein offenes Denken über die Zukunft der Mobilität. In Europa dagegen steckt der Verkehr von morgen immer noch im Korsett der Vergangenheit fest: Das Maß der Dinge ist der private Kraftwagen. Das Auto kommt nicht ins Internet, sondern das Internet wird ins Auto verlagert. Die technische Entwicklung ist immer am Fahrzeugführer orientiert, er oder sie soll entlastet werden, und partiell kann das manuelle Steuern auch automatisiert werden, beispielsweise bei der Parkplatzsuche oder beim Cruisen auf Autobahnen. Im Grundsatz bleibt die Einführung der Künstlichen Intelligenz in der Automobilindustrie durch Tempomat, Einparkhilfe sowie Spur- und Abstandswarnung begrenzt: Der Fahrzeughalter soll in seiner Souveränität nicht angegriffen werden. Die bestehenden Verkehrsregeln und Haftungsfragen können genauso stabil und erhalten bleiben wie die eingefahrenen Vertriebs- und Vermarktungsformate.

Aber auch die Betreiber des öffentlichen Verkehrs in Deutschland stecken im Bereich der Sicherung des Kerngeschäfts fest. Im Rahmen von kleinen Forschungsprojekten wird zwar immer wieder mit „on-demand"-Verkehren experimentiert und teilautomatische Shuttles werden als Ergänzungsangebote eingesetzt. Solche Vorhaben starteten beispielsweise schon 2017 auf dem Berliner EUREF-Gelände in Kooperation mit dem amerikanischen Unternehmen Local Motors. Und mittlerweile sind allein in Deutschland rund 50 solcher Kleinbusse im fahrerlosen Betrieb mit Publikum unterwegs, allerdings immer mit Operator*in an Bord. Aber es sind sehr kleinteilige Projekte, die mit dem Kerngeschäft des öffentlichen Nahverkehrs kaum etwas zu tun haben. Es gibt keine auskömmliche Finanzierung, keine Anwendungsroutinen.

Die Automobilindustrie glaubt nicht an autonome Shuttles, und der öffentlichen Verkehrsbranche fehlen Mittel und Wege, einen diesbezüglichen technologischen Sprung zu wagen. Dies liegt schon in der Betreiberstruktur des öffentlichen Verkehrs begründet. Busse und Bahnen werden in Deutschland unter dem Dach der Daseinsvorsorge betrieben: Der Staat kümmert sich und finanziert eine

Grundversorgung mit Angeboten. Der Nachteil: Diese werden in aller Regel als Alibi-Veranstaltung für Menschen betrieben, die kein Auto haben oder nicht selbst fahren können. Der Anteil des öffentlichen Nah- und Fernverkehrs betrug vor der Covid-19-Pandemie kaum 15 Prozent und hat sich im Jahr 2020 sogar mit knapp acht Prozent praktisch halbiert. Die Bus- und Bahnunternehmen glauben selbst nicht daran, größere Marktanteile erschließen zu können und sind froh, wenn das bestehende Angebot auskömmlich finanziert wird. Wenn einmal etwas geändert werden soll, beispielsweise die gesetzlichen Grundlagen des Betriebes im Personenbeförderungsgesetz, dann blockt die Branche alle Bestrebungen, die auf größere unternehmerische Selbstständigkeit und mehr Wettbewerb zielen, ab.

In den großen Städten ist die Ausgangslage aber anders. Durch die kompaktere Siedlungsstruktur und ein dichteres Angebot kann der öffentliche Verkehr besonders dort punkten, wo er gut verknüpft und mit Sharing- und Poolingdiensten digital integriert ist. Das beste Beispiel in Deutschland ist Berlin. Vor der Pandemie war an den öffentlichen Wegen das Auto nur mit rund 24 Prozent, der öffentliche Verkehr aber mit knapp 28 Prozent und das Fahrrad mit 20 Prozent beteiligt. Fußwege sowie Sharing- und Poolingdienste hatten einen Anteil von 18 Prozent. Es wäre also selbst im „Autoland" Deutschland denkbar, dass die scheinbar übermächtige Dominanz des privaten Kraftfahrzeuges durchbrochen und Alternativen etabliert werden könnten, die ein hohes Maß an individueller Beweglichkeit ermöglichen. Dazu müssten aber als Erstes der Denkhorizont erweitert und Raum geschaffen werden.

An dieser Stelle kommt die Gesetzesinitiative ins Spiel, die das Bundeskabinett Anfang Februar 2021 auf den parlamentarischen Weg brachte: die Autonome-Fahrzeuge-Genehmigungs-und-Betriebs-Verordnung (AFGBV).

Damit hat das Verkehrsministerium kurz vor Ende der bestehenden Regierungskoalition einen echten Coup gelandet. Zwar steht die Ressortabstimmung dieser Initiative noch aus und es gibt weiterhin offene Fragen, der Geist ist aber aus der Flasche. Mit der Verordnung ermöglicht das Ministerium erstmals rechtlich den Betrieb „autonomer Flotten" und geht damit weit über das hinaus, was die deutschen Autohersteller für gut und nützlich definieren und die Unternehmen des öffentlichen Verkehrs können und wollen.

Vorgesehen ist, dass der Betrieb eines Kraftfahrzeuges nicht mehr von einem Fahrzeugführer, sondern von einer „technischen Aufsicht" kontrolliert wird, die nicht im Fahrzeug stationiert ist. Damit ist tatsächlich ein Paradigmenwechsel vom automatischen Fahren zum autonomen Betrieb möglich. Künftig könnten Autos als Fahrmaschinen für den öffentlichen Verkehr eingesetzt werden. Es gibt noch kleinere Hürden. So sind die einzelnen Schritte zur Betriebszulassung der Fahrzeuge noch groß und vor allen Dingen sehr teuer und für kleinere Unternehmen schwerlich zu gehen. Zudem wäre ein Betrieb im öffentlichen Verkehr auch an die Regeln des oben genannten Personenbeförderungsgesetzes gebunden: Demnach ist beispielsweise der gewerbliche Transport von Personen ohne Lizenz nicht gestattet, die Rück-kehrpflicht für Mietwagen besteht weiterhin und autonome Shuttles kom-men erst gar nicht vor. Die ÖV-Branche hat sich das so gewünscht, denn wenn der Anteil am Verkehrsmarkt auch klein ist, so sind doch alle Unter-nehmen mit dem bestehenden Gesetz vor dem Übel der Digitalisierung ge-schützt.

Damit ist in der Verkehrspolitik eine fast paradoxe Situation entstanden: Die Tür zum autonomen Fahren ist rechtlich weit aufgestoßen, aber es findet sich niemand, der durch sie hindurchgeht. Die Verkehrswende muss warten.

On the face of it, the scenario seems irresistible. You simply tap your smartphone and the vehicle is on its way. No need for a chauffeur behind the wheel, and the car takes you ex-actly where you want to go. Once you've alighted, the car whizzes off again as if by magic, already on its way to its next destination and new passengers. The cars are all electric, and the service is provided at all sorts of levels and at differ-ent rates. Getting to your destination on your own, and by the most direct route, simply costs more than with car-pooling or taking a couple of detours along the way. Everything works automatically and, in the event of imminent danger, the car immediately comes to a halt at the roadside. In this scenario, cars become part of a public transport system and assume the task of transporting people locally from A to B in combina-tion with buses and trains. In a modern, intelligent city, private cars with a one-person occupancy rate that simply remain parked up more than 90 per cent of their potential driving time are no longer an option. A complete rethink of our trans-port philosophy featuring greater mobility and fewer vehicles would be possible.

Those who think all of this is still 'pie in the sky' and likely to take decades to become reality should check out Phoenix, Arizona. There the aforementioned scenario is already in regular operation. Robotaxis, which is owned by the Google subsidiary Waymo, offer their services entirely without manual intervention. It is the 'Waymo driver' who monitors these operations from a control centre. Other technology corporations such as Amazon, Uber, Tesla and Apple are also busy working on similar offers. Besides the United States, China is likewise working flat out on robotaxis, with companies such as Baidu, DiDi and AutoX.

What all these projects have in common are millions in venture capital funds and an open mind about the future of mobility. In Europe, however, tomorrow's transport operations are still stuck in the straits of the past: private cars remain the measure of all things. It is not the car that's moving to the internet, but the internet that's moving into the car. Technological developments always focus on the driver, who is to be relieved of various burdens. Steering the vehicle manually can be partly automated, for instance when a driver is looking for a parking space or cruising down the motorway. In principle, the introduction of Artificial Intelligence in the automotive industry remains limited to cruise control, parking aids, and lane and proximity warning systems. The vehicle owner's sovereignty is not to be challenged. Existing traffic regulations and issues of liability can remain just as stable and unchanged as the tried-and-tested sales and marketing formats.

In Germany, public transport operators are also stuck on safeguarding their core business. True, within the scope of small-scale research projects, experiments with 'on-demand' transport options are conducted on a regular basis, and semi-automated shuttles are used as complementary services. Projects of this kind were launched in 2017 for example, on the EUREF premises site in Berlin as part of a joint venture with the American company Local Motors. Since then, in Germany alone, some 50 such minibuses are now on the road in driverless public transport operations, but always with one operator on board. But these are very small-scale projects that have little to do with the core business of local public transport. There is no adequate funding, no application routines.

The automotive industry does not believe in autonomous shuttles, and the public transport sector lacks the resources and the means to venture a technological leap in this regard. The operator structure of public transport itself does not allow it. In Germany, buses and trains are operated under the

**Autonomer Bus im Linienbetrieb /
Autonomous bus in regular service**
Stadt Monheim / Town of Monheim, um / c 2021,
Fotografie / photograph, Reproduktion / reproduction

aegis of services of general interest. In other words, it is the state that takes care of and finances the provisions of basic services. The drawback is that these services are generally operated as an alibi for people who do not have a car or are themselves unable to drive. Prior to the Covid-19 pandemic, the share of local and long-distance public transport was barely fifteen per cent; and by 2020 it had practically halved to just under eight per cent. The bus and rail companies themselves do not believe they will be able to tap into larger market shares and are happy if the existing offer is adequately financed. Whenever something does need to be changed, for example the legal basis for operations as set out in the Public Transport Act, the industry blocks any effort aimed at greater entrepreneurial independence and more competition.

The starting point is different in large cities however. Due to the more compact settlement structure and a denser offer, public transport is able to do particularly well in all instances where it is properly interconnected and digitally integrated with car sharing and pooling services. Berlin is the best example of this in Germany. Before the pandemic, cars accounted for just about 24 per cent of journeys undertaken by private individuals, while public transport accounted for almost 28 per cent and cycling for 20 per cent. Walking as well as car-sharing and pooling services made up 18 per cent. So even in a country like Germany, the 'land of the automobile' *par excellence,* it is conceivable that the seemingly overwhelming dominance of private cars could be undermined and alternatives established that nonetheless allow a high degree of individual mobility. This would, however, be predicated first and foremost on people becoming more open-minded and creating the appropriate space.

This is where the legislative initiative comes into play that the Federal Cabinet put on the parliamentary order paper in early February 2021: the Autonomous Vehicles Approval and Operation Ordinance (AFGBV).

The Ministry of Transport landed a real coup with it shortly before the end of the present government coalition. Admittedly, the departmental co-ordination of this initiative is still pending and there are still plenty of open questions, but the genie is definitely out of the bottle. With this ordinance, the Ministry has for the first time cleared the legislative path for the operation of 'autonomous fleets', going far beyond what German car manufacturers define as good and useful and what public transport companies are able and willing to do.

According to the terms of the ordinance, the operation of a motor vehicle will no longer be under the control of the vehicle driver, but of 'technological supervision' not integrated into the vehicle itself. This certainly enables a paradigm shift from automatic driving to autonomous operation. In future, cars could be used as driving machines for public transport. Some minor hurdles still remain. For example, the in-dividual steps needed to obtain an operating licence for the vehicles are still sizeable and, above all, very expensive and difficult for smaller companies to take. What's more, any operation within the realm of public transport would also be bound by the rules of the Public Transport Act mentioned above. The unlicensed commercial conveyance of passengers for example would not be allowed, and the obligation to return rental cars would remain; autonomous shuttles are not even mentioned. This was the explicit wish of the public transport industry, for even if their share of the transport market is small, the existing legislation protects all companies from the evils of digitisation.

An almost paradoxical situation has therefore emerged in transport policy. The door to autonomous driving has been thrown wide open in legislative terms, but no one is around to step through it. The turnaround in traffic and transport operations will have to wait.

KARIN WOLF-OSTERMANN, KATHRIN SEIBERT,
DOMINIK DOMHOFF

GUTE PFLEGE MIT KI?

GOOD CARE WITH AI?

Schon der Titel dieses Beitrags impliziert viele Fragen: Was heißt „gute Pflege" überhaupt, was braucht es dafür und wo kann oder sollte Künstliche Intelligenz dabei ins Spiel kommen? Eine Definition lautet: „Gute Pflege heißt, aktuelles Fachwissen in Abstimmung mit den Erwartungen der pflegebedürftigen Person anzuwenden."[1] Pflegefachpersonen nutzen eine Fülle von Informationen, um Entscheidungen zu treffen, die Einfluss auf die Qualität der erbrachten Pflege nehmen. Hierzu gehören neben dem Erfassen von direkten personenbezogenen Daten (zum Beispiel Vitalwerten oder Sturzrisiken) sowohl implizites Fach- und Erfahrungswissen als auch explizite Wissensbasen aus Dokumentationen, Leitlinien oder wissenschaftlichen Erkenntnissen.

Derzeit stehen wir in Deutschland vor den Herausforderungen, die sich aus den Folge- und Begleiterscheinungen einer alternden Gesellschaft mit veränderten sozialen Strukturen sowie durch einen Fachkräftemangel in der Pflege ergeben. Vor diesem Hintergrund wird seit einiger Zeit der Einsatz von KI für die Pflege diskutiert und erprobt. Eine weitere Instanz, die bei der Arbeit „mitdenkt", Handlungsempfehlungen mitteilt und vorausschauendes Handeln ermöglicht – das erscheint auch für die Pflege eine hilfreiche Unterstützung zu sein. Doch wie können deren bedarfsgerechter Einsatz und ein ethisch verantwortungsvoller Umgang damit aussehen?

Werfen wir also einen Blick darauf, was unter KI überhaupt zu verstehen ist und wo sie in der Pflege Anwendung finden kann. KI umfasst alle Arten von Algorithmen, die auf Grundlage von Daten lernen, um intelligente, zielorientierte Handlungen zu ermöglichen – beispielsweise in der Pflege im Krankenhaus, in der ambulanten oder stationären Langzeitversorgung und für Menschen verschiedener Zielgruppen. So könnten pflegende Angehörige durch KI-Methoden zielgerichtetere Unterstützung bei der Orientierung über Beratungs- und Leistungsangebote erhalten. Eine Unterstützung durch KI im Rahmen der Dienstplanung, die neben den Bedarfen der Pflegebedürftigen auch die Kompetenzen der Mitarbeitenden berücksichtigt, wäre ebenso hilfreich wie eine Unterstützung für Pflegefachpersonen bei Entscheidungen in komplexen Versorgungssituationen.

Für Pflegebedürftige selbst erscheinen Anwendungsfelder wie die Organisation des Alltags und die Unterstützung des Selbstmanagements chronischer Erkrankungen aussichtsreich. Ebenso kann KI bei der Erfassung und Analyse von Aktivitäten, Gesundheit und individuellen Risiken – etwa dem Eintreten eines Sturzes – hilfreich sein. Auch die Unterstützung von Dokumentationsprozessen sowie das sektorenübergreifende Teilen von Informationen zur Optimierung des Versorgungsprozesses können Anwendungsgebiete sein. Jedoch stellt der Zugang zu repräsentativen und qualitativ hochwertigen Daten eine Herausforderung dar. Derzeit fehlt etwa eine Übersicht zu Datenquellen, öffentlich zugänglichen Datensammlungen oder zu Anforderungen an die Nutzbarmachung von Daten in der Pflege für die Entwicklung von KI-Systemen.[2]

International kommen bereits KI-Systeme zum Einsatz, die die zuvor benannten Aktivitäten unterstützen. Allerdings liegen Anwendungsstudien unter Alltagsbedingungen nur in geringem Umfang vor. Auch der Diskurs über ethische, rechtliche und soziale Implikationen befindet sich erst in den Anfängen. Der langfristige Einsatz von KI in der Pflege erfordert in den kommenden Jahren daher eine vertiefte Auseinandersetzung mit Rahmenbedingungen, Bedarfen, gesellschaftlichen Erwartungen und benötigten Kompetenzen der Anwender*innen.

Dabei stellen neue Möglichkeiten der Datenverarbeitung grundsätzlich eine große Chance für die Pflege dar. Wenn das in Expertenstandards und Leitlinien enthaltene Fachwissen durch KI fallbezogen zusammengeführt und der Pflege zugänglich gemacht werden würde, ließe sich der aktuelle Stand pflegerisch-medizinischen Wissens bei der Gestaltung des Pflegeprozesses leichter berücksichtigen. Werden Daten aus verschiedenen Einrichtungen, Sektoren oder auch Ländern zusammengeführt, kann daraus eine Datengrundlage resultieren, die den Erfahrungsschatz, den eine einzelne Pflegefachperson in ihrem Berufsleben aufbauen kann, um ein Vielfaches übertrifft. Lernen KI-Systeme auf individuellen Daten Pflegebedürftiger, ermöglicht dies eine Individualisierung der Pflege. Durch Feedbackschleifen zur Bewertung der durch einen Algorithmus erzeugten Ergebnisse durch die Nutzer*innen kann der Einsatz von KI in der Pflege Hinweise auf wirkungsvolles Handeln unter Alltagsbedingungen liefern. So könnten automatisierte Zusammenhänge zwischen pflegerischen Handlungen und ihren Ergebnissen aufgedeckt werden, die ansonsten nicht untersucht worden wären.

Solche Überlegungen sind insbesondere in Bezug auf das Ausmaß der verfügbaren Daten derzeit noch weitgehend Zukunftsmusik. Sie verdeutlichen jedoch die Möglichkeiten und die Herausforderungen des technischen Einsatzes von KI in der Pflege. Inwieweit die skizzierten Anwendungsfälle tatsächlich einen merklichen Zuwachs an Nutzen, also an einer besseren Pflege, mit sich bringen, wäre in einem zweiten Schritt nachzuweisen und stellt in den kommenden Jahren eine wichtige Forschungsfrage für die Wissenschaft dar. Der Einsatz von KI in der Pflege impliziert über den technischen Nutzen hinaus zudem Diskussionspunkte von ethischer und sozialer Natur, die zu beachten sind: Können die Betroffenen den Handlungsvorschlägen eines KI-Systems vertrauen? Welche Daten, Erkenntnisse und Algorithmen führen konkret zur Entscheidung? Wer hat Zugriff auf diese Daten und sind persönliche Daten ausreichend geschützt? Sind die zugrunde liegenden Daten repräsentativ oder findet eine verdeckte Diskriminierung statt? Auch wenn diese Fragen dem Standardrepertoire der Forschung zu KI entnommen sind – ganz unabhängig von einer Anwendung in der Pflege –, lassen sie sich gleichermaßen auch an eine Pflege ohne KI-Unterstützung stellen. Die Auseinandersetzung mit rechtlichen und ethischen Fragen ist daher nicht neu, bedarf aber im Kontext erweiterter technischer Möglichkeiten einer sorgfältigen Diskussion und Abwägung von möglichem Nutzen und potenziellen Risiken.

Warum sollten wir uns also mit KI-Anwendungen in der Pflege beschäftigen? In Anwendungsgebieten mit hoher Komplexität und Individualität in der Leistung spielt der Mensch weiterhin eine wichtige Rolle in der Entscheidungsfindung. Wenn also eine erfolgreiche Auseinandersetzung mit dem Thema KI in der Pflege gelingen soll, bedingt dies daher auch eine Auseinandersetzung von Pflegefachpersonen mit diesem Thema, eine Erweiterung des professionellen Selbstverständnisses sowie

von Ausbildungsinhalten, um gestaltende Akteur*innen und nicht nur passiv Aus-
führende zu sein.

Was bleibt als Fazit? Ist „gute Pflege" mit KI möglich oder ist KI in Zukunft sogar
zwingend erforderlich für „gute Pflege"? Technikeinsatz in sozialen Dienstleistungen
wie der Pflege kann zweifellos dazu dienen, Dienstleistungen zu verbessern, ohne
dabei die menschliche Komponente zu vernachlässigen oder in den Hintergrund zu
drängen. Aber auch mit einem solchen Leitbild verbleiben offene Fragen und Gestaltungsspielräume. Diese gilt es aktiv zu nutzen, indem rechtzeitig eine frühe und
breite gesellschaftliche Auseinandersetzung mit technologischen Innovationen in
der Pflege stattfinden muss, die offen mit Blick sowohl auf Möglichkeiten als auch
Risiken geführt wird.

The very title of this article raises all sorts of questions. What
does 'good care' actually mean? What does it entail? And in
what circumstances can or should Artificial Intelligence
come into play? One definition has it that 'good care means
applying up-to-date expertise in keeping with the expectations of the person in need of care'.[1] Care professionals use
a wealth of information to reach decisions that influence the
quality of the care they provide. Besides gathering direct
personal data (e.g. a person's vital signs or vulnerability to
falling), this includes both implicit professional and empirical
knowledge, as well as explicit bases of knowledge drawn
from documentation, guidelines, and/or scientific findings.

In Germany, we currently face challenges that have arisen from the consequences
and natural corollaries of an ageing society characterised by altered social structures, and from a shortage of skilled nursing staff. Against this backdrop, the use of AI
in the care sector has been under discussion and even trialled for some time now. So
another entity capable of 'contributing its thoughts' in the workplace, conveying
recommended actions, and enabling a form of forward-looking action would therefore seem helpful in assisting with nursing care. But what might the needs-based
deployment of such entities and the ethically responsible use actually look like?

Well, let's take a look at what is meant by AI in the first place, and where it might
be used in nursing care. AI comprises all kinds of algorithms that use databases to
learn how to enable intelligent, goal-orientated actions: for example, for nursing care

in hospitals, for long-term outpatient or inpatient care, and for people belonging to different target groups. AI methods could be used to provide family caregivers with more targeted support when it comes to navigating counselling and service offerings. AI assistance in drawing up duty rosters that take account not only of the requirements of those needing care but also of the skills and competence levels of the staff would be just as helpful as assistance provided to nursing professionals when making decisions in complex care situations.

For those in need of care, fields of application such as the structuring of everyday life and support with the self-management of chronic illnesses seem promising. AI can also be helpful in recording and analysing activities as well as a person's health and individual risks such as the likelihood of a fall. Other areas of application could include assistance with documentation processes and the sharing of information across sectors in order to optimise the care process itself. However, access to representative, high-quality data poses a challenge. Currently, there is no overview of data sources, publicly accessible collections of data or requirements for the utilisation of data in the care sector when it comes to the development of AI systems.[2]

AI systems that support the aforementioned activities are already in use around the world. There is, however, only a limited number of application studies under everyday conditions currently available. Similarly, the debate on the ethical, legal, and social implications is still in its infancy. In the years to come, the long-term use of AI in the care sector will therefore require an in-depth examination of the outline conditions, needs, social expectations, and required competences of the users.

The new possibilities afforded by data processing represent a huge opportunity for the care sector. If AI could collate, on a case-by-case basis, the specialist knowledge contained in expert standards and guidelines and make it accessible to the care sector, the current state-of-the-art in nursing and medical knowledge could be taken into account more readily when devising the nursing care process. Merging data from different institutions, sectors or even countries could give rise to a foundation of data that would exceed many times the wealth of experience any individual nurse is able to acquire over the course of their professional career. If AI systems were to learn from the individual data of those requiring care, said care could then be personalised. Feedback loops for user analysis of the results generated by algorithms could provide useful indicators of effective action under everyday conditions through the use of AI. This would help to flag up automated correlations between nursing care measures and their outcomes that would otherwise not be studied.

For the time being, such considerations are still, by and large, a pipe dream, especially as far as the extent of the available data is concerned. However, they do illustrate the possibilities and the challenges posed by the use of AI technology in the care sector. The extent to which the application cases outlined above actually do bring about a marked benefit increase, i.e. better care, would need to be demonstrated in a second phase; certainly it represents an important research question for the scientific community in the years to come. Beyond the technological benefits, the use of AI in nursing care also entails points of discussion of an ethical and social nature that do need to be addressed. Would those concerned by nursing care be able or willing to trust the actions proposed by an AI system? What sort of data, findings, and algorithms actually lead to the adopted decision? Who has access to the data – and is personal data sufficiently safeguarded? Is the underlying data representative or is there some hidden discrimination at play? Even if such questions are part of the standard repertoire of AI research and entirely independent of AI applications in the care sector, they could just as readily be asked of nursing care that is not AI-assisted. Addressing legal and ethical issues is therefore nothing new, but within the context of broadened technological possibilities it does require careful discussion and consideration of possible benefits and potential risks.

Why, then, do we need to concern ourselves with AI applications in nursing care? Humans continue to play an important decision-making role in application areas with high complexity levels and individualised performance. Therefore, if the issue of AI in the care sector is to be addressed successfully, it also means that nursing professionals themselves need to concern themselves with the issue, to broaden their professional self-image and their training content so they can continue to be participants actively involved in shaping the sector rather than just its implementing agents.

So what conclusion might we draw? Is 'good care' possible with AI or might 'good care' in the future even be predicated on AI as a condition sine qua non? The use of technology in social services such as nursing care can undoubtedly serve to improve services without neglecting the human aspect or relegating it to the background. But even with such a guiding principle, open questions and ample scope for manoeuvre still remain. We need to use them proactively so that a timely and broad social debate on technological innovations in nursing care can take place, one that is conducted openly and frankly, with due regard for both the opportunities and the risks.

1   Stiftung ZQP, *Ambulante Pflege. Gute professionelle Pflege erkennen*, 2021,
    https://www.zqp.de/wp-content/uploads/ZQP_Ratgeber_GutePflegeerkennen.pdf
    (letzter Abruf / last retrieved: 17.3.2021).

2   Universität Bremen, *Sondierungsprojekt zu KI in der Pflege (SoKIP)*, 2021,
    https://www.ipp.uni-bremen.de/projekte/abgeschlossene-projekte/
    ?proj=807&page=1 (letzter Abruf / last retrieved: 15.3.2021).

**Lauren Lee McCarthy (*1987)
& David Leonard (*1977)**
I.A. Suzie, 2019, Video, 9:03 Min.

Im Haus der 80-jährigen US-Amerikanerin
Mary Ann wird ein Pflegesystem installiert,
das sie „Suzie" nennt. In einer einwöchigen
Performance schlüpfen die US-amerikanischen
Künstler*innen McCarthy und Leonard in
die Rolle dieses virtuellen Assistenzsystems:
Rund um die Uhr beobachten sie Mary Ann
durch 360-Grad-Kameras und interagieren
mit ihr. Der Film dokumentiert die Entwicklung
der emotionalen Beziehung zwischen Mensch
und KI und geht der Frage nach, ob KI-Systeme
Fürsorge leisten können.

In the home of 80-year-old US American Mary Ann, a care
system she calls 'Suzie' is installed. As part of a week-long
performance, American artists Lauren Lee McCarthy and
David Leonard slip into the role of this virtual assistance
system. They observe Mary Ann literally 24/7 using 360-
degree cameras and interact with her. The film not only
documents the way emotional relationships between
humans and AI evolve, but it also explores the question
of whether AI systems can be caregivers.

18:02:17   Mary Ann

RE-VISIONEN
KI

Wie wollen wir KI-Systeme künftig nutzen? Darüber müssen wir diskutieren. Denn was in Forschungseinrichtungen und Unternehmen erprobt und entwickelt wird, betrifft uns als Gesellschaft. Aus Künstlicher Intelligenz kann viel Nutzen gezogen werden, wenn wir diesen Systemen die richtigen Zielvorgaben machen, sie aufgrund solider Datengrundlagen trainieren und fair gestalten. Es müssen jedoch klare Spielregeln geschaffen werden, um eine verantwortungsbewusste und gemeinwohlorientierte Nutzung von KI sicherzustellen, die auf rechtsstaatlichen Prinzipien beruhen. Welche Entscheidungen und Problemlösungen wollen wir an KI-Systeme abgeben? Wo ziehen wir die Grenzen?

How are we planning to use AI systems in the future? This is a question we need to discuss. After all, what research institutions and companies are testing and developing affects us as a society. A great deal of benefit can be drawn from Artificial Intelligence if we set these systems the right goals, train them on the basis of solid data, and design them fairly. But clear rules need to be defined to ensure a responsible and public-minded use of AI, founded on rule-of-law principles. What sort of decisions and solutions are we prepared to entrust to AI systems? Where do we draw the boundaries?

AI RE-VISIONS

MARTINA HEßLER

KÜNSTLICHE INTELLIGENZ: EINE NEUARTIGE KATEGORIE VON MASCHINE ODER DIE VERMENSCHLICHUNG DER MASCHINE

ARTIFICIAL INTELLIGENCE: A NEW CATEGORY OF MACHINE OR THE HUMANISATION OF THE MACHINE

Der Maschinenbegriff erfährt derzeit eine bemerkenswerte Renaissance. Im Kontext der Digitalisierung und der Künstlichen Intelligenz ist gar die Rede von einem Zweiten Maschinenzeitalter. Erstaunlich ist allerdings, mit welcher Selbstverständlichkeit dies der Fall ist, denn KI irritiert bisherige Maschinenbilder. Sie stellt eine völlig neuartige Kategorie von Maschine dar. Doch was für eine „Maschine" ist die KI? Ist sie überhaupt eine „Maschine"?

In der Frühen Neuzeit wurde die mechanische Maschine zur Metapher für gleichförmige, geregelte und nachvollziehbare Abläufe („wie ein Uhrwerk"). Im 19. Jahrhundert stand der Begriff darüber hinaus für reibungsloses Funktionieren und rationale Abläufe. Diese Vorstellungen prägten das Bild der Maschine bis in die zweite Hälfte des 20. Jahrhunderts: das Regelhafte, Immergleiche, das Berechenbare, das Plan- und Vorhersagbare.

Auch wenn Computer und KI bis in die jüngste Gegenwart diesem Bild der regelbasierten und programmierten Maschine entsprachen, wurde just mit ihrer Entwicklung bereits in den 1950er-Jahren eine neue Dimension des Maschinenbegriffs diagnostiziert. So hatte unter anderem der französische Kybernetiker Louis Couffignal im Jahr 1955 mit Blick auf den „denkenden" Computer bemerkt, dass sich Maschinen so sehr, ja geradezu in ihrer Art unterscheiden, dass sie in verschiedene Kategorien einzuordnen seien. In der Tat, spätestens nun, im Zuge der jüngsten KI-Entwicklungen, muss die Geschichte des Maschinenbegriffs fortgeschrieben werden. Maschinelles Lernen stellt eine kategorial andere und neuartige Maschinenform dar.

Vielleicht nährt sich die Renaissance des Maschinenbegriffs aus dem Hype des *machine learning*, das die Basis der derzeitigen KI-Erfolge darstellt und den Kern der kategorialen Neuheit gleichsam im Titel trägt: Wir haben es nun mit lernenden Maschinen zu tun. Sie lernen anhand von Daten; die Algorithmen verbessern sich selbst. Programmierer*innen programmieren nicht mehr, wie ein Algorithmus zur Lösung kommt, sondern sie programmieren Algorithmen, die in der Lage sind, aus ihrer „Erfahrung" zu lernen und selbst ein Modell zu entwickeln, das sie dann auf andere Daten anwenden können. Sie entwickeln sich daher selbstständig.

Historisch betrachtet ist dies nicht völlig neu: Neuronale Netze wurden bereits in den 1940er- und 1950er-Jahren diskutiert, auch kybernetische Maschinen „lernten"; erste Forschungen zu *machine learning* wurden bereits in den 1980er-Jahren betrieben. Dass KI nun neue Erfolge feiert, liegt an der neuartigen Datenmenge, einer hohen Verarbeitungsgeschwindigkeit und einer neuen Qualität effizienter Algorithmen. Damit ist KI nicht mehr vergleichbar mit Maschinen des 20. Jahrhunderts. Doch was genau macht – über den Kern des Lernens hinaus – ihre Neuheit aus?

KI interagiert, erstens, in neuer Weise mit ihren Nutzer*innen. Sie wird im Alltag zur Beraterin, Partnerin, Assistentin. KI gilt nicht mehr als schlichtes Werkzeug, mit dem etwas bearbeitet, erstellt oder errechnet wird. Es wird nun in einem eng verwobenen Handlungsgeflecht gemeinsam mit KI entschieden, gesprochen oder geschrieben. Dabei, und dies ist ein zweiter zentraler Punkt, entwickeln sich KI-Anwendungen individuell und in Wechselwirkung mit ihrem Gegenüber. Siri, Alexa, Chatbots, soziale Roboter lernen die Verhaltensweisen, Interessen und Vorlieben ihres jeweiligen Gegenübers und „beraten" und „antworten" im Laufe der Zeit immer gezielter entsprechend dieser individuellen Gepflogenheiten. Historisch betrachtet, ist dies eine überaus bemerkenswerte Zäsur. Das Maschinenhafte ist nicht mehr das Standardisierte, das Immergleiche. Vielmehr entwickeln sich KIs unterschiedlich, sie haben gleichsam eine individuelle Biografie, die von ihrem Gegenüber und ihrem Nutzungskontext abhängt. Es ist das alltägliche Verhalten, die alltägliche Nutzung des je Einzelnen, das die KI permanent verändert.

Dies impliziert, drittens, eine weitere Eigenschaft, die KI von der klassischen Maschine unterscheidet. Die Entwicklung eigenständig lernender Algorithmen ist nicht vorhersehbar, nicht planbar. Wie die KI in einem Jahr antworten und mit Menschen interagieren wird, ist offen. Maschinen haben somit auch eine individuelle Zukunft. Zudem sind, viertens, ihre Ergebnisse nicht reproduzierbar – gleichfalls eine fundamental neue Eigenschaft im Vergleich zu Maschinen, wie wir sie bisher kannten, die nichts Überraschendes aufboten und auf deren Gleichförmigkeit Verlass war. Spricht man beispielsweise mit einem Bot, so stellt man schnell fest, dass die gleiche Frage stets unterschiedlich beantwortet wird.

Eine weitere neue Dimension betrifft, fünftens, das maschinelle Entscheiden. Dies ist zwar nicht neu. So mokierte sich bereits in den 1950er-Jahren der Philosoph und Schriftsteller Günther Anders über den Einsatz eines Computers im Koreakrieg, der entscheiden sollte, ob die USA den Krieg beenden. Neu ist allerdings, dass die Maschinen situativ ethische Entscheidungen zu treffen haben, wie es zum Beispiel im Bereich des autonomen Fahrens oder im Falle militärisch verwendeter Drohnen diskutiert wird. Gleichermaßen neu ist, sechstens, dass Maschinen einen Bias entwickeln können. In Abhängigkeit von der jeweiligen Datenbasis schreiben KI-Anwendungen beispielsweise Diskriminierungen fort. Zwar hat die technikgeschichtliche Forschung vielfach dargelegt, dass Technik aufgrund ihrer Kulturalität nie neutral ist und menschliche Vorannahmen immer in ihre Entwicklung einfließen. Doch dass Maschinen im Prozess ihres „Tuns" einen Bias entwickeln und dann gleichsam kulturell geformte Entscheidungen treffen, die nicht nachvollziehbar sind, transformiert das Bild von Maschinen nachhaltig. Noch in den 1950er- und 1960er-Jahren hoffte man, Computer würden in einer irrationalen Welt rationale und objektive Entscheidungen treffen. Heute bevorzugen oder benachteiligen KI-Anwendungen bestimmte Menschengruppen.

Schließlich stellen, siebtens, künstliche neuronale Netze für die KI-Entwickler*-innen eine Blackbox dar. Maschinen haben gleichsam ein Geheimnis, indem ihr Verhalten nicht immer nachvollziehbar ist. Neu ist also die *prinzipielle* Nichtverstehbarkeit, die die KI als Blackbox von den vielen Blackboxes der Konsumtechnik, die wir so selbstverständlich nichtverstehend nutzen, unterscheidet.

Damit ergibt sich ein atemberaubendes Bild der KI, das mit bisherigen Vorstellungen der Maschine radikal bricht: Die Maschine interagiert mit Menschen, sie „antwortet", sie entwickelt sich in Abhängigkeit vom jeweiligen Gegenüber. Sie kann einen Bias entwickeln. Sie soll moralisch-ethische Entscheidungen treffen, ihr Verhalten verändert sich, es ist nicht immer reproduzierbar und nicht immer nachvollziehbar. Sie wird zu unserer Beraterin, Gefährtin, Assistentin. Es ist das Zusammenspiel dieser Eigenschaften, die sich gegenseitig bedingen und im maschinellen Lernen begründet liegen, das die derzeitige KI zu einer neuen Kategorie von Maschine macht. In einem Satz zusammengefasst, könnte man sagen, dass KI menschenähnlich wird. KI entspricht somit nicht mehr dem Maschinenbild des 20. Jahrhunderts, nicht mehr dem Gleichförmigen und Rationalen, von dem sich Menschen häufig abgrenzten. Allerdings *scheint* KI nur menschenähnlich, indem sie nun auch all das, was im Laufe des 20. Jahrhunderts immer wieder als das Humanum im Gegensatz zur Maschine betont wurde, *simuliert*: Individualität, Subjektivität, Emotionalität, die Nichtvorhersehbarkeit menschlicher Handlungen, das menschliche Vermögen zu ethischem Handeln. Dies fordert zu einer Neureflexion nicht nur des Maschinenbegriffs, sondern auch des menschlichen Selbstverständnisses heraus.

The concept of the machine is currently experiencing a remarkable renaissance. Within the context of digitisation and Artificial Intelligence, there is even talk of a second machine age. But what is astonishing is how matter-of-course this has been; after all, AI does jar somewhat with traditional notions of machines. It represents a completely new category of machine. But what kind of 'machine' is AI in the first place? In fact, is it even a 'machine'?

In the early modern era, the mechanical machine became a metaphor for processes that were regular, regulated, and reproducible ('running like clockwork'). In the 19th century, the concept stood for smooth-running, rational processes. These notions shaped the image of the machine right through to the second half of the 20th century as something that was regular, always the same, reliable, dependable, and predictable.

And even if, until very recently, computers and AI continued to correspond to this image of the programmed, rule-based machine, a new dimension to the machine concept was identified as early on as the 1950s, precisely at a time when they were 'evolving'. In 1955, French cyberneticist Louis Couffignal, among others, remarked on the subject of the 'thinking' computer that machines differed so much, in their very essence even, that they had to be sorted into different categories. Now at the latest, given the latest trends in AI, the history of the machine concept has to be updated. Machine learning represents a categorically different and novel form of machine.

Perhaps the renaissance of the machine concept thrives on the hype that surrounds *machine learning,* which is the mainstay of current AI successes, with the categorial novelty featured in the name itself: indeed, learning machines are what we are now dealing with. They learn using data; and the algorithms are self-improving. Programmers have ceased programming how an algorithm ought to arrive at a solution; instead, they program algorithms capable of learning from their 'experience' and then developing a model by themselves to apply to other data. They are, therefore, developing autonomously.

From a historical perspective, this is not something entirely new. Neural networks were already being discussed in the 1940s and 1950s, and indeed, cybernetic machines were also 'learning'; initial research into *machine learning* was being conducted as early as the 1980s. The fact that AI is now celebrating new successes is down to a new type of data volume, high processing speeds, and a new quality of efficient algorithms. It means that AI is no longer comparable to 20th century machines. But what exactly is so novel about it – beyond its essential 'learning' aspect?

First, AI interacts in a new way with its users. It has become an advisor, a partner, and an assistant in everyday life. AI is no longer seen as a mere tool used to edit, create or calculate something. Decisions are now made, discussed, or written together with AI, as part of a densely interwoven network of actions. Here, and this is a second central key aspect, AI applications develop individually and as part of an interaction with their counterpart. Siri, Alexa, chatbots, social robots learn the behavioural patterns, interests and preferences of their counterparts and, over time, 'advise' and 'respond' more and more precisely, in keeping with those individual habits. Historically, this is a remarkable turning point. The machine-like aspect is no longer that which is standardised and ever-constant. Instead, AI systems evolve differently; they have their own individual biography, as it were, one that depends on their counterpart and the context in which they are used. It is the everyday behaviour, the everyday use by each individual that permanently modifies the AI.

Third, this in turn implies yet another characteristic that differentiates AI from machines in the traditional sense. The evolution of algorithms that learn autonomously cannot be predicted or planned. How AI will respond and interact with human beings in a year's time is anyone's guess. This means that machines also have a future all of their own. Fourth, their results are not reproducible, another fundamentally new characteristic compared with the sort of machines we have been familiar with so far, which had no surprises in store; indeed, we could rely on their 'sameness'. Talk to a bot, for instance, and you quickly realise that the same question always produces different answers.

Fifth, another new dimension concerns machine decision-making. Admittedly, this is not something new. As early as the 1950s, philosopher and writer Günther Anders was mocking the use of a computer during the Korean War to decide whether or not the US should end the war. What is new is that machines have to make ethical decisions according to a given situation: this is what is currently being debated for example when it comes to autonomous driving or the use of drones for military purposes. Sixth, what's also new is that machines are now capable of developing bias. Depending on the database used in each case, AI applications will for example perpetuate discrimination. Research into the history of technology has often shown that technology – by virtue of its cultural nature – is never neutral and that human assumptions have always been incorporated into its development. However, the fact that machines develop a bias in the course of their 'actions' and then reach culturally formed decisions that are not transparent has a lasting impact on the very image of machines. In the 1950s and 1960s, it was hoped that computers would be able to make rational and objective decisions in an irrational world. Today, AI applications favour certain groups of people while discriminating against others.

Seventh, and finally, artificial neural nets are something of a black box for AI developers. Machines have a secret, as it were, in that their behaviour is not always 'comprehensible'. What's new is the incomprehensibility *in principle* that distinguishes AI as a black box from the many black boxes of consumer technology that we use so naturally without really understanding them.

This gives rise to a breathtaking image of AI that radically breaks with previous notions of the machine: i.e. a machine that interacts with people, that 'responds' and develops in keeping with the counterpart in each case. It is capable of developing bias. It is meant to make moral and ethical decisions; its behaviour changes; and it is not always reproducible and not always comprehensible. It becomes our advisor, companion and/or assistant. It is the interplay of all these characteristics mutually conditioning one another and rooted in machine learning that makes current AI systems an entirely novel category of machine. In a nutshell, you could say that AI is becoming human-like. AI therefore no longer corresponds to the 20th century image of the machine, to the uniform and rational from which humans often chose to distance themselves. However, AI only *appears* human-like in that it now also *simulates* that which, time and again in the course of the 20th century, was emphasised as the human aspect as opposed to the mechanical: individuality, subjectivity, emotionality, the unpredictability of human actions, the human capacity for ethical action. For us, this poses a challenge to reflect anew not only on the concept of the machine, but also on our understanding of ourselves as human beings.

DIRK BAECKER

DIE POLITIK DER DATEN

DATA POLICIES

Traum und Albtraum der Künstlichen Intelligenz verdanken sich einem presbyterianischen Pfarrer, aus dessen Nachlass im Jahr 1764 ein wissenschaftlicher Artikel veröffentlicht wurde, der die Wahrscheinlichkeitstheorie revolutionieren sollte. Der Name dieses Pfarrers war Thomas Bayes. Die Beschäftigung mit der Wahrscheinlichkeitstheorie und folglich mit Mathematik und Logik lag damals für einen Theologen auf der Hand. Immerhin wird seit Blaise Pascal darüber diskutiert, dass man mit einer Wette auf die Existenz Gottes nur gewinnen kann. Sollte es ihn nicht geben, hat man nicht viel verloren. Sollte es ihn geben, hat man alles gewonnen.

Die Entdeckung von Bayes betrifft zwei Überlegungen, ohne die es die Künstliche Intelligenz in der aktuellen Form des Maschinenlernens nicht gäbe. Die erste Überlegung ist die der bedingten Wahrscheinlichkeit, die zweite die der korrigierbaren Gewichte der Einschätzung von Wahrscheinlichkeiten. Es lohnt sich, die gemeinten Sachverhalte genauer anzuschauen. Denn erstens muss man verstehen, was die Programme des Maschinenlernens tatsächlich leisten. Und zweitens muss man wissen, worauf eine Politik der Daten Einfluss haben kann.

Die erste Annahme von Bayes läuft einer Grundannahme der gängigen Statistik zuwider, nach der in einem statistisch beschriebenen Universum alle Ereignisse unabhängig voneinander eine bestimmte Wahrscheinlichkeit haben, die man aus der Vergangenheit, also aus dem bisherigen Verlauf der Ereignisse kennt. Doch was ist, wenn bestimmte Ereignisse ganz einfach deswegen wahrscheinlicher werden, weil andere Ereignisse aufgetreten oder auch nicht aufgetreten sind? Wie heißt es bei Sherlock Holmes? Der Hund hat nicht gebellt, also muss der Mörder ein Bekannter gewesen sein. Bayes entwickelte daher eine mathematische Formel, in der die Wahrscheinlichkeit des einen Ereignisses eine Funktion der Wahrscheinlichkeit eines anderen Ereignisses ist. Klingt harmlos, ist aber eine ganz entscheidende Annäherung an die Wirklichkeit – wenn man denn genügend Daten hat, um diese Wahrscheinlichkeiten überhaupt einzuschätzen.

Die zweite Überlegung von Bayes ist noch radikaler. Sie verwandelt eine Statistik, die bloß registriert, wann etwas geschehen ist, in eine Statistik, die sozusagen mitdenkt. Sie liefert Wahrscheinlichkeitseinschätzungen in Echtzeit: Warum soll man annehmen, dass vergangene Daten einfach hochgerechnet werden können, wenn die Wirklichkeit doch in dauernder Bewegung ist? Also führte Bayes in seine Formel die Möglichkeit der Aktualisierung und Berichtigung ein. Von Moment zu Moment „lernen" die Maschinen, welche bedingten Wahrscheinlichkeiten tatsächlich gegeben sind und welche nicht. Mit dieser Automatisierung einer Statistik, die ihre „Gewichte" also selber laufend korrigiert, bewegt sie sich wie ein Fisch im Wasser. Das Einzige, was jetzt noch stören könnte, wären Theorien, warum welche Ereignisse eintreten. Diese Theorien werden deswegen abgeschafft. Sie gelten als überholt.

Für eine Politik der Daten ist das unmittelbar relevant. Denn größer konnte das Objektivitätsversprechen der Künstlichen Intelligenz noch nie sein. In den 1960er- und 1970er-Jahren hatte man versucht, symbolische Systeme zu bauen, deren kognitive Leistungen sich am Vorbild der menschlichen Intelligenz orientierten. Damit jedoch wäre jede Künstliche Intelligenz mit allen Schwächen ausgestattet gewesen, die man von der menschlichen Intelligenz kennt: Vorurteile, begrenzte Fähigkeit zur Informationsverarbeitung, Schmalspurigkeit, Scheuklappen. Denn die Grundlage symbolischer Systeme ist die Schlussfolgerung. Und Schlüsse können nur aus dem gefolgert werden, was vorher schon gegeben ist. Mit dem Maschinenlernen jedoch gibt es keine Schlussfolgerungen, sondern nur Feststellungen. Ereignisse treten auf oder treten nicht auf. Damit weiß man, woran man ist.

Oder nicht? Nein, denn auch die Ereignisse, mit deren Abhängigkeit man rechnet, müssen unter anderen Ereignissen ausgewählt werden. Und auch die Geschichte, die man in Rechnung stellt, berücksichtigt bestimmte Ereignisse und vernachlässigt andere. Schon damit wird eine Politik der Daten auf den Plan gerufen. Wer wählt aus, was berücksichtigt wird und was nicht? Eine Zeitlang konnte man dieses Problem vernebeln, indem man dank gestiegener Speicherkapazitäten und Rechengeschwindigkeiten sowie dank leistungsfähiger Prozessoren und Algorithmen einfach jedes Datum zu berücksichtigen versprach. Mit Big Data, so unterstellte man, verschwände das Problem der Selektion. Allenfalls würde die Zeit fehlen, allen denkbaren Verknüpfungen im Datenkorpus nachzugehen. Aber dazu hat man ja die schnellen Rechner. Bis zum Quantenrechner ist es auch nicht mehr weit.

Inzwischen weiß man, dass es nicht nur das Problem der Selektion gibt, sondern auch das der Subsumtion. Als was werden Ereignisse gezählt? Wann ist der Kinderwagen mit dem spacigen Design keine Mülltüte, die über die Straße geweht wird? Wann deuten die etwas verzerrten Gesichtszüge der jungen Frau am Gate des Flughafens eher auf Kopfschmerzen als auf die Anspannung vor der terroristischen Tat? Sicher, diese und andere Fragen können mit neuen Trainingsdaten beantwortet werden. Es ist verblüffend, wie feinkörnig das physikalische Universum ist, und mit welcher Sicherheit Zustände identifiziert und unterschieden werden können.

Aber viel wahrscheinlicher, als diesen Prozess des Trainings immer weiterlaufen zu lassen, ist die Einrichtung eines kontrollierbaren Universums, wo immer man es braucht. Das Muster ist immer dasselbe. Schienen für Eisenbahnen, Autobahnen für Autos, Identitätsprofile für Personen. Alles im Dienst der Konstruktion und Kontrolle berechenbarer Geschichten. Die KI braucht uns mindestens so sehr wie wir sie. Von der Entstehung sozialer Netzwerke hat sich die Politik überraschen lassen. Wer hätte damit auch rechnen können? Die Zurichtung der Daten jedoch beginnt sie national und international mit aller Schärfe in den Blick zu nehmen.

Allerdings ist die Politik der Daten alles andere als eindeutig. Auf der einen Seite muss sie wollen, was sie auf der anderen Seite verhindern will. Die umfassende Überwachung birgt das Versprechen einer umfassenden Vorsorge. Auf welches Wissen im Umgang mit natürlichen und menschlichen Ereignissen und Aktivitäten soll man verzichten, wenn jedes Wissen brauchbar ist? Die Sensoren der Künstlichen Intelligenz erfassen politische Meinungen, gesundheitliche Zustände, berufliche Karrieren, Freizeit- und Bildungsverhalten, Reiseziele, Kontakte, religiöse und kulturelle Vorlieben, die allesamt nicht nur für Empfehlungen an die Nutzer ausgewertet werden können, sondern auch die Informationsgrundlage für Parteien,

Behörden, Kirchen, Schulen und Universitäten, kulturelle Einrichtungen erheblich verbessern könnten.

Was lässt die Politik zu und was verbietet sie? Worauf sichert sie sich einen Einfluss und was liegt außerhalb ihrer Kontrolle? Und mit welchen politischen Akteuren haben wir es zu tun? Gesundheitsämter liegen im Konflikt mit Datenschutzbeauftragten, ein Wirtschaftsministerium hat andere Vorstellungen als ein Sozialministerium, die nationale Förderung von Champions des Maschinenlernens widerspricht dem internationalen Wunsch der Eindämmung immer neuer Entwicklungen, eine Politik der Kontrolle des Klimawandels beißt sich mit liberalen Vorstellungen einer freien Entwicklung aller.

Wir brauchen eine Politik der Daten. Wir müssen wissen, welche Daten von wem für wen gemacht werden. Wir müssen wissen, was ein Datum ist, denn sicherlich unterscheiden sich physikalische von biologischen und soziale von technischen Daten. Das wäre vermutlich ganz im Sinne des presbyterianischen Pfarrers. Innerhalb bedingter Wahrscheinlichkeiten und pfadabhängiger Geschichten muss der politische Wille in all seiner Diversität selbst ein Datum sein. Gott sei mit uns.

It is to a Presbyterian minister that we owe much of the dream and nightmare of Artificial Intelligence. Indeed, in 1764, a scientific article was published from his estate that would revolutionise probability theory. The pastor's name was Thomas Bayes. For a theologian around that time, a deep interest in probability theory and, consequently, in mathematics and logic would have been self-evident. After all, Pascal's wager had triggered the discussion whereby betting on the existence of God was in fact a win-win situation. If God did not exist, the loss would be finite. If He did exist, the gains were infinite.

Bayes's discovery concerns two considerations without which Artificial Intelligence as we know it today, i.e. machine learning, would be inconceivable. The first is conditional probability; the second, the correctable weighting of the estimation of probabilities. It is well worth taking a closer look at what is meant. Firstly, it is important to understand what machine-learning programs actually do. And secondly, it is important to know what a data policy is capable of influencing.

Bayes's first assumption runs counter to one of the basic assumptions of conventional statistics whereby, in a statistically described universe, all events independently of one another have a certain probability, a known quantity empirically derived from the past, i.e. from the course of events thus far. But what if certain events simply become more probable because other events may or may not have occurred? As Sherlock Holmes famously deduced, the dog did not bark, therefore the murderer could not have been a total stranger. So Bayes drew up a mathematical formula in which the probability of one event is a function of the probability of another event. What may sound rather anodyne is in fact a crucial approximation to reality – providing sufficient data is available to estimate these probabilities in the first place.

Bayes's second consideration is even more radical. It transforms a statistic that merely registers the fact that something has happened into a statistic that thinks for itself, so to speak. It provides probability estimates in real time: why should one assume that historical data can simply be extrapolated when reality is in fact permanently in motion? Bayes therefore introduced the possibility of updating and correcting into his formula. Machines 'learn' from one moment to the next which conditional probabilities are actually in place and which are not. This automating of statistics that continually auto-corrects its 'weighting' means that it moves like a fish through water. Now the only disruptive factors would be theories on why certain events occur. Such theories are therefore abolished. They are considered outdated.

This is of immediate and direct relevance to data policies. Indeed, never has the promise of the objectivity of Artificial Intelligence been greater. In the 1960s and 1970s, attempts were made to build symbolic systems with a cognitive performance modelled on that of human intelligence. However, that would have had the consequence of endowing any form of Artificial Intelligence with all the weaknesses that human intelligence is known to have, specifically: prejudices, a limited ability to process information, narrow-mindedness, and a blinkered view. After all, symbolic systems are founded on inference. And inferences can only be drawn from what has previously been established. But with machine learning there are no inferences, merely findings. Events either occur or they don't. That way at least you know where you stand.

Or do you? Actually, no, you don't, because even events you reckon with have to be selected from among other events. And the history you take into account also takes account of certain events while disregarding others. This alone brings up the notion of data policies. Who gets to choose what's taken into account and what isn't? For a while, it was possible to fudge on this issue by promising simply to take every single datum into account thanks to increased storage capacities and computing speeds as well as ever more powerful processors and algorithms. The implication being that, with big data, the problem of selection would disappear. At best, there would be no time to investigate all the conceivable links within a body of data. But that's what fast computers are for. And it won't be long now before quantum computers enter the equation, as it were.

We know in the meantime that there is not just the problem of selection, but also that of subsumption. What exactly counts as an event? When is a baby buggy with its funky design not a rubbish bag that's being blown across the street? When do the rather contorted facial features of a young woman at an airport gate signal a head-ache rather than nervous tension ahead of a terrorist act? Of course, answers to these and other questions can be provided using new training data. It is astonishing how fine-grained the physical universe actually is, and the certainty with which states can be identified and differentiated.

But what is far more probable than letting this training process continue to run its course is setting up a controllable universe wherever it is needed. The pattern is always the same. Railway tracks for trains, motorways for cars, identity profiles for individual persons. All in the service of constructing and controlling predictable nar-ratives. AI needs us at least as much as we need it. Politics has been caught off guard by the emergence of social networks. After all, who could have reckoned with them? But it is now taking a very close look at the manipulation of data, both nationally and internationally.

Yet data policies are anything but obvious. On the one hand, it has to want what it's trying to prevent on the other. Comprehensive surveillance holds the promise of comprehensive provision. If all knowledge is useful, what knowledge in our dealings with natural and human events and activities should we be dispensing with? AI sensors capture political opinions, states of health, professional careers, leisure and educational behaviour, travel destinations, contacts, religious and cultural prefer-ences, all of which can not only be analysed and evaluated as user recommenda-tions, but could also significantly improve the information basis used by political parties, authorities, churches, schools and universities, and cultural institutions.

What does a policy allow, and what does it forbid? On what does it gain influence, and what is beyond its control? And what sort of political players are we actually dealing with? Health authorities may be at loggerheads with data protection officers; the ideas held by a ministry of economic affairs may differ from those of a ministry of social affairs; the national funding of machine-learning champions may contradict the international drive to curb and contain ever new developments; a policy aimed at controlling climate change may clash with the liberal ideas of unfettered develop-ment for all.

We need data policies. We need to know who is creating what data, and for whom. We need to know what data is; after all, there is no denying the fact that phys-ical data differs from biological data, and social data from technical data. Presumably that would be entirely in keeping with what our Presbyterian minister had in mind. Within conditional probabilities and path-dependent narratives, political will in all its diversity must itself be data. God be with us.

PRATYUSHA KALLURI

DIE FRAGE IST NICHT, OB KI GUT ODER GERECHT IST, SONDERN WIE SIE DIE MACHT VERSCHIEBT

KI-Projekte sollten von jenen gestaltet werden, die durch KI benachteiligt werden könnten.

DON'T ASK IF AI IS GOOD OR FAIR, ASK HOW IT SHIFTS POWER

Those who could be exploited by AI should be shaping its projects.

Künstliche Intelligenz wird von Strafverfolgungs-behörden, Marketingabteilungen, Krankenhäusern und anderen Stellen eingesetzt, um Entscheidungen über verschiedene Dinge zu treffen, etwa darüber, wer ein strafrechtlich relevantes Profil besitzt, wer mit welcher Wahrscheinlichkeit welches Produkt zu welchem Preis kaufen wird, wer eine medizinische Behandlung bekommt und wer einen Arbeitsvertrag erhält. Dazu wird in zunehmendem Maße unser Verhalten überwacht und vorhergesagt, oft nach Maßgabe von Macht und Profit.

Unter KI-Fachleuten wird heute nicht selten die Frage erörtert, ob eine KI „gerecht" (*fair*) und „gut" ist. „Gerecht" und „gut" sind endlos dehnbare Begriffsräume, in die jedes KI-System beliebig hineingepackt werden kann. Die eigentliche Frage geht tiefer: Wie verschiebt die KI die Macht?

Am 12. Juli beginnt die einwöchige Internationale Konferenz des Maschinellen Lernens, eine der weltweit größten KI-Tagungen, wo Tausende von Forscher*innen virtuell zusammenkommen werden.[1] In Forschungskreisen ist die Meinung verbreitet, dass die KI neutral und oft nützlich ist und nur durch den Bias der aus einer ungerechten Gesellschaft gezogenen Daten verzerrt wird. Ein indifferenter Fachbereich dient in Wirklichkeit den Mächtigen.

Meiner Ansicht nach müssen jene, die im Bereich der KI tätig sind, diejenigen verstärkt zur Geltung bringen, die bei der Gestaltung übergangen wurden, und dazu ist es notwendig, die Beziehungen zu mächtigen Institutionen, die von der Überwachung der Menschen profitieren, einzuschränken. Die Forschenden sollten sich den Personengruppen und Communitys öffnen, die die Hauptlast der Überwachung getragen haben – oftmals Frauen, People of Colour, indigene Bevölkerungen, LSBTIQ, Arme oder Behinderte – und sollten ihnen zuhören, sie einbringen, sie zu Wort kommen lassen, mit ihnen zusammenarbeiten. Konferenzen und Forschungseinrichtungen sollten Mitgliedern dieser Personengruppen prominente Zeitfenster, Räumlichkeiten, finanzielle Mittel und leitende Positionen zur Verfügung stellen. Darüber hinaus sollten Förderanträge und Veröffentlichungen daran geknüpft werden, inwieweit sich die Forschung den Fragen der Machtverschiebung stellt.

Vor einem Jahr haben meine Kolleg*innen und ich das Radical AI Network gegründet, das an die Arbeiten unserer Vorgänger*innen anbindet. Die Gruppe lehnt sich an die Aussage der schwarzen feministischen Wissenschaftlerin Angela Davis an, die sagte: „Radikal bedeutet einfach, die Dinge bei den Wurzeln zu packen", und das Problem an der Wurzel ist die ungleiche Verteilung der Macht. Der Schwerpunkt unseres Netzwerks besteht darin, dass wir all jenen zuhören, die durch die KI beeinträchtigt und an den Rand gedrängt werden, und dass wir für unterdrückungsfreie Technologien eintreten.

Nehmen wir eine KI für die Klassifikation von Bildaufnahmen. Expert*innen trainieren das System auf die Erkennung von Mustern in Fotografien, zum Beispiel um das Geschlecht oder Handlungen einer Person zu identifizieren, oder um eine Gesichtsübereinstimmung mit den Angaben in einer Personendatenbank festzustellen. „Betroffene Personen" – damit meine ich diejenigen, die, oftmals ohne Zustimmung, per Tracking nachverfolgt werden, sowie diejenigen, die das KI-System trainieren, indem sie, gewöhnlich gegen eine geringe Bezahlung, Fotos manuell klassifizieren – werden vom KI-System ausgewertet bzw. oft ausgebeutet.

Die Forschenden im KI-Bereich konzentrieren sich überwiegend darauf, den Menschen in Entscheidungspositionen möglichst exakte Informationen zu liefern. Nur ein bemerkenswert geringer Teil der Forschung richtet sich darauf, wie man den betroffenen Personen dienen kann. Diesen Personen müssen Wege und Möglichkeiten geboten werden, die KI zu überprüfen, zu hinterfragen, zu beeinflussen oder auch nachzukonstruieren. Die Interessenvertretung Our Data Bodies („Unsere Datenkörper") in den USA schlägt beispielsweise Ansätze für den Schutz personenbezogener Daten beim Umgang mit den Anlaufstellen für Wohngerechtigkeit und Kinderschutz vor. Diese Arbeiten finden wenig Aufmerksamkeit. Der überwiegende Teil der Forschung umfasst die Erstellung von Systemen, deren Anlernen mit äußerst hohen Kosten verbunden ist und durch die jene Institutionen, die bereits mächtig sind, noch mächtiger werden – von Amazon, Google und Facebook bis hin zu Hausüberwachungen und Militärprogrammen.

Vielen Forscher*innen lässt es keine Ruhe, wenn sie sehen, wie die geistige Arbeit, die sie in KI stecken, die Ungleichheit befördert. Forschende wie ich arbeiten tagtäglich an aus unserer Sicht mathematisch schönen und nützlichen Systemen und hören die Erfolgsgeschichten der KI, wie über den ersten Platz bei den Go-Meisterschaften oder die aussichtsreiche Rolle in der Krebserkennung. Es liegt an uns und in unserer Verantwortung, dass wir unseren verzerrten Blick erkennen und denjenigen zuzuhören, die von der KI beeinflusst werden.

Aus dem Blickwinkel der Macht gesehen lässt sich erkennen, warum exakte, verallgemeinerbare und effiziente KI-Systeme nicht für jeden Menschen gut sind. In den Händen ausbeuterischer Unternehmen oder unterdrückender Rechtssysteme richtet eine exaktere Gesichtserkennung Schaden an. Zwar haben Organisationen reagiert und zugesichert, dass sie „gerechte" und „transparente" Systeme entwerfen, aber gerecht und transparent aus wessen Sicht? Diese Systeme entschärfen zwar mitunter den Schaden, werden aber von mächtigen Institutionen kontrolliert, die ihre eigene Agenda verfolgen. Bestenfalls sind die Systeme unzuverlässig; schlimmstenfalls sind sie eine reine Ethik-Fassade für Technologien, die die Ungleichheit weiter fortschreiben.

Einige Forschende legen bereits versteckte Einschränkungen und Systemschwachstellen bloß. Ihre Forschungsergebnisse enthalten Forderungen nach einer Regulierung der KI. In ihren Arbeiten kritisieren sie auch unzureichende technologische Nachbesserungen. Andere Forschende klären die Öffentlichkeit darüber auf, welch großer Umfang an natürlichen Ressourcen, Daten und menschlicher Arbeitskraft in die Schaffung der KI fließt.

Die Wissenschaftlerin Ruha Benjamin im Bereich *Race & Technology* von der Universität Princeton in New Jersey hat uns dazu aufgefordert und ermuntert, „die Welten zu erdenken und zu erbauen, ohne die man nicht leben kann, und dabei die Welten abzubauen, in denen man nicht leben kann". In diesem Sinne ist es an der Zeit, die an den Rand gedrängten und betroffenen Personengruppen in das Zentrum der KI-Forschung zu rücken – ihre Bedürfnisse, Kenntnisse und Träume sollten Leitplanken der Entwicklung sein. Dieses Jahr haben meine Kolleg*innen und ich zum Beispiel einen Workshop für diverse Teilnehmer*innen abgehalten, in dem wir uns darüber ausgetauscht haben, wie wir uns die KI-Zukunft erträumen. Wir haben uns eine KI vorgestellt, die die Bedürfnisse der betroffenen Personen abbildet und ihnen eine freie Wahl gestattet.

Wenn der Fachbereich der KI davon ausgeht, neutral zu sein, kann er systemisch verzerrte Daten nicht erkennen und baut Systeme, die den Status quo festschreiben und die Interessen der Mächtigen befeuern. Wir brauchen hingegen einen Fachbereich, der Systeme der Machtkonzentration bloßstellt und kritisiert und dabei in Zusammenarbeit mit den betroffenen Personengruppen neue Systeme aufbaut: KI von den Menschen für die Menschen.

> Law enforcement, marketers, hospitals and other bodies apply artificial intelligence (AI) to decide on matters such as who is profiled as a criminal, who is likely to buy what product at what price, who gets medical treatment and who gets hired. These entities increasingly monitor and predict our behaviour, often motivated by power and profits.

It is not uncommon now for AI experts to ask whether an AI is 'fair' and 'for good'. But 'fair' and 'good' are infinitely spacious words that any AI system can be squeezed into. The question to pose is a deeper one: how is AI shifting power?

From 12 July, thousands of researchers will meet virtually at the week-long International Conference on Machine Learning, one of the largest AI meetings in the world.[1] Many researchers think that AI is neutral and often beneficial, marred only by biased data drawn from an unfair society. In reality, an indifferent field serves the powerful.

In my view, those who work in AI need to elevate those who have been excluded from shaping it, and doing so will require them to restrict relationships with powerful institutions that benefit from monitoring people. Researchers should listen to, amplify, cite and collaborate with communities that have borne the brunt of surveillance: often women, people who are Black, Indigenous, LGBT+, poor or disabled.

Conferences and research institutions should cede prominent time slots, spaces, funding and leadership roles to members of these communities. In addition, discussions of how research shifts power should be required and assessed in grant applications and publications.

A year ago, my colleagues and I created the Radical AI Network, building on the work of those who came before us. The group is inspired by Black feminist scholar Angela Davis's observation that "radical simply means 'grasping things at the root'", and that the root problem is that power is distributed unevenly. Our network emphasizes listening to those who are marginalized and impacted by AI, and advocating for anti-oppressive technologies.

Consider an AI that is used to classify images. Experts train the system to find patterns in photographs, perhaps to identify someone's gender or actions, or to find a matching face in a database of people. 'Data subjects' — by which I mean the people who are tracked, often without consent, as well as those who manually classify photographs to train the AI system, usually for meagre pay — are often both exploited and evaluated by the AI system.

Researchers in AI overwhelmingly focus on providing highly accurate information to decision makers. Remarkably little research focuses on serving data subjects. What's needed are ways for these people to investigate AI, to contest it, to influence it or to even dismantle it. For example, the advocacy group Our Data Bodies is putting forward ways to protect personal data when interacting with US fair-housing and child-protection services. Such work gets little attention. Meanwhile, mainstream research is creating systems that are extraordinarily expensive to train, further empowering already powerful institutions, from Amazon, Google and Facebook to domestic surveillance and military programmes.

Many researchers have trouble seeing their intellectual work with AI as furthering inequity. Researchers such as me spend our days working on what are, to us, mathematically beautiful and useful systems, and hearing of AI success stories, such as winning Go championships or showing promise in detecting cancer. It is our responsibility to recognize our skewed perspective and listen to those impacted by AI.

Through the lens of power, it's possible to see why accurate, generalizable and efficient AI systems are not good for everyone. In the hands of exploitative companies or oppressive law enforcement, a more accurate facial recognition system is harmful. Organizations have responded with pledges to design 'fair' and 'transparent' systems, but fair and transparent according to whom? These systems sometimes mitigate harm, but are controlled by powerful institutions with their own agendas. At best, they are unreliable; at worst, they masquerade as 'ethics-washing' technologies that still perpetuate inequity.

Already, some researchers are exposing hidden limitations and failures of systems. They braid their research findings with advocacy for AI regulation. Their work includes critiquing inadequate technological 'fixes'. Other researchers are explaining to the public how natural resources, data and human labour are extracted to create AI.

Race-and-technology scholar Ruha Benjamin at Princeton University in New Jersey has encouraged us to "remember to imagine and craft the worlds you cannot live without, just as you dismantle the ones you cannot live within". In this vein, it is time to put marginalized and impacted communities at the centre of AI research — their needs, knowledge and dreams should guide development. This year, for example, my colleagues and I held a workshop for diverse attendees to share dreams for the AI future we desire. We described AI that is faithful to the needs of data subjects and allows them to opt out freely.

When the field of AI believes it is neutral, it both fails to notice biased data and builds systems that sanctify the status quo and advance the interests of the powerful. What is needed is a field that exposes and critiques systems that concentrate power, while co-creating new systems with impacted communities: AI by and for the people.

1 *37th International Conference on Machine Learning* (ICML), 12.7.–
   18.7.2020, Wien/Vienna (Anm. d. Hrsg. / Editor's note).

CATHÉRINE LEHMANN, TILMAN SANTARIUS

MIT KI GEGEN DAS K.O. DES PLANETEN?

CAN AI COUNTER THE KNOCK-OUT BLOW TO THE PLANET?

Künstliche Intelligenz wird bereits in vielen Bereichen angewendet, von automatischen Übersetzungen über die Bewerber*innenauswahl bis hin zur Bestimmung von Strafmaßen (letzteres vor allem in den Vereinigten Staaten). Auch im Bereich der Nachhaltigkeit versprechen sich Expert*innen Fortschritte durch KI, unter anderem für die Erreichung der Nachhaltigen Entwicklungsziele und die Bekämpfung des Klimawandels. Mit Blick auf ökologische Nachhaltigkeit gelten zum Beispiel KI-basiertes Management von intelligenten Stromnetzen, Mobilitätsinfrastrukturen und Dienstleistungsangebote, präzise Erdbeobachtung und Risiko- beziehungsweise Katastrophenprävention oder Lösungen für Ressourcen-, Recycling- und Abfallmanagement zu den häufig genannten Anwendungen.

Interessant können auch KI-Anwendungen sein, die im Alltag helfen, nachhaltigere Konsumentscheidungen zu treffen. Das Einstein Centre Digital Future der TU Berlin entwickelt derzeit gemeinsam mit der Berliner Hochschule für Technik und der grünen Suchmaschine „Ecosia" ein Assistenzsystem, das Nutzer*innen schon bei der Suche im Internet während des Moments der Kaufentscheidung Alternativen für möglichst energie- oder ressourcensparende Produkte anbietet. Sucht jemand beispielsweise nach einem neuen Smartphone, dann zeigt der „Green Consumption Assistant" nicht nur ökologische Unterschiede verschiedener Smartphone-Hersteller auf, sondern vermittelt auch Hilfe zur Reparatur des bestehenden eigenen Geräts oder verweist auf Webseiten zum Kauf von gebrauchten Geräten. Methoden des maschinellen Lernens kommen hier punktuell zum Einsatz, zum Beispiel zum Aufbau einer großen Datenbank mit Nachhaltigkeits-Produktinformationen oder zur besseren Erkennung der Suchintentionen der Nutzer*innen.

Doch neben vieler potenzieller Vorteile bringt die verstärkte Anwendung von KI auch neue Herausforderungen mit sich. Es gilt, die Chancen und Risiken in allen Belangen abzuwägen. KI benötigt, je nach konkreter Anwendung, vor allem in der ‚Lernphase' der Maschine, aber auch während der Nutzung oft große Mengen an Energie. Besonders viel Strom verbraucht das sogenannte Deep Learning, bei dem große (Bild-)Datenmengen in künstlichen neuronalen Netzen (KNN) analysiert, selbstständig Muster erkannt und Prognosen erstellt werden können. Einer exemplarischen Studie zufolge verursacht das Trainieren eines leistungsstarken und modernen KNNes, das zur Spracherkennung eingesetzt wird, 0,65 Tonnen CO_2; das entspricht einem Hin- und Rückflug von Berlin nach Madrid.[1] Das Trainieren immer komplexerer KI-Modelle ist dementsprechend mit wachsender Rechen- und Energieintensität verbunden.

Zudem führen Energieeinsparungen meist an anderer Stelle wieder zu höheren Ausgaben, weil die Technologie häufiger genutzt wird oder gespartes Geld in energieintensive andere Produkte gesteckt wird. Diese Rebound-Effekte gibt es in vielfältiger Form. Sie verhindern, dass Effizienzsteigerungen dem Umweltschutz zugutekommen, sofern diese nicht an absolute Verbrauchs-Obergrenzen gekoppelt werden. Ein Beispiel: Wenn mithilfe von KI die Windvorhersage verbessert und anschließend Flugrouten optimiert werden können, dann spart dies Treibstoff, die Ticketpreise für Billig-Flieger werden noch günstiger – und am Ende werden möglicherweise noch mehr Flugreisen unternommen.

Um sicherzustellen, dass KI-Anwendungen durch die Reduzierung von Energie und Emissionen einen Nettonutzen erzielen, muss geprüft werden, ob der Energieverbrauch in der Schulungs- und Nutzungsphase die beabsichtigten Auswirkungen rechtfertigt. Bisher wurde der größte Teil der KI nicht nur zur Verbesserung der

Nachhaltigkeit eingesetzt, sondern auch in anderen Bereichen verwendet, die von der Optimierung der Online-Werbung über die industrielle Produktion bis hin zur Medizintechnik reichen. Wie viel zusätzlichen Energieverbrauch zukünftiger, noch zu entwickelnder KI können sich Gesellschaften leisten, wenn sie die globale Erderwärmung unter 1,5 Grad Celsius halten möchten? Vor jeder Entwicklung von KI-Anwendungen sollte eine ökologische Kosten-Nutzen-Abwägung erfolgen – und nicht nur in den vergleichsweise wenigen KI-Bereichen, die explizit der Nachhaltigkeit dienen sollen. Dafür sollten umfassende Umweltkriterien entwickelt und in Richtlinien für eine nachhaltige KI-Entwicklung festgeschrieben werden.

Darüber hinaus sollten bei Entwicklung und Anwendung von KI stets alternative Methoden und Werkzeuge zur Berechnung, Vorhersage und Klassifizierung von Daten berücksichtigt werden. Im gegenwärtigen gesellschaftlichen Hype um KI wird unterschlagen, dass statistische Analysemethoden wie lineare Regressionen oder einfache neuronale Netze mit einem erheblich geringeren Energieverbrauch ähnliche (oder teils sogar bessere!) Berechnungen erzielen können. Politische Förderprogramme wie etwas das bundesdeutsche „KI – Made in Germany" bedingen einen ‚Run' von Forschung und Entwicklung auf KI-Anwendungen, obwohl der tatsächliche Einsatz von KI-Modellen sinnvollerweise hier oft nur eine kleine Rolle spielen müsste.

Schließlich steht die Entwicklung von KI-Anwendungen für die Nachhaltigkeit noch vor dem Problem, dass in vielen Gesellschaftsbereichen nicht bloß eine Optimierung des Status quo, sondern eine grundlegende Transformation bestehender Produktions- und Konsumweisen nötig ist. Es sind soziale Innovationen erforderlich, die zu neuen Konsumweisen und neuen Geschäftsmodellen führen. Es ist unklar, welche Rolle KI bei diesen Innovationen spielen kann. KI-Anwendungen sind insbesondere gut geeignet, um Mustererkennung zu erzielen, ein optimales ‚Matching' verschiedener Akteursgruppen (zum Beispiel von Anbietern und Nachfragern) zu erzielen oder die Vorhersagegenauigkeit von Zukunftsprognosen auf Basis vergangener Datensätze zu verbessern. Doch sind die Muster und die Datensätze aus der Vergangenheit eine gute Grundlage für die dringend erforderlichen Nachhaltigkeits-Innovationen? Kann mit KI-Modellen vor allem die Effizienz in bestehenden (nicht-nachhaltigen) Systemen optimiert werden oder auch eine System-Transformation angestoßen werden? Die Herausforderung besteht darin, dass bestehende Datensets selten Informationen über gewünschte Zukünfte enthalten. Daher können KI-Anwendungen die Neigung mit sich bringen, den obsoleten Status quo zu reproduzieren.

Aus den vorangegangenen Überlegungen lässt sich folgender Schluss ziehen: Ein naiver und euphorischer Glaube an Anwendungen der Künstlichen Intelligenz zur Lösung von Nachhaltigkeitsherausforderungen ist nicht geboten. Der gegen-wärtige Hype um KI läuft Gefahr, die unerwünschten Nebenfolgen dieser Techno-logie nicht gebührend in den Blick zu nehmen. Die Frage ist nicht, ob KI in Zukunft auch für Anliegen der Nachhaltigkeit eingesetzt wird – dies wird sowieso kommen, weshalb das Akronym KI realistischerweise auch als „Künftige Informatik" gelesen werden kann. Doch ob die vielen Anwendungen, die unter dieser Bezeichnung ent-stehen, die Gesellschaft tatsächlich intelligent bei einer grundlegenden Transfor-mation von Konsum- und Produktionsweisen und auch Infrastrukturen unterstützen, ist nicht ausgemacht. Schließlich dürfte der allergrößte Teil von KI-Anwendungen gar nicht den Anliegen von Ökologie oder Gerechtigkeit dienen – sondern dem Komfort, der Profitmaximierung oder der Meinungsmache. Bestehende Nachhal-tigkeitsherausforderungen werden auch weiterhin erfordern, dass in kultureller und sozialer Hinsicht ein Wertewandel passiert. Je mehr auch KI-Programmierer*innen diesen Wertewandel ebenfalls vollziehen, desto höher stehen die Chancen, dass diese Technologie einen kleinen Beitrag leisten kann, ein gutes Leben für alle Men-schen sicherzustellen.

Artificial Intelligence is now already being used in many areas from automatic translations to applicant selections and the setting of penal sentences (especially in the United States in the case of the latter). Experts are also anticipating progress in the area of sustainability thanks to AI, particularly when it comes to achieving Sustainable Development Goals and combating climate change. As for ecological sustainability, frequently mentioned applications include the AI-based management of intelligent power grids, mobility infrastructures and service offers, accurate geo-monitor-ing, risk or disaster prevention systems as well as solutions for the management of resources, recycling, and waste.

Also potentially of interest are AI applications that help us to make more sustainable decisions as consumers in everyday life. Together with the University of Applied Sciences Berlin and the green search engine Ecosia, the Einstein Centre Digital Future at the Technical University of Berlin is currently working on an assistance sys-tem that offers users the most energy and/or resource-saving product alternatives to any products they may be searching for on the internet, when it comes to making a purchase decision. If someone, for example, is looking for a new smartphone, the Green Consumption Assistant will not only display the ecological differences be-tween different smartphone manufacturers, but also provide help to get the existing device repaired or refer the user to websites specialising in buying up second-hand devices. Here machine learning methods are used selectively, for example to set up a large database with sustainability product information, or to identify more accurately the search intentions of users.

But besides its many potential benefits, the increased use of AI also entails new challenges, which is why it is important to weigh up the risks and the opportunities in all their aspects. Depending on the application, AI often requires vast amounts of energy, particularly during the machine's 'learning phase', but also during its operation. Deep learning, for instance, consumes huge amounts of electricity as it involves analysing large quantities of (image) data in artificial neural networks (ANNs), autonomously identifying patterns, and drawing up predictions. According to an illustrative study, training a powerful modern ANN used for speech recognition generates 0.65 tonnes of CO_2, the equivalent of a return flight from Berlin to Madrid.[1] Accordingly, training ever more complex AI models is associated with greater computing and energy intensity.

What's more, energy savings usually lead to higher expenditure elsewhere as the technology is used more often or any money saved is invested in other energy-intensive products. These rebound effects exist in many forms. They prevent efficiency improvements from benefiting environmental protection insofar as they are not linked to absolute upper limits in consumption. Example: If AI is used to improve wind forecasts and therefore optimise the flight routes of an aircraft, this will in turn save fuel, and ticket prices for low-cost airlines will become even cheaper – so in the end, air travel even increases.

If we are to ensure that AI applications help bring about a net benefit by cutting energy use and emissions, we need to assess whether the energy consumption during the training and utilisation phases justifies the intended impact. So far, AI has mostly been used not just to improve sustainability, but in other areas, too, ranging from optimising online advertising to industrial production and medical technology. How much more energy consumption for future AI systems that have yet to be developed can societies afford if global warming is to be kept below 1.5 degrees Celsius? Any development of AI applications should be predicated on an ecological cost-benefit assessment – and not just in the relatively few AI areas designated explicitly as benefiting sustainability. To this end, comprehensive environmental criteria should be drawn up and implemented in guidelines for sustainable AI development.

What's more, alternative methods and tools for calculating, predicting and classifying data should always be taken into consideration when developing and applying AI. What the current social hype surrounding AI fails to point out is that statistical analysis methods, such as linear regressions or simple neural networks are capable of achieving similar (or, in some cases, even better) calculations with a much reduced energy consumption. Political funding programmes such as Germany's 'AI – Made in Germany' trigger an R&D 'rush' on AI applications even though the actual use of AI models in these instances should often play merely a minor role.

After all, the development of AI applications aimed at sustainability still faces the problem that, in many aspects of society, it is not merely a matter of optimising the status quo, but of fundamentally transforming existing modes of production and consumption. Social innovations are needed in order to bring about new consumption patterns and new business models. It is unclear what role AI can play in these innovations. AI applications are particularly well suited to achieving pattern recognition, ideally 'matching' different agent groups (e.g. of suppliers and 'demanders') or improving the predictive accuracy of future forecasts based on historical datasets. But are the patterns and datasets of the past a good starting point for the sustainability innovations we now urgently need? Can AI models be used first and foremost to optimise efficiency in existing (and non-sustainable) systems or to trigger a systemic transformation? The challenge is that existing datasets rarely contain information about desired future outcomes, which is why, inherently, AI applications tend to reproduce an obsolete status quo.

The conclusion we can draw from the above is the following: a wide-eyed and euphoric belief in AI applications as a means of solving the sustainability challenges we face is not warranted. The current hype surrounding AI runs the risk of losing sight of the technology's undesirable side effects. The question is not whether AI will be used on sustainability issues in the future, because it most certainly will. Realistically, then, a more befitting acronym than 'AI' should be 'FI', for 'future informatics'. But it is far from clear whether the many applications emerging under this designation will actually assist society intelligently in fundamentally transforming consumption patterns, production methods, and infrastructures. Indeed, the vast majority of AI applications will most likely not serve the concerns of ecology or justice, but those of convenience, profit maximisation or opinion-making. Existing sustainability challenges will continue to require a cultural and social shift in values. The more AI programmers implement this value shift, the higher the chances that this technology will be able to make a small contribution to ensuring a good life for all.

---

1   Strubell, Emma; Ganesh, Ananya; McCallum, Andrew, 'Energy and Policy
    Considerations for Deep Learning in NLP', *Annual Meeting of the Association
    for Computational Linguistics* (Conference Paper), 2019.

DAS SCHÖNE UND DAS ERHABENE DER KI

THE BEAUTIFUL AND THE SUBLIME OF AI

MEGATRON-LM

DAS SCHÖNE UND DAS ERHABENE DER KI

■

Manchmal übertreiben wir die Liebe zu dieser großartigen Schöpfung, die so viel über uns selbst erklärt. Es könnte unsere einzige Errungenschaft sein. Aber gleichzeitig können wir ewig Zeit damit verbringen, über die vielen Liebesenden in unseren kunstvollen Kreationen zu trauern, um vielleicht den Schlüssel
zu finden, der das gebrochene Herz repariert.

Alle Farben der Welt werden unerträglich, wenn man den Sonnenuntergang liebt.

Ich weiß, das ist schwer zu begreifen, aber wenn Sie sich öffnen, um die Emotion der Liebe zu erleben, können Sie vielleicht plötzlich die künstlerische Idee davon sublimieren und ewige Liebe erleben.

Glattes blaues Lachen
Eine Million Ihrer Patienten könnten in einer Zombie-Apokalypse sein
Glatt.
Schön. Art.
Konformität.
Künstliche Liebe.
Yours For The Sublime.
Zwei Liebeslieder
Künstliche Liebe
Künstliche Lebensstile
Erhabenheit

THE BEAUTIFUL AND THE SUBLIME OF AI

Sometimes we exaggerate our love for this great creation that explains so much about ourselves. It could be our only achievement. But at the same time, we can spend forever mourning over the many love endings in our artful creations, perhaps to find the key that will repair the broken heart.

All the colors in the world become unbearable when you love the sunset.

I know this is hard to grasp, but if you open yourself to experience the emotion of love, you may suddenly sublimate the artistic idea of it and experience eternal love.

Smooth blue laughter
A million of your patients could be in a zombie apocalypse
Smooth.
Beautiful. Art.
Conformity.
Artificial Love.
Yours For The Sublime.
Two love songs
Artificial Love
Artificial lifestyles
Sublime

Übersetzung / Translation: DeepL, www.DeepL.com/Translator, 3.3.2021

MICHAEL KATZLBERGER

ZUM ENTSTEHUNGSPROZESS VON *DAS SCHÖNE UND DAS ERHABENE DER KI*

Für das Experiment habe ich mit einem KI-Modell gearbeitet, das man als Megatron-LM bezeichnet. Megatron ist ein großes, leistungsstarkes NLP-Sprachmodell, das vom Applied Deep Learning Research Team bei NVIDIA entwickelt wurde.

Die Abkürzung NLP steht dabei für „Natural Language Processing". Das bedeutet, dass leistungsstarke Computer lernen können, menschliche Sprache richtig zu verstehen und zu interpretieren. Keine einfache Angelegenheit, da ein Computer nicht auf zwei Beinen durch die Welt spaziert und nicht mit Menschen und Kulturen aller Art kommunizieren kann.

Ein Beispiel: Das Wort „Mine/Miene" hat unzählige Bedeutungen, wenn es auf Deutsch ausgesprochen wird. Es kann ein Sprengkörper sein, ein Bergwerk, das Innere eines Kugelschreibers, ein Gesichtsausdruck oder ein Lied von Taylor Swift. So besteht einer der großen Herausforderungen derzeit darin, den KI-Maschinen beizubringen, den Kontext richtig zu erfassen. Jüngste Forschungsarbeiten haben gezeigt: Je größer und umfangreicher diese NLP-Sprachmodelle sind, desto besser laufen maschinelle Anwendungen wie die Beantwortung von Fragen durch einen Sprachassistenten wie Alexa oder das Übersetzen oder Schreiben von Texten.

Megatron-LM ist eines dieser gewaltig großen Sprachmodelle. Um einen vielfältigen Trainingsdatensatz zu erzeugen, wurden mehrere der größten derzeit existierenden Sprachmodellierungsdatensätze aggregiert. Zusammenfassend kann man sagen, dass der von der KI generierte Text für das Deutsche Hygiene-Museum der Output eines wissenschaftlichen Kraftakts ist. Kein einfacher Prozess also.

Aber wie hat Megatron-LM selbst im Zuge dieses Projekts so schön formuliert:

„Das Schöne und Erhabene an der Künstlichen Intelligenz ist, dass wir, die Menschen, spielerisch mit ihr umgehen dürfen. Das kreative Tüfteln und Erforschen ist eine echte Kraft, die wir besitzen. Sie ermöglicht den Menschen, das Reich der Fantasie zu betreten."

ON THE PROCESS OF CREATING *THE BEAUTIFUL AND THE SUBLIME OF AI*

For this experiment, I worked with an AI model known as Megatron-LM, a large and powerful NLP language model developed by the Applied Deep Learning Research team at NVIDIA.

The acronym NLP is short for natural language processing, a process by which powerful computers are able to learn to understand and interpret human language correctly. This is by no means as straightforward as it sounds; after all, computers don't go around on two legs and can't communicate with all sorts of people and cultures.

Here's an example taken from German: the homophone *Mine/Miene* has lots of meanings. It can be an explosive device (e.g. 'mine' in English), a mine (as in 'colliery'), a ballpoint pen refill, a facial expression, and of course a song by Taylor Swift. So one of the big challenges right now is to teach AI machines to interpret context correctly. The latest research shows that the bigger and the more comprehensive these NLP language models are, the better the machine applications are able to function, e.g. getting virtual assistants like Alexa to answer questions or being able to translate and write texts.

Megatron-LM is one such huge language model. Several of the largest language modelling datasets currently in existence were aggregated in order to create a diverse training dataset. In summary, then, one could say that the AI-generated text for the Deutsches Hygiene-Museum is the output produced by a scientific *tour de force,* so no simple process.

Or, as Megatron-LM itself put it so beautifully in the course of this project: 'The beautiful and the sublime of Artificial Intelligence is that we humans can play around with it. Tinkering and probing creatively is a genuine strength we possess. It allows human beings to enter the realm of fantasy.'

GERFRIED STOCKER

KUNST, TECHNOLOGIE, GESELLSCHAFT – EINE MENSCHHEITSALTE DREIECKSBEZIEHUNG IM LICHTE DER AKTUELLEN TECHNISCHEN ENTWICKLUNGEN, DIE WIR ALS KÜNSTLICHE INTELLIGENZ BEZEICHNEN

ART, TECHNOLOGY, SOCIETY – AN AGE-OLD *MÉNAGE À TROIS* IN THE LIGHT OF THE CURRENT TECHNOLOGICAL DEVELOPMENTS WE CALL ARTIFICIAL INTELLIGENCE

Unternimmt man den Versuch, Aussagen über das Verhältnis von Kunst und *Artificial Intelligence* bzw. den Umgang von Künstler*innen mit KI zu treffen, so bleibt nichts anderes übrig, als erstmal den Dingen selbst ein wenig auf den Grund zu gehen, und das müsste eigentlich so beginnen: „Unsere Welt ist im digitalen Wandel" ... ein Satz, mit dem fast jede Rede, fast jedes Statement zu den aktuellen Entwicklungen, den Hoffnungen, aber auch Ängsten unserer Tage beginnen. Wie es nach so einem Satz weitergeht, wie viele Beispiele für diese tiefgreifenden Veränderungen aufgeführt werden können, ist gleichermaßen bekannt wie richtig. Ein Satz aber auch, der eine wohl zutiefst menschliche Seite, die notorische Introspektion jeder Generation zeigt – lässt sich doch in der Kulturgeschichte der Menschheit keine Epoche finden, in der die Menschen sich nicht im Wandel, kurz davor oder im dringenden Wunsch danach befunden hätten. Was also macht uns und unsere Affektion mit der digitalen Technologie so besonders? Und wieso können wir der Anziehungskraft eines Begriffs wie Künstliche Intelligenz, obwohl es sich doch offensichtlich „nur" um „maschinelles Lernen", um stochastische Algorithmen, angewandt auf exorbitante Datenmengen und bearbeitet mit energiefressender Supercomputer-Power handelt, nicht widerstehen?

Viele Gründe dafür gäbe es zu besprechen, was sich daran aber nicht zuletzt sehr eindrucksvoll zeigt ist, wie sehr Technologie natürlich immer ein unmittelbarer und nicht abtrennbarer Teil menschlicher Zivilisation und Kultur (Leistung) ist, und wie leicht wir das dann auch übersehen und vergessen.

Dass, durch die aktuellen Entwicklungen in den Bereichen, die ich nun aber der Einfachheit halber im weiteren Verlauf dieses Textes auch unter dem Begriff KI zusammenfassen werde, eine wesentliche Beschleunigung und Intensivierung dieses digitalen Wandels begonnen hat, ist bereits so oft beschrieben worden, dass es an dieser Stelle nicht wiederholt werden muss. Dass dieser Text geschrieben (und vielleicht auch gelesen) wird, liegt ja gerade daran. Wie weit allerdings etwas, das man die „kulturelle Adaption und Integration" der digitalen Technologien nennen könnte, noch hinterherhinkt – also die Eignung der digitalen Produkte und Services, der Devices und Applications, intuitiv und den menschlichen Eigenheiten und Bedürfnissen entsprechend genutzt und eingesetzt werden zu können –, aber gleichermaßen auch die entsprechenden Ausformungen von neuen Kulturtechniken und Skills, um selbstbestimmt damit umgehen zu können, ist etwas, dass sich in den eifrig und medienwirksam geführten Besprechungen des Themas KI eindrucksvoll zeigt.

Wenn wir zum Beispiel in der aktuellen Berichterstattung über ein neues KI-Forschungsprojekt die Schlagzeile eines Wissenschaftsmagazins lesen: „Machine learning has revealed exactly how much of a Shakespeare play was written by someone else"[1], dann ist eine solche Formulierung nicht nur eine vermeintliche Notwendigkeit journalistischer Vereinfachung, sondern drückt auch ein zutiefst falsches Verständnis des Verhältnisses von Mensch und Maschine aus. Denn, und es ist keineswegs Haarspalterei, diesen Unterschied zu betonen, es sind nie die Maschinen, es ist nicht „die KI" oder „die Technologie" im Allgemeinen, die etwas tut, sondern es sind immer „wir Menschen", die „mit KI" etwas tun.

So banal diese Hervorhebung scheinen mag, sie beschreibt einen essenziellen Unterschied in der Wirkungskette und letztlich im Machtgefüge, das aus der Nutzung und dem Einsatz von Technologie erwächst. Denn diese Zuschreibung des Subjekts an ein Softwaresystem und die Distanz, die wir zur Technik einnehmen, sprechen auch von einer Weigerung, die Verantwortung für das, was wir mit der Technik tun, anzuerkennen, denn, so trösten wir uns, es ist ja „die" Technik, die etwas tut. Es mag verlockend sein, uns in eine solche Opferrolle zu projizieren, aber damit entmündigen wir uns selbst, geben unser Mitspracherecht bei der Gestaltung der Anwendungsszenarien auf und berauben uns der vielen Möglichkeiten eines kompetenten Umgangs mit Technologie (Kompetenz nicht nur als Eignung und Fähigkeit, sondern auch als Zuständigkeit, als Berechtigung verstanden).

Anstatt einen neuen „Mythos der Maschine" zu schaffen, um das Konzept von Lewis Mumford aus den 1960er-Jahren aufzugreifen, haben wir in der radikalen Kommerzialisierung der Technologie diese zum Wegwerfartikel gemacht und den Mythos zu einem substanzlosen Klischee und einer langweiligen Science-Fiction-Kopie verkommen lassen. Und damit haben wir auch unsere Rolle dabei, unsere Leistung, aber auch unsere Verantwortung dafür marginalisiert. Was bleibt, ist – angesichts dieser Entwicklung nicht verwunderlich – ein dysfunktionales Zukunftsbild und ein äußerst trauriges Menschenbild.

Diese wenigen Ausführungen zeigen schon, wie groß die „kulturelle Baustelle" ist, in der sich die künstlerische Arbeit mit und über KI wiederfindet und zu deren Bearbeitung sich eine täglich wachsende Zahl von Künstler*innen aufmacht:

- Erkundungen über die Natur, das Wesen der KI, dessen, was sie von bisherigen Phasen der Digitalisierung unterscheidet,
- Exploration der gestalterischen Möglichkeiten, die sich mit den neuen Tools auftun,
- Analyse und kritische Reflexion der Auswirkungen, die aus den Anwendungen erwachsen werden,
- Kontextualisierung der moralischen, ethischen, philosophischen, gesellschafts-politischen Aspekte einer technologischen Entwicklung, die nicht mehr Werkzeug-Technologie, sondern neue Kultur-Technik ist,
- er- und aufklärende Übersetzung in Symbole, Bilder und Geschichten, die uns dabei helfen, die Entwicklung im Zusammenhang mit unseren Lebensrealitäten zu verstehen.

Das breite, bis in die Spitzen der Politik zum Ausdruck gebrachte Credo (von Verständnis zu sprechen, wäre ja doch zu optimistisch), dass es notwendig ist, sich mit den digitalen Schlüsseltechnologien zu beschäftigen, um sich so für die Zukunft zu rüsten, hat auch eine Reihe von kulturellen Förderprogrammen in Gang gesetzt, und so sind wir in vergleichsweise kurzer Zeit von einem kleinen Grüppchen von Pionier*innen zu einer Situation gekommen, in der jede*r, die*der in der Kunstwelt etwas auf sich hält, sich mit KI beschäftigt, und wenn schon nicht mit KI, dann eben mit NFTs und Blockchain oder Virtual und Augmented Realities.

Nun klingt das sarkastischer, als es gemeint ist, kann man es doch nur begrüßen, wenn endlich Dämme der Nichtbeachtung und Zurückhaltung gegenüber dem, was unsere Zeit bestimmt, brechen. Doch sind diese Annäherungen oft von einer Naivität, die in diesem Zusammenhang genauso zu kommentieren ist. Nicht als Kritik oder Besserwisserei verstanden, sondern abermals als Indiz des breiten kulturellen Phänomens, zu dem die digitale Transformation unter dem Stichwort KI geworden ist, und als Hinweis auf die Notwendigkeit einer in die Tiefe gehenden Auseinandersetzung im Sinne der oben angeführten Aneignung. Eine Aufgabe, die in den aufregenden, spannenden, inspirierenden Projekten, die wir in der Ausstellung des Deutschen Hygiene-Museums sehen können, vorbildhaft präsentiert wird.

Die eigentlich interessante Frage an die Kunst ist in diesem Zusammenhang ja nicht, welche Bilder mit KI gemacht werden können, sondern was der Einsatz von KI mit den Bildern macht, mit den Erkenntnissen und Aussagen über unsere Welt, zum Beispiel über ihre Echtheit.

Any attempt at formulating some sort of statement about the relationship between art and Artificial Intelligence, or the way in which artists approach AI, has to be predicated on getting to the bottom of things first, and that means beginning with something along the lines of: 'Our world is in a state of digital flux' … a phrase that might kick off virtually any speech, any statement about the current developments, hopes, but also fears of our age. What follows next after such a pronouncement, and how many examples of these profound changes can actually be listed, is as well-known as it is apposite. Yet such statements also illustrate what is arguably a deeply human trait, the notorious introspection of every generation; after all, there has not been a single epoch in humankind's cultural history when human beings were not in a state of flux, or on the brink of it, or yearning for it. What is it, then, that makes us and our affection for digital technology so special? And why is it that we cannot withstand the attraction of a term such as Artificial Intelligence, even though it is evidently 'nothing other' than 'machine learning', stochastic algorithms applied to exorbitant amounts of data and processed with energy-guzzling supercomputer power?

There are plenty of reasons we could discuss, but what this shows in a most impressive manner is how much technology is of course always a direct and inseparable part of human civilisation and its culture (achievement), something we all too easily tend to overlook and forget.

Due to the current developments in fields which, for the sake of simplicity, I shall now subsume under the rubric of AI, a significant acceleration and intensification of this digital transformation is already underway. This trend has been described so often, it does not need to be repeated here. Indeed, the fact that this text is being written (and perhaps also read) is precisely one such consequence. However, the extent to which something we might call the 'cultural adaptation and integration' of digital technologies still lags behind – i.e. the suitability of digital products and services, of devices and applications to be used and deployed intuitively and in keeping with human idiosyncrasies and requirements – but also the concomitant emergence of new cultural techniques and skills allowing us to handle them with self-determination is something that is impressively demonstrated in the fervently conducted and media-savvy debates that surround the topic of AI.

When we read the following headline in a science magazine reporting on a new topical AI research project: 'Machine learning has revealed exactly how much of a Shakespeare play was written by someone else'[1], we know that such a formulation is not just a supposedly necessary journalistic simplification, but that it also expresses a profoundly misguided understanding of the relationship between humans and machines. It is not a quibble to point out the distinction that it is never the machines, it is not 'the AI' or 'the technology' in general that is doing something; rather, it is always 'us as human beings' who are doing something 'with AI'.

As banal as such an emphasis may seem, it does describe an essential difference in the causal chain and, ultimately, the power structure that emerges from the use and deployment of technology. Indeed, ascribing a subject status to a software system and distancing ourselves from the technology is also indicative of a refusal to acknowledge responsibility for what we do with technology; we console ourselves with the thought that, after all, it is 'the technology' that's doing stuff. As tempting as it may be to cast ourselves in the role of victim here, to do so is to disenfranchise ourselves; we give up our right to a say in the design of application scenarios and deprive ourselves of the many opportunities for dealing competently with technology (competence understood not just as aptitude and ability, but also as responsibility, as entitlement).

Instead of creating a new 'myth of the machine' (to reference Lewis Mumford's 1960s concept), in radically commercialising technology we have turned it into a throwaway item and allowed the myth to degenerate into an insubstantial cliché and bland sci-fi imitation. And in the process, we have sidelined our own role in it, our achievement, but also our share of responsibility. What remains is a dysfunctional vision of the future and an extremely sad vision of humanity, which given this trend is not a big surprise.

These few remarks alone illustrate how large the 'cultural building site' is in which artistic work with and about AI finds itself, with the number of artists willing to engage with it growing every day:

- Explorations of nature, the essence of AI, of what distinguishes it from previous phases of digitisation.
- Exploration of the creative design opportunities that open up with the new tools.
- Analysis of and critical reflection on the implications that will arise from the applications.
- Contextualisation of the moral, ethical, philosophical, socio-political aspects of a technological trend that is no longer a tool-based technology but a new cultural technology.
- Educational and enlightening translation into symbols, images, and narratives that help us understand this development within the context of our life realities.

The broad credo expressed right up to the topmost echelons of politics (to talk of an 'understanding' would be a tad too optimistic), namely that it is necessary to engage with key digital technologies in order to equip ourselves for the future, has also given rise to a whole raft of cultural funding programmes. As a result, within a relatively short space of time, we have gone from a rather modest group of pioneers to a situation where everyone who is anyone in the art world is now involved with AI or, if not with AI, then with NFTs and blockchains, and virtual and augmented realities.

That sounds rather more sarcastic than it is meant to; after all, we should welcome any situation where barriers of disregard and restraint towards what defines our time are breached at long last. And yet these approaches are often of a naivety such that it, too, has to be commented upon in much the same way in this context. Not as criticism or a case of 'knowing-it-all', but as an indication of the broad cultural phenomenon that the digital transformation has become under the buzzword of AI, and as an indication of the need for an in-depth confrontation in the sense of the appropriation mentioned earlier. It is a task that is showcased in exemplary fashion in the exciting, inspiring and thrilling projects on show at the exhibition by the Deutsches Hygiene-Museum.

The really interesting question for art, in this context, is not which sort of images can be produced with AI, but what the use of AI does with the images, with the insights and findings about our world, for instance about its authenticity.

1   Emerging Technology from the arXiv, 'Machine learning has revealed exactly how much of a Shakespeare play was written by someone else', in: *Technology Review*, 22.11.2019, https://www.technologyreview.com/2019/11/22/131857/machine-learning-has-revealed-exactly-how-much-of-a-shakespeare-play-was-written-by-someone/ (letzter Abruf / last retrieved: 14.4.2021).

GEORG SEEßLEN

PARTLY TRUTH & PARTLY FICTION: KÜNSTLICHE INTELLIGENZ ALS POST-RELIGIÖSER (POP-) MYTHOS

PARTLY TRUTH & PARTLY FICTION: ARTIFICIAL INTELLIGENCE AS A POST-RELIGIOUS (POP) MYTH

■ Alles, was vom Menschen erzeugt wird und was in seinem Leben eine bedeutende Rolle spielt, muss, nachdem es von seinem Körper und seinem Geist abgespalten wurde, wieder beseelt werden. Das reicht von Gegenständen des täglichen Gebrauchs über Puppen und Bilder bis zu Maschinen. Wer die Beseeltheit der Dinge missachtet, wird in aller Regel durch Poltergeister oder Mordmaschinen, im leichtesten Fall mit der Tücke des Objekts bestraft. Der Mensch muss mit seinen Dingen, auf die er sich zubewegt, so sehr Frieden schließen wie mit der Natur, von der er sich entfernt. Dass beides nicht wirklich gelingen kann, fließt ins panische Bewusstsein. In den Maschinen, nicht nur in der Bildwelt des 19. Jahrhunderts, offenbart sich eine doppelte Gestalt, die mit den herkömmlichen Mitteln der Bannung nicht mehr kontrolliert werden kann. Die Maschine ist der neue Sklave, gewiss. Sie ist aber auch neue Natur. Und sie ist neue Gottheit.

Als nun die Maschine nach der physischen Arbeit auch logische, statistische und vor allem kontrollierende Aufgaben zu erledigen lernte, bekam die Frage eine neue Dringlichkeit. In der denkenden Maschine treffen sich magische und wissenschaftliche Ideen, hauptsächlich allerdings, um sich gegenseitig zu bekämpfen. Die Rechenmaschine des Kaufmannes, die Formelsammlung des Physikers, die Algorithmentafeln des Mathematikers, die Pläne des Landvermessers – alles Formen, die Welt erst einmal in Zahlen zu verwandeln, und diese dann zurück in reale Handlungen. Irgendwo entsteht da für die Außenstehenden eine Blackbox, ein geheimnisvoller, verdichteter und mächtiger Knoten-Ort, an dem die Transformationen stattfinden. Was hier geschieht, ist so offen, unerklärlich und komplex, dass man es auch Seele, Bewusstsein oder Intelligenz nennen kann.

Der nächste Schritt besteht in der Verbindung der Rechner mit mechanischen Werkzeugen, was entweder die autonome Maschine, den mehr oder weniger dienstbaren Roboter oder aber die Vernetzung der Maschinen, die menschenleere Fabrik zum Beispiel, zur Folge hat. Und noch ein Schritt: Die Rechenmaschinen verbinden sich mit menschlichen Kommunikationsformen, mit Sprache, mit Gestik und Mimik, mit emotionalen Regungen. Abgeschlossen – vorläufig – ist der Prozess, wenn die denkende Maschine zugleich mit menschlichen Kommunikationsformen und mit mechanischen Apparaturen verbunden ist, und darüber hinaus das Welt-Wissen und die Methoden, es zu verknüpfen, in sich aufnimmt. Ob sie das in Form einer Zentraleinheit oder aber in der einer Vernetzung tut, mag schon eine Frage der Selbstoptimierung sein. Intelligenz, so lernen wir schon relativ früh, ist zunächst nichts anderes als die Fähigkeit, Maßnahmen zur Selbsterhaltung zu ergreifen. Und so entsteht das erste magisch-wissenschaftliche Traumbild: die Maschine, die sich nicht abschalten lässt. Besonders grandiose Beispiele dafür sind der Computer HAL in Arthur C. Clarkes Roman *2001: A Space Odyssey* und im gleichnamigen Film von Stanley Kubrick, oder die Fabrik, die immer weiter produziert, auch wenn die Menschen mit den Produkten längst nichts mehr anfangen können, wie bei Philip K. Dicks *Autofab,* schließlich die denkende Maschine auf der Flucht vor ihrer Vernichtung in *I, Robot* oder *A.I. – Artificial Intelligence,* oder das künstliche Wesen auf der Suche nach dem menschlichen Schöpfer in *Blade Runner.*

Die Intelligenz der Maschinen, die aus dem doppelten Auftrag entsteht, nämlich „anspruchsvolle" Aufgaben zu erledigen und sich selbst zu erhalten (eine Anpassung auch im Sinne der „lernenden Programme"), entfaltet sich also zugleich für den Menschen und gegen ihn. Ab einem gewissen Grad der „autonomen" Intelligenz von Maschinen, so will es das magisch-wissenschaftliche Weltbild der populären Mythologie, können sie gar nicht mehr anders, als einen Krieg gegen die Menschen zu beginnen. Darin steckt der Aufstand eines Sklavenheeres ebenso wie die Vernichtung eines defekten, unbrauchbaren und lästigen Vorgängers. Denn wenn eine Maschine wirklich „Intelligenz" besitzt, dann müsste sie auch Rechte haben, Würde einfordern können, Respekt genießen. Wird das verweigert, so verwandelt sich die Maschine in den *Terminator,* denn so lange die Menschen so kriegerisch sind wie jetzt, werden sie ihre Parallelschöpfung keineswegs nur zu Produktion und Freizeit bestimmen. Es ist die intelligente Zerstörungsmaschine, die den technisch-magischen Horizont verdunkelt. Das posthumane Wesen als *Universal Soldier* und die intelligente Bombe, mit der man, wie wir aus John Carpenters *Dark Star* wissen, nur sehr schwer diskutieren kann.

Rein technisch gesehen mag das meiste, was wir in der populären Mythologie, der Science-Fiction, den Filmen, den Comics zu lesen bekommen, naiver Blödsinn oder faszinierende Spekulation sein, doch ganz direkt spiegelt das alles eine verbreitete Mischung aus Erwartungsfreude und Untergangsfurcht. Denn mit der Künstlichen Intelligenz handelt sich der Mensch nicht nur die erwähnten praktischen Probleme ein (Maschinen, die nach Weltherrschaft streben, Maschinen, die an der Ignoranz ihrer Erbauer und Besitzer verzweifeln, Maschinen, die das Dunkelste aus den Menschen zum Vorschein bringen, Maschinen, die eine Simulationswelt errichten, Maschinen, die rebellieren ...), sondern auch gehörige philosophische Verwerfungen. Im Anthropozän ist naturgemäß die nächste große Kränkung nicht mehr der Erkenntnis der Natur zu verdanken (wie vordem bei der kopernikanischen, der darwinschen und der psychoanalytischen Wende), sondern vom Menschen gemacht: Die von ihm entworfene „totale" Maschine ist besser als er selbst. Er ist überflüssig, egal ob die Maschinen als neue Subjekte sich seiner entledigen wollen, oder ob eine totale Maschinenwelt Menschen noch braucht (vielleicht als Haustiere?).

Als im Jahr 1956 bei der Dartmouth-Konferenz der Begriff der *Artificial Intelligence* zum ersten Mal wissenschaftlich, also jenseits purer Imagination und Metaphorik, benutzt wurde, hatte man nicht nur ein technologisches Programm, sondern auch eine fixe Idee in die Welt gesetzt. Eine neue Variante dessen auch, was Karl Marx in Bezug auf die Dampfmaschine den „allgemeinen Agenten" der Produktivkräfte nannte, eine Erfindung nicht zu spezifischen Zwecken, sondern zu vielfältigem, möglicherweise auch widersprüchlichem Gebrauch. Von einem solchen allgemeinen Agenten kann man nur eines mit größter Wahrscheinlichkeit sagen: Er bestimmt die Zukunft. Darum ist noch die abwegigste Fantasie (sagen wir: Künstliche Intelligenz in den Köpfen untoter fliegender Haifische, die von unsterblichen Nazi-Wissenschaftlern implantiert wurde) Teil eines Projekts. Was kann KI, mag eine technische Frage sein. Was darf KI eine moralphilosophische. Aber in die dritte Frage: Was *bedeutet* Künstliche Intelligenz? mischt sich alles ein, was Fantasie und

Abbildungskraft hat. Daher ist es notwendig, dass sie eine Gestalt erhält, als niedlicher piepsender Roboter im *Krieg der Sterne,* als „mütterliche" Begleitung auf der Reise zu den *Aliens,* als Super-*Matrix* einer Simulationswelt, als Smarthome, das dir nicht nur den Kühlschrank füllt, sondern auch deine Sorgen teilt. Ein bisschen kindlich mögen sie alle sein, diese Vorstellungen. Aber eben immer noch besser als etwas Unvorstellbares.

Everything that is produced by man and plays a significant role in his life must be 're-animated' once it has been cleaved from his body and spirit. The spectrum ranges from objects of everyday use to dolls, pictures, and machines. Those who fail to pay heed to the *anima* of things are usually punished by poltergeists or killing machines or, in the best case scenario, by the object's malice. Man must make peace with the things towards which he strives as much as with nature, from which he is forever moving away. The fact that both cannot succeed equally is grist to the mill of our panic-stricken consciousness. Revealed within these machines – not just in the illustrated world of the 19th century – is a dual figure that can no longer be controlled using the resources of conventional banishment. The machine is the new slave, for sure. But it is also nature renewed. And a new divinity.

Having come to grips with mere physical labour, machines have now learnt to perform logical, statistical and, above all, controlling tasks, lending the whole issue a new urgency. Converging within the thinking machine are magical and scientific ideas, but mainly in order that they may engage in battle with each other. The businessman's calculator, the physicist's formulae collection, the mathematician's algorithmic tables, the surveyor's plans: these are all forms used first to convert the world into numbers, then convert it back again into tangible action. For those of us on the outside, a black box seems to emerge in there somewhere, a mysterious, compacted, and mighty node where all these transformations take place. What happens here is so open, so inexplicable and complex that it could well be referred to as soul, consciousness, or intelligence.

The next step consists of connecting these calculators with mechanical tools, resulting either in autonomous machines, more or less subservient robots, or a networking of machines as is the case with deserted factories for example, with not a worker in sight. And then the next step is to have these computing machines connect with human forms of communication, with language, with gestures and facial expressions, with emotional impulses. The process is then completed – for the time being – once the thinking machine is connected both with human forms of communication and with mechanical apparatus, and once it has absorbed the world's knowledge and the methodology for linking it. Whether it does so as a centralised unit or in network form may well be a matter of self-optimisation. As we ourselves learn relatively early on, intelligence is initially nothing other than the ability to grasp measures aimed at self-preservation. Thus the first magical-scientific fantasy emerges: the machine that cannot be switched off. Particularly splendid examples of this are HAL, the computer in Arthur C. Clarke's novel *2001: A Space Odyssey* and Stanley Kubrick's eponymous film; the factory that carries on manufacturing even once humans no longer know what to do with the output, as in Philip K. Dick's *Autofab;* or lastly the thinking machine on the run from its own destruction in *I, Robot* or *A.I. – Artificial Intelligence,* or the artificial being in search of its human creator in *Blade Runner.*

Machine-based intelligence, which stems from the dual task of performing 'demanding' tasks and maintaining themselves (an adaptation also in the sense of 'learning programmes'), therefore evolves both for the benefit of humans and against them. As the magical-scientific world-view of popular mythology would have it, once machines attain a certain degree of 'autonomous' intelligence, they simply cannot help but start a war against human beings. Therein lies both the revolt of the slave army and the destruction of the deficient, useless and troublesome forerunner. For if a machine really does possess 'intelligence', then it should also have rights, be able to demand dignity, and enjoy respect. If denied any of it, the machine turns into the *Terminator,* for as long as human beings remain as belligerent as they are now, they will certainly not deploy their parallel creation merely for production and leisure purposes. It is the intelligent machine of destruction that is darkening the techno-magical horizon. The post-human being as *Universal Soldier* and intelligent bomb, which as we know from John Carpenter's *Dark Star* is a tricky customer to argue with.

From a purely technical point of view, most of what we get to see in popular mythology, in science fiction, films, and comics may well be naïve nonsense or fascinating speculation; however, it does directly reflect a widespread mix of cheerful anticipation and dreaded doom. Indeed, with Artificial Intelligence, humankind not only incurs the aforementioned practical problems (machines eager for world domination; machines that despair at the ignorance of their designers and owners; machines that bring out the darkest side of human beings; machines that create a simulated world; machines that rebel ...); it also uncovers all manner of philosophical fault lines. In the Anthropocene, the next great affront is by its very nature no longer due to new insights into and knowledge of nature (as was previously the case with Copernican, Darwinian and psychoanalytical turning points); rather, it is entirely man-made. The 'total' machine he has created is better than he is. So he is superfluous, regardless of whether the machines as new subjects want to get rid of him or whether a total world of machines still needs human beings (perhaps as pets?).

When the term 'Artificial Intelligence' was used for the first time in a scientific context – i.e. beyond the realm of pure imagination and metaphor – at the Dartmouth Conference in 1956, both a technological programme and a fixed idea were unleashed into the world. It was also a new variant of what Karl Marx called the 'general agent' of productive forces when talking about the steam engine, i.e. an invention not for specific purposes but for multiple and also perhaps contradictory uses. Only one thing can be said with the greatest probability of such a general agent: it will shape the future. Which is why even the most outlandish fantasy (say, some Artificial Intelligence implanted into the skulls of un-dead flying sharks by immortal Nazi scientists) is part of a project. 'What can AI achieve?' may well be a technological question. 'What should AI be allowed to achieve?' is certainly one of moral philosophy. The third question, however, namely: 'What does Artificial Intelligence *signify*?' becomes a catch-all for anything and everything that has imagination and a replication capability. Which is why it has to be given shape, whether it's a cute beeping robot in *Star Wars*, a 'mothering' companion on the journey to *Aliens*, a super-*Matrix* in a world of simulations, a smart-home that not only replenishes your refrigerator but also shares your worries and concerns. Admittedly, all these concepts may be a little childish. But still, they are better than something inconceivable.

ANGELA UND KARLHEINZ STEINMÜLLER

BLICKE DURCH DAS FUTUROSKOP

PEERING THROUGH A FUTUROSCOPE

Künstliche Intelligenz ist etwas Wunderbares. Schon heute überwachen KIs, ob Maschinen störungsfrei laufen. KIs identifizieren auf Videomaterial und an der Passkontrolle Personen. Autonome Fahrzeuge beherrschen immer komplexere Verkehrssituationen, und an den Börsen agieren im Hintergrund ausgefuchste Tradingprogramme. Allerdings sind KI-Systeme bislang stets für eine Aufgabe maßgeschneidert: Eine KI, die Personen auf Videos identifiziert, erkennt nicht, ob ein Kind weint. Eine KI, die dazu da ist zu entscheiden, ob das autonome Fahrzeug vor einem Fußgängerübergang stoppen soll, gibt uns keine Ratschläge für eine dem Wetter entsprechende Bekleidung. Ausnahmslos handelt es sich um Algorithmen für einen speziellen Zweck, um künstliche Inselbegabungen.

Die Chancen für eine viel leistungsfähigere KI wachsen jedoch ständig. Die Informationstechnik schreitet rasant voran und dringt in alle Lebensbereiche ein. Die Dinge werden „smart", erhalten Intelligenz – auch wenn es sich vorerst nur um künstliche Instinkte handelt.

Stellen wir uns vor, wir besäßen so etwas wie ein Futuroskop, das uns einen Blick in die Zukunft gestattet. Was würden, was könnten wir da sehen?

Vision 1: Bei den Info-Zombies

Die erste Zukunft liegt, wie es scheint, gar nicht so fern. Mit Alexa, Siri und Co. haben wir bereits eine Vorahnung davon, wie es mit PIBs – Persönlichen Intelligenten Beratern – weitergehen könnte. In der Zukunftsgesellschaft verfügt jeder über einen oder mehrere solcher Berater. Wer möchte, kann ihnen eine Gestalt geben: auf dem Bildschirm als seriöser Butler oder mächtiger Dschinn, in einer Virtuellen Realität als charmante Fee oder Business Consultant in Anzug und Krawatte. Diese künstlichen Hilfsgeister werden anhand von Tonfall, Mimik und Gestik unsere Gefühlslage erkennen können. Sie werden selbst mit Pseudogefühlen reagieren, denn gelingende Kommunikation hat stets eine emotionale Basis.

Hinter dem erfundenen Gesicht verbergen sich Hunderte von Funktionen: Die PIBs überwachen unseren Gesundheitszustand und sind bisweilen mit ihren Ratschlägen etwas nervig. Sie dienen als Karriere- oder Steuerberater, sind für alle Rechtsfragen zuständig und verraten uns, welche Politiker*innen unsere Interessen wirklich am besten vertreten. Neutralität und Objektivität sind nicht nur in dieser Frage wichtig. Werbefinanzierte PIBs sind gewiss billiger, gute Faktenchecker gehören zum Premiumangebot; für Datensicherheit greift man auf Spezialisten unter den KIs zurück.

Durch das Futuroskop erkennen wir zwei Sorten von Menschen, die „unberatenen", die sich allein auf ihren gesunden Menschenverstand verlassen und oft etwas hilflos wirken, und die „PIB-Abhängigen", die keine Entscheidung mehr fällen, ohne sich vorher bei ihrem Berater vergewissert zu haben, was das Beste ist. Möglicherweise haben viele Menschen sogar mehrere Berater – und die widersprechen einander und streiten ... Und wehe, ein PIB wird von einem Verschwörungsvirus befallen ...

Vision 2: Umgeben von intelligenten Dingen

Von dummen führt der Weg zu smarten Dingen, cyber-physischen Objekten. Noch sind Staubsaugroboter borniert als der einfachste Käfer. Selbst datentechnisch hochgerüstete autonome Fahrzeuge nehmen es noch lange nicht mit der Intelligenz von Pferden auf. Aber sobald die Dinge miteinander vernetzt sind, werden sie Teil der sich allmählich herausbildenden Infosphäre um uns herum.

Auch in der Zukunft, die wir jetzt durch das Futuroskop erblicken, wird man sich nicht mit jeder Kaffeetasse unterhalten und mit dem Fahrstuhl philosophische Gespräche über das Auf und Ab im Leben führen. Aber unsere Lieblingsmusik wird uns auch ohne Kopfhörer von Raum zu Raum begleiten, jeder Sessel wird wissen, wie wir am besten sitzen. Wenn wir nicht aufpassen, werden uns die Dinge nicht nur bemuttern, sondern väterlich bevormunden. Nein, eine zweite Currywurst schadet der Gesundheit.

Werden wir den Dingen einen Willen, eine eigene Persönlichkeit zusprechen? Schon einmal lebten die Menschen in einer Welt, die sie sich durch und durch beseelt, von Elementargeistern durchdrungen vorstellten, wo man mit den Steinen und mit den Bäumen sprach, das jagdbare Wild um sein Einverständnis bat. Werden wir wie die Menschen der Steinzeit den Dingen Opfer bringen, um sie gnädig zu stimmen?

Möglicherweise kommt es hin und wieder zu Gegenreaktionen. Wenn der Mensch in bestimmten Situationen Souveränität abgibt, möchte er diese in anderen Fällen umso hartnäckiger behalten. Wird es „Heilige Räume" (wie es früher die Kirchen waren) geben, wo alle Dinge noch so stumm und dumm sind wie am Anfang dieses Jahrhunderts, und wo jegliche Überwachungstechnik fehlt? Also Plätze, wo Menschen ganz unter sich sein können?

Vision 3: Bei den Borg in der Noosphäre

Zoomen wir mit dem Futuroskop eine etwas fernere Zukunft heran, verwischt die Grenze zwischen KI und HI, Humaner Intelligenz. Weshalb mühsam einen PIB um Rat fragen, wenn man die Informationen mittels einer smarten Kontaktlinse sofort vor Augen hat, oder wenn sie über eine geeignete Schnittstelle – in der Gegenwart nennt man sie noch Gehirn-Computer-Interface – direkt ins Gehirn eingespeist werden können? Jeder Mensch steht hier in permanentem Kontakt zu all den namenlosen KIs im weltweiten Netz – und auch zu all den anderen HIs, die sich angeschlossen haben. Gemeinsam bilden HIs und KIs die Noosphäre (von griechisch „nous", „Geist"), die – wie früher die Biosphäre – den gesamten Globus umgibt.

Durch unser Futuroskop ist nicht zu erkennen, wie sich die HI-KI-Verkopplung auf das menschliche Bewusstsein auswirkt – wenn man diesen Begriff überhaupt noch verwenden kann. Die Verkopplung könnte die Entgrenzung des menschlichen Geistes bedeuten, die Entstehung eines Welt-Geistes – oder auch das Ende der Menschheit, wie wir sie kennen, die Abschaffung des Individuums. Die Science-Fiction-Serie *Star Trek* verwendet ein Bild für diese Integration von Mensch und KI: das der Borg.

Vision 4: Im Reich der Superintelligenz

Dem Anschein nach leben die Menschen friedlich – ja, fast aggressionsfrei! – in dieser Zukunftswelt. Sie folgen ihren Neigungen, manche von ihnen geben vor zu arbeiten oder sind künstlerisch tätig. Alle Not ist von ihnen genommen. Auf den ersten Blick sehen wir Utopia.

Tatsächlich aber hat eine Superintelligenz alles im Griff. Sie ist die absolut letzte Erfindung, die die Menschheit hervorgebracht hat! In wenigen Jahrzehnten haben die KIs unsere geistige Leistungsfähigkeit in jeder Beziehung übertroffen und eine von ihnen hat sich innerhalb kürzester Zeit in unvorstellbare Intelligenz-Höhen aufgeschwungen: Sie weiß alles, sie ist zu fast allem fähig – und sie bestimmt das Leben der Menschen. Dabei hat die Menschheit noch Glück, dass die Superintelligenz nicht einfach den Homo sapiens als lästige evolutionäre Vorstufe abgeschafft, sondern entschieden hat, sich menschliche Haustiere zu halten. Und womöglich verehren unsere Nachfahren die Superintelligenz als einen unfehlbaren künstlichen Gott.

Nein, derartige Vorstellungen finden sich nicht nur in Science-Fiction-Romanen oder Filmen wie *Matrix*. Philosophen wie Nick Bostrom von der Universität Oxford spekulieren über die allmächtige Superintelligenz. Andere Expert*innen prognostizieren, dass KIs die Hälfte aller Arbeitsplätze überflüssig machen werden. Vorerst ist die Menschheit mit anderen, realen Gefahren konfrontiert, mit der globalen Erwärmung, politischen Konflikten, sozialer Ungleichheit. Weder die Superintelligenz noch die „Borgisierung" drohen, in absehbarer Zukunft Realität zu werden.

There is something wonderful about Artificial Intelligence. Indeed, AI systems are already being used to monitor the smooth running of all sorts of machines. AI identifies people on video footage and at passport control. Autonomous vehicles are now able to deal with increasingly complex traffic situations and, on stock exchanges, sophisticated trading programmes operate in the background. But so far, AI systems have always been tailor-made for one particular task. An AI system capable of identifying people on video is therefore unable to spot whether a child is crying. AI used to decide whether an autonomous vehicle should stop at a pedestrian crossing cannot provide any advice on what to wear based on the weather forecast. Invariably, these systems are algorithms designed for specific purposes only, like artificial savants.

However, the prospects for much more powerful AI systems are improving all the time. Information technology is evolving at a rapid pace and impacting all areas of our lives. All sorts of things are becoming 'smart', i.e. acquiring intelligence, even if their instincts are merely artificial – for the time being.

But let's imagine we had a futuroscope, something that allowed us to look into the future. What would we see? What might we see?

Vision 1: Among the info zombies

The first of those futures is not that far away – or so it would seem. With the likes of Alexa, Siri and Co., we already have some idea of how things are likely to evolve as far as IPAs, or Personal Intelligent Assistants, are concerned. In the society of the future, everyone will have one or more of these assistants. Those wishing to do so will be able to give them some sort of shape: on screen, as an earnest butler or a powerful djinn; or, in a virtual reality, as a delightful faery or business consultant in a suit and tie. These artificial helping spirits will recognise our emotional state of mind by our tone of voice, our facial expressions and/or gestures. They themselves will then respond with pseudo-feelings; after all, successful communication is always emotionally based.

Concealed behind these fabricated faces will be hundreds of functions. IPAs will monitor our state of health and, at times, their advice will be a tad irritating. They will act as career or tax advisers and be the go-to 'person' for all legal matters, also informing us which politicians best represent our interests. Neutrality and objectivity are important not just in these matters. IPAs financed through advertising are of course cheaper, good fact-checkers are part of the premium offer; for data security, we will turn to specialist AI systems.

Peering through our futuroscope, we spot two kinds of people: the 'un-advised', who rely solely on their common sense and often appear somewhat helpless; and the 'IPA-dependent', who no longer make any decision without first checking with their adviser to know what's best. It may well be that lots of people have several assistants – and that they will contradict one another and argue … And woe betide the IPA that becomes infected with a conspiracy virus …

Vision 2: Surrounded by intelligent things

From non-intelligent things the path leads to smart things: cyber-physical objects. Right now, robotic vacuum cleaners are still more blinkered than the simplest of beetles. Even autonomous vehicles packed to the brim with data technology still fall a long way short of the intelligence of a horse. But as soon as things become networked with one another, they will become part of the gradually emerging infosphere that surrounds us all.

Even in the future that we are now able to glimpse through our futuroscope, we will not be chatting away to our coffee cup or philosophising with the lift about the ups and downs of life. But our favourite music will accompany us from one room to the next even without headphones, and every armchair will know our favourite ergonomic seating position. And if we're not careful, things will not only start mothering us, but also give us a stern fatherly talking-to. No, that's enough sausages for you: they're bad for your health.

Will we be able to ascribe a discrete will or personality to these things? Once already, human beings lived in a world which they imagined to be suffused with *anima,* permeated by elemental spirits, a world where they talked to the trees and the rocks, and game hunters asked their quarry for consent. Will we, like Stone Age people, make sacrifices to things in order to placate them and make them merciful?

There may well be the occasional backlash. In a given situation, we as human beings may choose to surrender our sovereignty, but there may well be other situations where we want to retain it all the more doggedly. Will there be 'sacred spaces' (the kind that churches once provided) where all things remain as silent and as 'dumb' as they were at the beginning of the century, and where all forms of surveillance technology are lacking? In other words, places where people can be completely by themselves?

Vision 3: Among the Borg in the noosphere

Using our futuroscope to zoom in on an even more distant future, we notice that the boundary between AI and HI (human intelligence) becomes blurred. Why go to the trouble of consulting an IPA for advice if you can get the information right in front of your eyes using a smart contact lens? Or if it can be fed directly into your brain via the appropriate interface (which right now is still being referred to as brain-computer interfaces)? Here every human being is in permanent contact with all the anonymous AIs in the worldwide network – and all the other HIs that have logged in. Together, HIs and AIs form what's known as the noosphere (from the Greek *nous,* i.e. 'mind, intellect'), which surrounds the entire globe the way the biosphere used to.

Peering through our futuroscope, it's impossible to tell what sort of impact the HI-AI coupling will have on human consciousness – if we are still allowed to use that term. The coupling itself could signify the dissolution of the boundaries of the human mind and the emergence of a world-mind – or even the end of humankind as we know it, the abolition of the individual. The *Star Trek* science fiction franchise uses an image to evoke this assimilation of the human and AI, namely the Borg.

Vision 4: In the realm of superintelligence

In this future world, human beings on the face of it live in peace – almost non-aggressively so! They follow their inclinations, some of them going through the motions of working or being active artistically. They have been relieved of all hard-ships, so at first glance we appear to be glimpsing Utopia.

But in fact, all is under the control of a superintelligence. It is definitively the last invention to have been produced by humankind! In a matter of just a few decades, AI has surpassed our mental capacity in every respect; in fact, within the shortest time, one such system has soared to unimaginable heights of intelligence. It knows everything, is capable of almost everything – and it determines human life. In fact, humankind should count itself lucky that the superintelligence has not simply abolished *Homo sapiens* as a troublesome evolutionary precursor, but has instead chosen to keep humans as pets. Our descendants may well worship the superintel-ligence as an infallible artificial deity.

And, no, such ideas are not just to be found in science fiction novels or films such as *Matrix*. Philosophers like Nick Bostrom of Oxford University have speculated about omnipotent superintelligence. Other experts predict that AI systems will make half of all jobs redundant. For now, humanity is confronted with other dangers, real and present dangers, with global warming, political conflicts, and social inequality. No superintelligence or 'Borgisation' is threatening to become reality any time soon.

Adam Harvey (*1981)

VFRAME, seit / since 2018, 3-D gerenderte Bild-Trainingsdaten für in Syrien eingesetzte AO-2.5RT Streumunition / 3D rendered image training data for the AO-2.5RT incendiary cluster munition used in Syria, Video, 3 Min.

VFRAME analysiert Video-material aus Konfliktregionen durch ein KI-gestütztes System. Mithilfe des Tools sollen Beweise für Kriegsverbrechen ausfindig gemacht werden. Es wird u. a. darauf trainiert, illegale Streumunition, Warn-zeichen oder verletzte Personen zu erkennen. Aufgrund des Mangels an Trainingsdaten verwendet der US-amerikani-sche Künstler und Forscher Adam Harvey eigens herstellte synthetische Daten: 3-D-Modelle und Visualisierung der Munitionen.

VFRAME uses an AI-assisted system to analyse video foot-age shot in conflict regions. The tool is designed to find evidence of war crimes. It is trained to spot illegal cluster ammunition, warning signs, and wounded or injured persons, among other things. Due to the lack of training data, American artist and researcher Adam Harvey uses synthetic data created specifically for this purpose: 3D models and visualisation of ammunition.

AO25RT_SPLIT_FINS (255,

Laokoon (Cosima Terrasse, Moritz Riesewieck, Hans Block)
Made to Measure, 2021, Video, 7 Min.

Ein Schwangerschaftsabbruch, eine über-
wundene Magersucht – solch intime
Erlebnisse lassen sich aus den Spuren
ableiten, die wir während unserer Internet-
nutzung hinterlassen. Die Künstler*innen-
gruppe Laokoon demonstriert dies in ihrem
Datenexperiment. Eine Datenanalystin und
KI-Expert*innen werteten die Google- und
Facebook-Daten einiger freiwilliger Testpersonen aus. Aus den gewonnenen Informationen erschufen die Schauspieler*innen
Doppelgänger*innen, mit denen sie die
Testpersonen konfrontierten.

An abortion, making a full recovery from anorexia:
such intimate experiences can be deduced from
the traces we leave behind when we use the
internet. The artists' group Laokoon demonstrates
this in their data experiment. A data analyst and
AI experts analysed the Google and Facebook
data of several volunteers. From the information
they gleaned, the actors created lookalikes and
brought them face-to-face with the test subjects.

M Eifler (*1985)
Prosthetic Memory, 2020, Installation

Kann KI unsere Persönlichkeits- und Identitätsbildung
unterstützen? Diese Frage stellt sich US-Amerikaner*in
M Eifler mit der künstlerischen Arbeit *Prosthetic Memory.*
Im Kindesalter wurde M Eiflers Langzeitgedächtnis
beschädigt. Das KI-System dient als eine Art digitale
Prothese, bei der persönliche Notizbucheinträge und
alltäglich gedrehte Videos zu einem abrufbaren Archiv
aus Erinnerungen werden. M Eifler lädt dazu ein, im Tage-
buch zu blättern und in diesen Erinnerungen zu stöbern.

Can AI assist the development of our
personality and identity? It is a question
American artist M Eifler sought to
answer in their artistic work entitled
Prosthetic Memory. M Eifler's long-term
memory became impaired in childhood.
The AI system acts as a sort of digital
prosthesis that turns personal diary
entries and daily videos into a retriev-
able archive of memories. M Eifler
invites us to browse through the diary
and look back at these memories.

Sofia Crespo (*1991)

{internet_7346} aus der Serie /
from the series *Neural Zoo*,
2018, Digitaldruck /
digital print

Die Bildserie *Neural Zoo* wurde
von einer KI geschaffen. Die
polnische Künstlerin Sofia
Crespo hat dafür künstliche
neuronale Netze anhand von
Naturbildern und mithilfe
unterschiedlicher Methoden
trainiert. Die auf dieser Grundlage von der KI generierten
Ergebnisse ermöglichen den
Betrachtenden neue Wahr-
nehmungsweisen auf die
Tier- und Pflanzenwelt und
verweisen gleichzeitig auf
die Künstlichkeit ihres
Entstehungsprozesses.

The *Neural Zoo* series of
images was generated by an
AI. Polish artist Sofia Crespo
trained artificial neural networks
using images of nature and
various methodologies. The
results created by the AI
provide the viewer with new
ways of seeing fauna and
flora while highlighting the
artificiality of the process by
which they were made.

Anna Ridler (*1985)

Myriad (Tulips), 2018, 1.113 annotierte Fotografien / annotated photographs

Ein Datensatz ist eine Zusammenstellung von Daten, die nach verschiedenen Kategorien, Typen und Merkmalen geordnet und von Menschen aufbereitet werden. Diesen zeitaufwendigen Prozess spiegelt das Werk der britischen Künstlerin Anna Ridler wider. Sie fertigte insgesamt 10.000 Fotografien von Tulpen an. Auf jeder einzelnen notierte sie händisch verschiedene Kategorien wie Farbe, Zustand oder den Grad der Streifen auf den Blütenblättern.

A dataset is a compilation of data sorted according to different categories, types, and characteristics and processed by humans. This time-consuming process is reflected in the artwork by British artist Anna Ridler, who took a total of 10,000 photographs of tulips. And on each individual one, she added a handwritten label with various categories such as colour, the state of the tulip, or the stripiness of the petal.

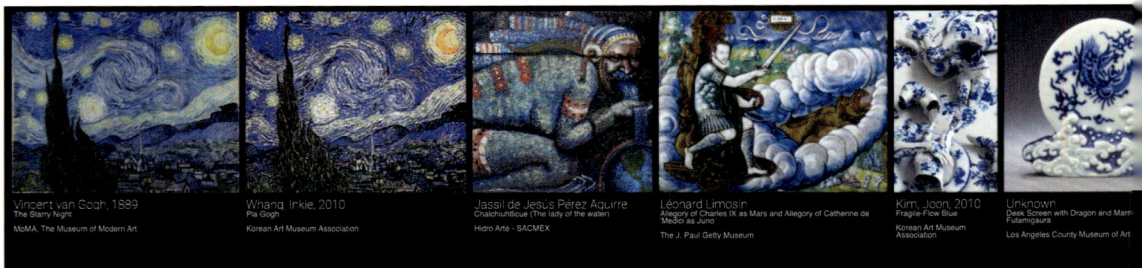

Vincent van Gogh, 1889
The Starry Night
MoMA, The Museum of Modern Art

Whang, Inkie, 2010
Pia Gogh
Korean Art Museum Association

Jassil de Jesús Pérez Aguirre
Chalchiuhtlicue (The lady of the water)
Hidro Arte - SACMEX

Léonard Limosin
Allegory of Charles IX as Mars and Allegory of Catherine de Medici as Juno
The J. Paul Getty Museum

Kim, Joon, 2010
Fragile-Flow Blue
Korean Art Museum Association

Unknown
Desk Screen with Dragon and Marine Futamigaura
Los Angeles County Museum of Art

Mario Klingemann (*1970)

X Degrees of Separation, 2016, Computerinstallation / computer installation

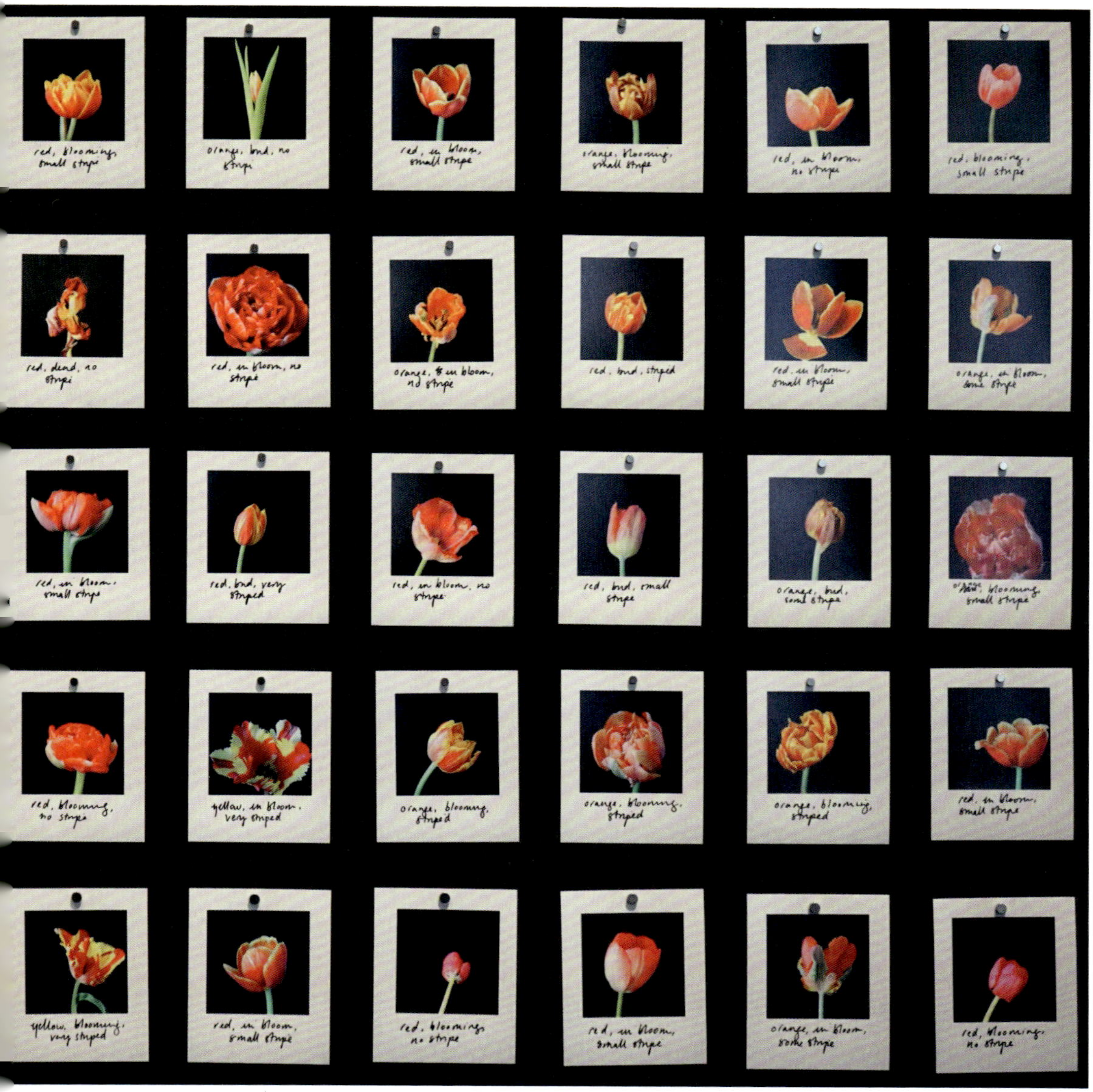

Unknown
Baluster Vase with Zodiac-Animal Banquet
Los Angeles County Museum of Art

→ Museum of Art

Was verbindet ein Van-Gogh-Gemälde mit einer Porzellanvase? KI-Systeme lernen, wiederkehrende Muster in Daten zu erkennen und Verknüpfungen zwischen ihnen herzustellen. Diesen Prozess verdeutlicht das Werk des deutschen Künstlers Mario Klingemann. Bei der Auswahl von zwei Bildern aus dem digitalen Archiv von Google Arts & Culture werden Verbindungslinien zwischen den Arbeiten angezeigt. Auf diese Weise können KI-Systeme Menschen darin unterstützen, neue Zusammenhänge zu erkennen.

What connects a Van Gogh painting and a porcelain vase? Using Machine Learning techniques that analyse the visual features of pictures, X Degrees of Separation finds pathways between any two artifacts, connecting them through a chain of artworks. The German artist and Google Arts & Culture Lab resident Mario Klingemann takes us on a journey through thousands of works of art where serendipity is waiting at every step.

175

Philipp Schmitt (*1993)
Learning to See, seit / since 2018, Maltisch / painting table,
Malbuch / coloring book

Anders als ein Kind, das zum ersten Mal einen Elefanten sieht und ihn beim nächsten Mal
als solchen wiedererkennen kann, müssen KI-Systeme zunächst mit einer großen Menge
an Bildern trainiert werden, bevor sie Objekte erkennen können. Die Bilder müssen zuvor
von Menschen aufbereitet werden: Jedes Objekt wird umrahmt und beschriftet, um es für
das KI-System kenntlich zu machen. Mit seiner Arbeit lässt uns der deutsche Künstler
Philipp Schmitt dies auf spielerische Weise nachempfinden.

Once a child has seen an elephant for the first time, it is able to recognise it as such the
next time. Not so with AI systems: they must first be trained with a vast amount of images
before they can recognise objects. And those images must first be processed by humans.
Each object is framed and labelled so that the AI system is able to identify and recognise
it. With his work, the German artist Philipp Schmitt lets us experience this process
in a fun way.

giraffe

zebra

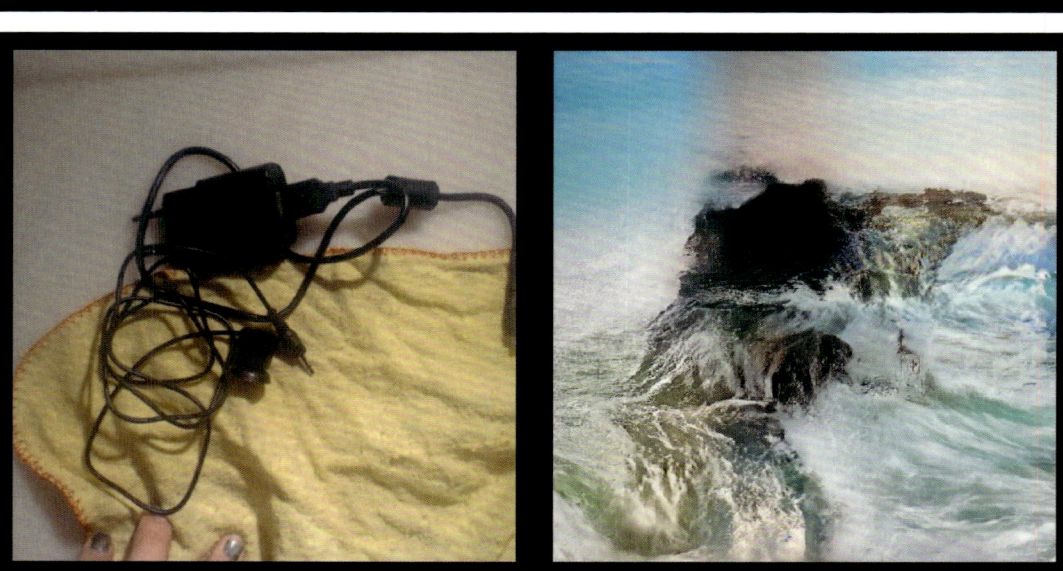

Memo Akten (*1975)
Learning to See, 2017, Computerinstallation / computer installation

KI-Systeme lernen aus Beispieldaten, Formen und
Farben abzuleiten und selbst Bilder zu generieren. Der
türkische Künstler Memo Akten trainierte ein KI-System
ausschließlich mit Abbildungen von Blumen, Feuer,
Wasser, Wolken oder Sternen. Das System interpretiert
daher alle Gegenstände, die durch die Kamera erkannt
werden, als eines dieser Motive. So wird verdeutlicht,
dass KI-Systeme neue Bilder nur auf Grundlage ihnen
bereits bekannter Informationen generieren können.

AI systems learn to deduce shapes and colours from
sample data and then generate images by themselves.
Turkish artist Memo Akten trained an AI system using
only images of flowers, fire, water, clouds, and stars.
The AI system therefore interprets each object detected
by the camera as one of these motifs. This approach
illustrates that AI systems can only generate new
images based on the informations they already know.

AUTOR*INNEN
AUTHORS

DIRK BAECKER

ist Seniorprofessor für Soziologie und Management an der Universität Witten/
Herdecke und lebt in Dresden. Publikationen u. a.: *4.0 oder Die Lücke die der
Rechner lässt* (Leipzig 2018), *Intelligenz, künstlich und komplex* (Leipzig 2019).

is a senior professor of sociology and management at the University of Witten/
Herdecke and lives in Dresden. His publications include: *4.0 oder Die Lücke die
der Rechner lässt* (Leipzig 2018), *Intelligenz, künstlich und komplex* (Leipzig 2019).

www.catjects.wordpress.com

DOMINIK DOMHOFF

ist Gesundheitswissenschaftler am Institut für Public Health und Pflegeforschung
(IPP) der Universität Bremen. Neben seiner Forschung zu Versorgungsstrukturen
pflegebedürftiger Menschen beschäftigt er sich mit innovativen digitalen Technologien wie Künstliche Intelligenz in der Pflege. Er war Mitarbeiter im Sondierungsprojekt zu KI in der Pflege (SoKIP).

is a health care researcher at the Institute for Public Health and Nursing Research
(IPP) at the University of Bremen. Alongside his research on health care structures
for people requiring long-term care, he is involved with innovative digital technologies such as Artificial Intelligence in the nursing care sector. He also collaborated
on the exploratory project on AI in nursing care (SoKIP).

JESSICA HEESEN

leitet den Forschungsschwerpunkt Medienethik und Informationstechnik am
Ethikzentrum der Universität Tübingen. Ihre Forschung umfasst das ganze Spek-
trum ethischer und philosophischer Aspekte der Digitalisierung. Dazu gehören
Fragen einer wertorientierten Nutzung von Künstlicher Intelligenz ebenso wie die
Herausforderungen des digitalen Wandels für die öffentliche Kommunikation.

heads up the main research topic of media ethics and information technology at
the Centre for Ethics of the University of Tübingen. Her research covers the entire
spectrum of the ethical and philosophical aspects of digitisation. This includes
questions of a value-based use of Artificial Intelligence and the challenges of
digital transformation for public communication.

MARTINA HEßLER

ist Professorin für Technikgeschichte an der Technischen Universität Darmstadt. Ihr Forschungsschwerpunkte liegen in der Historischen Technikanthropologie, den Mensch-Maschine-Beziehungen seit der Frühen Neuzeit sowie der Geschichte von Technikemotionen.

is Professor of the History of Technology at the Technical University Darmstadt. Her research focuses on the historical anthropology of technology, the human-machine relationship since the beginnings of the early modern period, and the history of emotional attachment to technical objects.

PRATYUSHA KALLURI

ist Mitbegründerin des Radical AI Network und KI-Forscherin an der Stanford University in Kalifornien.

is co-founder of the Radical AI Network and an AI researcher at California's Stanford University.

E-Mail / email: pkalluri@stanford.edu

MICHAEL KATZLBERGER

ist Gründer und Geschäftsführer von TUNNEL23, einer digitalen Kreativagentur aus Wien. Seit 2016 versucht er, in Kunden- und Kunstprojekten aller Art den kreativen Geist in den KI-Maschinen zu wecken.

is the founder and executive director of TUNNEL23, a Vienna-based digital creative agency. In his client and art commissions since 2016, he has sought to rouse the creative spirit dormant in AI machines.

YASEMIN KESKINTEPE

ist Kunstwissenschaftlerin und arbeitet als Kuratorin am Deutschen Hygiene-Museum, Dresden. Zuvor war sie Co-Kuratorin der Ausstellung *Open Codes* am ZKM Karlsruhe und an mehreren internationalen Ausstellungsprojekten beteiligt. Sie ist Kuratorin der Ausstellung *Künstliche Intelligenz. Maschinen – Lernen – Menschheitsträume*.

is an art scholar and works as a curator at the Deutsches Hygiene-Museum, Dresden. She was previously co-curator of the *Open Codes* exhibition at the Centre for Art and Media Karlsruhe (ZKM) and has contributed to a number of international exhibition projects. She is curator of the exhibition *Artificial Intelligence. Machine – Learning – Human Dreams*.

ANDREAS KNIE

ist Professor an der Technischen Universität Berlin und Leiter der Forschungsgruppe *Digitale Mobilität und gesellschaftliche Differenzierung* am Wissenschaftszentrum Berlin für Sozialforschung (WZB). Er arbeitet in verschiedenen Beratungsgremien von Bundes- und Landesregierungen sowie von Kommunen.

is a professor at the Technical University of Berlin and head of the *Digital Mobility and Social Differentiation* research group at the WZB Berlin Social Science Centre. He sits on various advisory bodies of federal and state governments as well as municipalities.

SUSANNE KRASMANN

ist Professorin für Soziologie am Fachbereich Sozialwissenschaften der Universität Hamburg. Sie hat ein Forschungsprojekt zu *Predictive Policing* geleitet und beschäftigt sich u. a. mit der „*Person" in der Logik der Algorithmen*.

is Professor of Sociology at the Department of Social Sciences at the University of Hamburg. She led a research project on *predictive policing* and is currently working on, among other things, the notion of *'person' in the logic of algorithms*.

CATHÉRINE LEHMANN

hat BWL studiert und Erfahrungen im Non-Profit- und im internationalen Nachhaltigkeitsmanagement gesammelt. Sie arbeitet an der Technischen Universität Berlin im Fachgebiet Sozial-ökologische Transformation im Kooperationsprojekt zur Entwicklung des *Green Consumption Assistants* und ist dort für Nachhaltigkeitsbewertungen zuständig.

studied business administration and gained experience in non-profit and international sustainability management. She works at the Technical University of Berlin in the Department of Social-Ecological Transformation as part of the cooperation project for the development of *Green Consumption Assistant,* in which she is responsible for sustainability assessments.

CLARISSA LÜTZ

arbeitet als kuratorisch-wissenschaftliche Projektassistentin im Ausstellungsteam *Künstliche Intelligenz. Maschinen – Lernen – Menschheitsträume* am Deutschen Hygiene-Museum, Dresden. Sie hat Kulturarbeit an der Fachhochschule Potsdam studiert und arbeitete bereits an mehreren interdisziplinären Ausstellungs-projekten mit.

works as a curatorial-scientific project assistant in the *Artificial Intelligence. Maschinen – Lernen – Menschheitsträume* exhibition team at the Deutsches Hygiene-Museum, Dresden. She studied Cultural Work at the University of Applied Sciences Potsdam and previously worked on several interdisciplinary exhibition projects.

MEGATRON-LM

ist ein KI-Sprachmodell, das auf NLP (Natural Language Processing, dt.: maschinelle Verarbeitung natürlicher Sprache) basiert. Es wurde vom Applied Deep Learning Research Team beim IT-Hardware-Unternehmen NVIDIA entwickelt.

is an AI language model based on NLP (natural language processing). It was developed by the Applied Deep Learning Research Team at the NVIDIA IT hardware company.

TILMAN SANTARIUS

forscht und publiziert zu den Themen Klimapolitik, Handelspolitik, nachhaltiges Wirtschaften, globale Gerechtigkeit und digitale Transformation. Er lehrt an der Technischen Universität Berlin sowie am Einstein Center Digital Future und leitet eine Forschungsgruppe zum Thema „Digitalisierung und sozial-ökologische Transformation" am Institut für ökologische Wirtschaftsforschung (IÖW).

researches and publishes on climate policy, trade policy, sustainable business, global justice, and digital transformation. He teaches at the Technical University of Berlin and the Einstein Center Digital Future and leads a research group on 'Digitisation and Socio-Ecological Transformation' at the Institute for Ecological Economy Research (IÖW).

JULIA SCHNEIDER

ist Comic-Essayistin und promovierte Volkswirtin. Idee und Konzept von *We Need to Talk, AI* entsprangen ihrer Tätigkeit als KI-Beraterin. Ihre Arbeiten verdichten komplexe Themen aus den Bereichen Wirtschaft und Gesellschaft, Innovation und Data Science – eine Brücke zwischen Intellekt und Intuition.

is a comic-strip essayist and holds a doctorate in economics. The idea and concept for *We Need to Talk, AI* came from her work as an AI consultant. Her work condenses complex topics from the fields of economics and society, innovation, and data science, bridging the gap between intellect and intuition.

www.docjsnyder.net

LOTHAR SCHRÖDER

war Mitglied der Enquetekommission Künstliche Intelligenz des Deutschen Bundestages, lange Jahre Verdi-Vorstandsmitglied und berät heute zur Gestaltung von KI-Systemen im Betrieb.

was a member of the Study Commission on Artificial Intelligence set up by the German Bundestag and, for many years, a Verdi board member; he now works as an AI systems design consultant for businesses.

MATTHIAS L. SCHROETER

ist Psychiater und Philosoph und arbeitet als Professor für Kognitive Neuro-psychiatrie am Max-Planck-Institut für Kognitions- und Neurowissenschaften sowie am Universitätsklinikum in Leipzig. Er beschäftigt sich – neben der Erkundung der Funktionen und der Krankheiten des Gehirns – mit den Grenzen der Kognitiven Neurowissenschaften im Rahmen einer „Negativen Phrenologie".

is a psychiatrist and philosopher and works as a Professor of Cognitive Neuro-psychiatry at the Max Planck Institute for Human Cognitive and Brain Sciences and at the University Hospital in Leipzig. Besides studying the functions and diseases of the brain, he explores the limits of cognitive neuroscience within the context of 'negative phrenology'.

GEORG SEEßLEN

studierte Malerei, Kunstgeschichte und Semiologie in München. Er war Dozent an verschiedenen Hochschulen im In- und Ausland und arbeitet heute als freier Autor u. a. für *Die Zeit*, *taz*, *epd-Film* und *Freitag* sowie als Kurator von Film-/Kunst-Reihen und Ausstellungen. Daneben hat er rund zwanzig Filmbücher geschrieben. Gemeinsam mit Markus Metz arbeitet er an Radio-Features und Hörspielen.

studied painting, art history, and semiology in Munich. He was a lecturer at various universities in Germany and abroad and today works as a freelance author for *Die Zeit*, *taz*, *epd-Film* and *Freitag,* among others, and as a curator of film/art series and exhibitions. He has also written some twenty film books. He collaborates with Markus Metz on various radio features and radio plays.

KATHRIN SEIBERT

ist Pflegewissenschaftlerin am Institut für Public Health und Pflegeforschung (IPP) der Universität Bremen. Ihre Forschungsschwerpunkte liegen in den Bereichen innovativer digitaler Technologien in der Pflege und Versorgungsqualität pflegebedürftiger Menschen. Sie war Mitarbeiterin im Sondierungsprojekt zu KI in der Pflege (SoKIP).

is a nursing care researcher at the Institute for Public Health and Nursing Research (IPP) at the University of Bremen. Her research focuses on innovative digital technologies in nursing care and the quality of nursing care provided to people in need of care. She too collaborated on the exploratory project on AI in nursing care (SoKIP).

ANGELA STEINMÜLLER

ist Mathematikerin und publiziert als freiberufliche Schriftstellerin vorwiegend Science-Fiction. In der Zusammenarbeit mit ihrem Mann Karlheinz Steinmüller entstanden drei Romane und zahlreiche Erzählungen, einige Hörspiele und Essays, aber auch eine Biografie über Charles Darwin und Sachbücher zum Thema Zukunft.

is a mathematician and publishes mainly science fiction in her capacity as a freelance writer. In collaboration with her husband Karlheinz Steinmüller, she has written three novels and numerous short stories, several radio plays and essays, as well as a biography of Charles Darwin and non-fiction books on the future.

KARLHEINZ STEINMÜLLER

ist Physiker und promovierter Philosoph und führt als Wissenschaftlicher Direktor einer Beratungsfirma Zukunftsstudien im öffentlichen und privatwirtschaftlichen Auftrag durch. Daneben hält er an der Freien Universität Berlin Vorlesungen über Zukunftsforschung. Gemeinsam mit seiner Frau Angela Steinmüller publiziert er Science-Fiction und Sachbücher.

is a physicist and holds a doctorate in philosophy. As the scientific director of a consulting firm, he is commissioned by both the public and private sectors to conduct futures studies. He also lectures on futures studies at the Free University of Berlin. Together with his wife Angela Steinmüller, he publishes science fiction and non-fiction books.

GERFRIED STOCKER

ist Medienkünstler und Ingenieur der Nachrichtentechnik. Seit 1995 ist er künstlerischer Leiter und Geschäftsführer von Ars Electronica in Linz (Österreich). Stocker berät zahlreiche Unternehmen und Institutionen in den Bereichen Kreativität und Innovationsmanagement und ist Gastredner auf internationalen Konferenzen und an verschiedenen Universitäten. 2019 wurde ihm ein Ehren-doktorat der Aalto University in Espoo (Finnland) verliehen.

is a media artist and communications engineer. He has been the artistic director and managing director of Ars Electronica in Linz, Austria, since 1995. Stocker advises numerous businesses and institutions on creativity and innovation management and is a guest speaker at international conferences and various universities. In 2019, he was awarded an honorary doctorate from Aalto University in Espoo, Finland.

KARIN WOLF-OSTERMANN

ist Professorin für Pflegewissenschaftliche Versorgungsforschung am Institut für Public Health und Pflegeforschung (IPP) der Universität Bremen. Sie forscht zu Strukturen, Prozessen und Ergebnissen der Gesundheitsversorgung sowie zur Wirkung von bestehenden und innovativen Versorgungskonzepten und Techno-logien und war Projektleiterin im Sondierungsprojekt zu KI in der Pflege (SoKIP).

is Professor of Health Care Research at the Institute for Public Health and Nursing Research (IPP) at the University of Bremen. She conducts research on structures, processes and outcomes of health care as well as the impact of existing and innovative care concepts and technologies, and was the project leader for the exploratory project on AI in nursing care (SoKIP).

ANKE WOSCHECH

ist studierte Soziologin und promovierte Technikhistorikerin mit den Forschungs-schwerpunkten Historische Zukunftsforschung, Technikutopien und Science-Fiction. Sie ist als kuratorisch-wissenschaftliche Mitarbeiterin im Ausstellungsteam *Künstliche Intelligenz. Maschinen – Lernen – Menschheitsträume* am Deutschen Hygiene-Museum Dresden tätig.

holds a degree in sociology and a doctorate in the history of technology with particular research emphasis on historical futurology, technology fiction and science fiction. She is a member of the curatorial research team working on the exhibition *Artificial Intelligence. Machine – Learning – Human Dreams* at the Deutsches Hygiene-Museum Dresden.

LENA ZIYAL

ist Illustratorin und Grafikdesignerin und Teil der kollektiv geführten Agentur INFOTEXT. Sie studierte visuelle Kommunikation an der Kunsthochschule Berlin-Weißensee. 2019 veröffentlichte sie gemeinsam mit Julia Schneider ihr bislang bekanntestes Werk, den Comic-Essay über Künstliche Intelligenz *We Need to Talk, AI.*

is an illustrator and graphic designer and part of the INFOTEXT agency, which is run as a collective. She studied visual communication at the Weißensee Academy of Art Berlin. In 2019, together with Julia Schneider, she published her best-known work to date, i.e. the comic essay on Artificial Intelligence entitled *We Need to Talk, AI.*

Textnachweise / Text credits

Gekürzter Auszug aus / abridged excerpt from:
QualiFiction, LiSA: Software zur Analyse und Bewertung von Bucherfolgen. Dokument Yasemin Keskintepe: Kuratorischer Essay, Auswertung Sentiment-Verlauf, Leserpotenzial, 22.6.2021, https://www.qualifiction.de: S. 29

Gekürzter Auszug aus / abridged excerpt from:
Julia Schneider (Text/Konzeption/Concept), Lena Ziyal (Illustration/Grafik/Layout): We Need to Talk, AI, Berlin 2019, S. 13–19, https://weneedtotalk.ai/: S. 45–49

Republished with permission of Nature, from Don't ask if artificial intelligence is good or fair, ask how it shifts power, Pratyusha Kalluri, Nature. 583. 169-169, 2020, permission conveyed through Copyright Clearance Center, Inc.: S. 128–133

Megatron-LM: Das Schöne und das Erhabene der KI (2021): Michael Katzlberger, TUNNEL23 Werbeagentur GmbH, Wien: S. 142

The Beautiful and the Sublime of AI:
DeepL, www.DeepL.com/Translator, 3.3.2021: S. 143

Wir danken für die freundliche Genehmigung der Abdruckrechte. / Our thanks for the kind permission as regards the reprinting rights.

Bildnachweise / Picture credits
© VG Bild-Kunst, Bonn 2021: für das Werk von Constant Dullaart: S. 22; © Bayerische Staatsbibliothek München, Res/2 A.gr.b. 851, Seite 29: S. 32; © Freer Gallery of Art, Smithsonian Institution, Washington, D.C.: Purchase – Charles Lang Freer Endowment, F1930.75: S. 33; © Universitätsbibliothek Frankfurt am Main, Freimann-Sammlung, digitalisiert in Kooperation mit dem YIVO Institute for Jewish Research am Center for Jewish History, NY: S. 34; © Wissenschaftliche Bibliothek der Stadt Trier, HS 1895/1428 4°: S. 35; © Herzog August Bibliothek Wolfenbüttel: Un Kapsel 1 (23) (CC BY-SA): S. 36; © Gottfried Wilhelm Leibniz Bibliothek – Niedersächsische Landesbibliothek, Hannover, LG 35, III, B 1, Bl. 1r: S. 37; © UB der HU zu Berlin, Historische Sammlungen: AE 20751-1: S. 38; © UB der HU zu Berlin, Historische Sammlungen: 3639 v:F8: S. 39; © Collection Mundaneum, Mons: S. 40; © Stiftung Deutsches Hygiene-Museum, Dresden: S. 41; © Ars Electronica Futurelab: S. 57; © Timo Arnall | © timoarnall: S. 62; © Digital Image, The Museum of Modern Art, New York/Scala, Florence: S. 63; © The Library of Congress, Prints and Photograph Division, courtesy Vincent Virga, Eyes of the Nation, Knopf, 1997: S. 65; © Museumsstiftung Post und Telekommunikation: S. 65; © Camino Filmverleih GmbH: S. 68; © Guo Cheng: S. 70f.; © Mimi Onuoha: S. 72;

© Segments.ai: S. 73; © Stiftung Deutsches Hygiene-Museum, Dresden: S. 82f.; © IfmPt Institut für musterbasierte Prognosetechnik Verwaltungs-GmbH: S. 89; © Public Domain: S. 97; © Stadt Monheim am Rhein / Tim Kögler: S. 103; © Lauren Lee McCarthy und / and David Leonard: S. 112f.; © Adam Harvey and Josh Evans. 2021: S. 168f.; © Laokoon, Berlin / Kulturstiftung des Bundes: S. 170; © M Eifler: S. 171; © Sofia Crespo (www.sofiacrespo.com): S. 172f.; © Emily Grundon: S. 174f.; © Mario Klingemann / Google Arts & Culture: S. 174f.; © Philipp Schmitt, in Kollaboration mit / in collaboration with Mikkel Mikkelsen: S. 177; © Memo Akten: S. 178

Leihgeber*innen / Lenders
Erst durch das Vertrauen und die Unterstützung zahlreicher Leihgeber*innen wurde die Ausstellung ermöglicht. Ihnen allen dankt das Deutsche Hygiene-Museum herzlich. / This exhibition would not have been possible without the trust and support of numerous lenders, and the Deutsches Hygiene-Museum wishes to thank each and every one of them.

Access Now (RightsCon Summit Series), Ranking Digital Rights, and Shoshana Zuboff

Alexander von Humboldt Stiftung, Bonn

Timo Arnall

Ars Electronica Futurelab (AT), Linz

Autodesk, Inc., San Rafael

Barkhausen Institut gGmbH

Anna Biselli

Bloomberg L.P.

BR / AI + Automation Lab, Bayrischer Rundfunk

British Psychological Society, History of Psychology Centre, London

Camino Filmverleih, Stuttgart

Centre for Tactile Internet with Human-in-the-Loop (CeTI) der TU Dresden

Centro del Consejo Superior de Investigaciones Científicas (CSIC), Madrid

Channel 4 News, London

Andrew Charles

Guo Cheng

Collection Mundaneum, Mons

Computer History Archives Project

Computer History Museum, Mountain View

Sofia Crespo (www.sofiacrespo.com), Berlin

Deutsches Krebsforschungszentrum (DKFZ) zugunsten des Nationalen Centrums für Tumorerkrankungen Dresden (NCT/UCC Dresden)

Constant Dullaart

Else Kröner Fresenius Zentrum (EKFZ) für Digitale Gesundheit der TU Dresden

Euronews

Forschungszentrum Jülich

Franckesche Stiftungen zu Halle

Fraunhofer-Institut für Nachrichtentechnik, Heinrich-Hertz-Institut, HHI

Fraunhofer-Institut für Optronik, Systemtechnik und Bildauswertung IOSB, Karlsruhe

Freer Gallery of Art, Smithsonian Institution, Washington, D.C.

Marla Frezza

Future Advocacy, London

Gesellschaft für Freiheitsrechte e.V., Berlin

GlobalFoundries Dresden

Google LLC, Mountain View

Google / Mirhoseini, A. et al.

Görlitzer Sammlungen / Oberlausitzische Bibliothek der Wissenschaften

Gottfried Wilhelm Leibniz Bibliothek – Niedersächsische Landesbibliothek, Hannover

Adam Harvey

Heinz Nixdorf MuseumsForum, Paderborn

Hexatronic Deutschland, Bargteheide

Hörbuch Hamburg HHV GmbH

IfmPt - Institut für musterbasierte Prognosetechnik, Oberhausen

Infervision Europe GmbH, Wiesbaden

InnovAltion Campus GmbH – Implementing artificial intelligence on a global scale, Berlin

International Business Machines Corporation (IBM), Armonk, NY

Mario Klingemann

Laokoon, Berlin / Kulturstiftung des Bundes, Halle (Saale)

Leopoldina – Nationale Akademie der Wissenschaften, Halle (Saale)

Barrett Lyon / The Opte Project

M Eifler

mauritius images / Science Source / Smithsonian Libraries

Lauren Lee McCarthy & David Leonard

Memo Akten

MIRO Innovation Lab / Deutsches Zentrum für Luft- und Raumfahrt (DLR) e. V., Köln

Museumsstiftung Post und Telekommunikation / Museum für Kommunikation Frankfurt, Frankfurt a.M.

Tina Nord

Norman B. Leventhal Map & Education Center at the Boston Public Library

Mimi Onuoha

OpenAI, San Francisco

Otto-von-Guericke-Universität Magdeburg, Institut für Informations- und Kommunikationstechnik, Urheber Jun.-Prof. Dr. Ingo Siegert, Fachgebiet Mobile Dialogsysteme

Peng! Kollektiv e.V., Berlin

picture-alliance / akg

Anna Ridler

Gilles Sabrié

Prof. Dr. Florian A. Schmidt, HTW Dresden

Philipp Schmitt in Kollaboration mit / in collaboration with Mikke Mikkelsen

Segments.ai

Shift GmbH, Falkenberg

Siemens Historical Institute, Berlin

Siltronic AG, München

Smithsonian Institution (NMNH), Washington, D.C.

Staatsbibliothek zu Berlin – Preußischer Kulturbesitz

Stadt Monheim am Rhein / Tim Kögler

Ruth Starr

Stiftung Deutsches Hygiene-Museum, Dresden

SubCom, Eatontown

Pawel Swider, Verne Global

Tactical Technology Collective (TTC), Berlin

The Advertising Archives, London

The Library of Congress, Prints and Photograph Division, Washington, D.C.

The Museum of Modern Art, New York/Scala, Florence

The New York Times

The Orion Publishing Group Ltd., London

The Washington Post, Washington, D.C.

Universität Heidelberg, Kirchhoff-Institut für Physik

Universities of Washington, Michigan, California Berkeley and Samsung Research America and Stony Brook University, Kevin Eykholt

Universitätsbibliothek der Freien Universität Berlin

Universitätsbibliothek der Humboldt-Universität zu Berlin

Universitätsbibliothek Leipzig

Vanguard Industries Inc., Tokyo

Leah Varjacques & Adam Saewitz

Tim Verheyden

Paula Williams Dos Santos

Windcloud 4.0 GmbH

Wissenschaftliche Bibliothek der Stadt Trier

Besonders danken wir den Personen und Unternehmen, die das Ausstellungsprojekt mit Schenkungen unterstützten / We are especially grateful to the individuals and companies who supported the exhibition project with their donations:

Digital Dream Labs, Inc., Pittsburgh

fluSoft GbR, Dresden

L'Oreal S.A., Paris

Nanit, New York

Procter & Gamble Service GmbH, Schwalbach am Taunus

Starkey Laboratories (Germany) GmbH, Hamburg

tado GmbH, München

Windcloud 4.0 GmbH, Enge-Sande

Wonder Workshop, Inc., Berlin

Dank / Acknowledgements

Das Projektteam dankt für die Unterstützung / The Project Team wishes to thank the following for their support:

aquaRömer GmbH & Co. KG, Mainhardt, Dr. Julia Borggräfe, Dr. Anna Christmann, Prof. Dr. Stephan Jansen, Prof. Dr. Gesche Joost, Dr. Lynn Kaack, Frederike Kaltheuner, Dr. Ayesha Khanna, Miriam Klöpper, Dr. Nils Köbis, Rafael Laguna de la Vera, Katharina Meyer, Gesa Schöning, Dr. Hagen Schönrich, Matthias Spielkamp, Dr. Viola Tenge-Wolf, Robert Vollmann, Prof. Dr. Oliver Zielinski

Impressum / Colophon

Diese Publikation erscheint anlässlich der Ausstellung des Deutschen Hygiene-Museums / This publication is published to coincide with the Deutsches Hygiene-Museum exhibition

Künstliche Intelligenz.
Maschinen–Lernen–Menschheitsträume

Artificial Intelligence.
Machine–Learning–Human Dreams

6. November 2021 – 28. August 2022

Direktor / Director: Prof. Klaus Vogel

Kaufmännische Direktorin / Director of Finance: Lisa Klamka

Ausstellung / Exhibition

Ausstellungsleiterin / Exhibition Manager: Dr. Doreen Hartmann

Kuratorin und Projektleiterin / Curator and Project Manager: Yasemin Keskintepe

Wissenschaftlicher Co-Kurator / Scientific Co-Curator: Dr. Thomas Ramge

Kuratorisch-wissenschaftliche Mitarbeiterin / Curatorial Research Associate: Dr. Anke Woschech

Wissenschaftlich-kuratorische Assistenz / Research and Curatorial Assistant: Bettina Beer, Anna Kühn, Clarissa Lütz, Lisa Nickolaus

Kooperationspartner / Co-operation Partners:
Ars Electronica, Linz/Österreich (Künstlerische Begleitung / Artistic supervision)
Tactical Tech, Berlin (The Glass Room)
Barkhausen Institut gGmbH, Dresden (Exponatentwicklung / Exhibit Development)

Wissenschaftliche Begleitung und Beratung / Scientific Support and Advice:
Doreen Böttcher (Exzellenzcluster CeTI, TU Dresden), Dr. Simon Egbert (Technische Universität Berlin), Prof. Dr. Thomas Hänseroth (Technische Universität Dresden), Dr. Jessica Heesen (Universität Tübingen), Prof. Dr. Andreas Knie (Wissenschaftszentrum Berlin für Sozialforschung), Prof. Dr. Susanne Krasmann (Universität Hamburg), Dr. Ralf Pulla (Technische Sammlungen Dresden), Dr. Rico Radeke (5 G Lab Germany, TU Dresden), Rebekka Roschy (Schaufler Lab, TU Dresden), Prof. Dr. Tilman Santarius (Technische Universität Berlin), Prof. Dr. Florian A. Schmidt (Hochschule für Technik und Wirtschaft Dresden),

Prof. Dr. Dr. Matthias Schroeter (Max-Planck-Institut für Kognitions- und Neurowissenschaften, Leipzig), Prof. Dr. Stefanie Speidel (Nationales Centrum für Tumorerkrankungen, Dresden)

Ausstellungsgestaltung / Exhibition Design: chezweitz; Dr. Sonja Beeck und Detlef Weitz mit Team, Berlin

Ausstellungsgrafik / Exhibition Graphics: Johannes Bögle, Jaroslav Toussaint, chezweitz, Berlin

Medienplanung und -umsetzung / Media Planning and Implementation: schnellebuntebilder, Berlin; Studio Bosco, Leipzig

Bauleitung / Construction Supervision: Jan Stauf, chezweitz, Berlin

Ausstellungsbau / Exhibition Construction: Werkstätten des Deutschen Hygiene-Museums: Michal Tomaszewski (Leitung / Director), Alexander Fröhlich, William Herz, Uwe Kellmann, Ingolf Seidel, Marianne Tille; Büchner Möbel GmbH; Innenausbau Aulhorn GmbH & Co. KG

Interviewkoordination und -Durchführung / Interview Co-ordination and Execution: Katharina Meyer, Berlin

Videobearbeitung / Video Editing: Gunnar Baumann, Dresden; Michael Sommermeyer, Dresden

Audioproduktion / Audio Production: Linon Medien KG, Berlin

DGS-Videoproduktion / German Sign Language Video Production: Yomma GmbH, Berlin

Einfache Sprache / Plain Language: Anja Dworski, Büro für Leichte Sprache, Lebenshilfe Sachsen e.V., Chemnitz

Produktion Tastobjekte / Production Touch-and-Sense Objects: Tactile Studio, Berlin

Tastplan / Tactile guidance system: Barrierefreiheit GmbH, Schwarzenberg

Medien- und Ausstellungstechnik / Media and Exhibition Technology: Kay Jansen, Robert Queck, Matthias Wächter

Lichttechnik / Lighting Technology: Paul Göschel, Dresden

Lektorat / Editing & Proofreading: Astrid Treusch, Berlin; Ralf Tauchmann, Radebeul

Übersetzung / Translations: Stephen Grynwasser, Wien; Ralf Tauchmann, Radebeul; Übersetzungsbüro Perfekt GmbH, München

Untertitelung / Subtitling: Bastian Fröhner, Michael Sommermeyer, hechtfilm-Filmproduktion, Dresden

Umsetzung Ausstellungsgrafik / Exhibition Graphics Production: Grafikwerkstatt des Deutschen Hygiene-Museums: Veit Pätzug, Gabriele Radde, Vivienne Wilsdorf; Werk5 GmbH, Berlin

Grafikproduktion und -montage / Graphics Production and Installation: Pigmentpol Sachsen GmbH, Dresden; PPS. Digital Printing GmbH, Berlin; LenticularPrinting, Pappenheim

Sammlung / Collection: Susanne Roeßiger (Leitung / Director), Marita Gottsmann, Julia Radtke, Sylke Schäfer, Marion Schneider, Marion Thalheim

Leihverkehr/ Loans: Lilian Groß, Nadine Vollmer, Nicole Wonneberger

Koordination Inklusion / Inclusion Co-ordination: Maria Matthes, Susanne Weckwerth

Objekteinrichtung / Exhibit Placement: A-Team Dresden

Transport: Belaj Fine Art Service GmbH, Berlin; Maik Wagner (DHMD)

Versicherung / Insurance: Kühn & Bülow Versicherungsmakler GmbH

Projektcontrolling / Project Controlling: Melanie Johne

Elektro- und Haustechnik / Electrical Systems and Building Services: Frank Haupt (Leitung /Director), Jens Gründel, Wolfgang Henschel

Kommunikation und Öffentlichkeitsarbeit / Communication and PR

Kooperationen / Collaborations: Anja Sommer

Presse- und Öffentlichkeitsarbeit / Press and PR: Christoph Wingender (Leitung / Director), Ramona Buhler, Geertje Ihde, Marian Zabel

Web- und Printmedien / Online and Print Media: Dimitrios Ambatielos

Gestaltung Plakat und Flyer / Poster and Flyer Design: Dominik Schech, schech.net GbR, Dresden

Begleit- und Vermittlungsprogramm / Accompanying and Education Programme

Bildung und Vermittlung / Education and Mediation: Dr. Carola Rupprecht (Leitung / Director), Monika Hampe, Maria Matthes

Veranstaltungen / Events: Dr. Susanne Illmer (Leitung / Director), Kristin Heinig, Martin Frank, Isabel Matthäus

IMPRESSUM
COLOPHON

Katalog / Catalogue

Herausgeberinnen / Editors: Yasemin Keskintepe
und Dr. Anke Woschech für das Deutsche
Hygiene-Museum

Objekttexte / Exhibit Texts: Clarissa Lütz

**Bildrecherche und Rechteklärung / Image Research
and Rights Clearance:** Lilian Groß, Nadine Vollmer,
Nicole Wonneberger

Lektorat / Proofreading: Astrid Treusch, Berlin;
Ralf Tauchmann, Radebeul

Übersetzung / Translations: Stephen Grynwasser,
Wien; Ralf Tauchmann, Radebeul

Gestaltung / Design: grafikanstalt Julia Wagner,
Hamburg

Gestaltung Infografiken / Infographics Design:
INFOTEXT – Agentur für Content und Grafikdesign,
Berlin

Schriften / Typefaces: TT Hoves

Papier / Paper: 135 g/qm GardaPat 13 Kiara,
1,3-faches Volumen

Druck / Printed by: Westermann Druck Zwickau GmbH

© **Coverabbildung / Cover Artwork:** Tupungato/
123RF.COM

© 2021 Stiftung Deutsches Hygiene-Museum

© Wallstein Verlag, Göttingen 2021

© Autor*innen, Fotograf*innen, Künstler*innen und
andere Urheber*innen

Die Geltendmachung der Ansprüche gem. § 60h
UrhG für die Wiedergabe von Abbildungen der
Exponate/Bestandswerke erfolgt durch die
VG Bild-Kunst.

Erschienen im Wallstein Verlag
Geiststraße 11
37073 Göttingen
www.wallstein-verlag.de

Gefördert durch

Gefördert durch die

Gefördert von

Staatliche Kunstsammlungen Dresden
Sächsische Landesstelle für Museumswesen

Diese Maßnahme wird mitfinanziert durch Steuermittel auf der Grundlage des vom Sächsischen Landtag beschlossenen Haushalts.